INDIAN SYSTEMS OF PSYCHOTHERAPY

INDIAN SYSTEMS OF PSYCHOTHERAPY

Prakash Veereshwar

KALPAZ

Published by

Kalpaz Publications
C-30, Satyawati Nagar,
Delhi – 110052
Ph.: 011-47034999, 9811692060
www.kalpazpublications.com
E-mail: kalpaz@hotmail.com

Distribution Network
gyanbooks.com
India, USA, Canada, UK, Australia, France

ISBN: 978-81-7835-078-3 (HB)

Reprint in India, 2024
First Published, 2002

Printed at: Gyan Press, Delhi.

Indian System of Psychotherapy
Author: Prakash Veereshwar

Published by

Kalpaz Publications
C-30, Satyawati Nagar,
Delhi – 110052
Ph.: 011-47034999, 9811692060
www.kalpazpublications.com
E-mail: kalpaz@hotmail.com

Distribution Network
gyanbooks.com
India, USA, Canada, UK, Australia, France

ISBN: 978-93-5722-419-2 (PB)

First Published, 2024

Printed at: Gyan Press, Delhi.

Indian System of Psychotherapy
Author: Prakash Veereshwar

Contents

Preface

This work has deep bearing on the Indian System of Psychotherapy whose birth may be traced back to about two thousand years. Although the modern generation has made much head way in the field of scientific research, the significance of Psychotherapy does subsist even till this day. The experts in the western world are in agreement about the effective efficacy of this system. Indeed its signifacance does lie in the fact that its healing practices have gone deep among the masses of India living in the far-flung regions of our sub-continent. In fact this system has inner inherent strength and vitality that checks several opposing factors from securing an edge over this system. It is well said that all that is old is not necessarily rubbish : it can prove to be as precious as gold.

The author has meticulously explored the healing powers of Ayurveda with a glaring hint on Yoga, now being practised in several countries of Europe, Asia and elsewhere. However the author emphasises the point that deep research in this regard is the call of the hour. The idea is to remove mental and physical ailments which make our humanity the pitiable victim.

The draft has been weaved into well-written eleven chapters, the emphasis being on Western veiws, the Vedas, Atharva Veda, Ayurveda, Samhtas, Yoga, Psychotherapy, salient features of Indian system, along with an exhaustive Bibliography.

Prakash Veereshwar

Introduction

Indian system of Psychotherapy is of very ancient origin. Its beginnings can be traced back to some two thousand years BC. The very special thing about it is that it still exists, even in the present age of scientific advancement. This precisely is what gives it credence over all other systems of medicine in the world. If it is so, there must be some vital factor present somewhere which makes it go on and on. To the people trained in the Western view of science, it may seem like superstition or witch-craft. But a deeper look at the whole phenomena leads one to wonder at the profound understanding of human nature contained in the rituals, and their practices. That some pseudo-medicine men, novices and quacks defraud the simple illiterate rural and tribal folks by their tricks—is a fact. But these people are not the real and trained practitioners, neither are they properly trained nor authorized to such practice. They just befool and cheat simple folts for their selfish ends. The real practices are still alive in certain temples of the country.

The main reason for the continuation of the system seems to be that it has been deeply ingrained in Indian psyche, that is why it has not been wiped out even by the onslaught of foreign science and medicine, that is why it has lasted for so long and still has deep influence on Indian masses, in some form or other. That it is alive and kicking is evident at temple healing practices today.

If a system can continue to influence such a large population for four millennia, it must have some inner inherent strength and vitality in it. The need is for a proper approach and a positive attitude towards it. All that is old is not necessarily rubbish, there may be gold in old. Now since the Western world is awakening to the wonders of Ayurveda, and the special healing powers of Yoga, we in India must try to explore and to rediscover the wonders of

Ayurveda and Yoga. Ayurveda started with Vedas 600 BC and Patanjali's Yoga Sutra is dated 150 BC.

The need of the hour is a proper research in this field, by the experts, to find out the truth behind it and to test it in the light of modern scientific knowledge. By going through the rigorous regimen of thorough scientific testing, the truth will come out of the chaff which has been accumulating with the passage of this long time. If properly examined and tested, Ayurveda can become a modern and scientific system, which can be India's unique contribution to the world of medicine. For example, take the case of Yoga. Yoga is an ancient Indian philosophy. It is a science as well as an art. If has been accepted and being used in modern psychotherapy throughout the world (ref. American psychiatrist and MD who has taken the name Swami Ajaya). Numourous studies of experiments on Yoga are available, proving the healing beneficial effects of Yogasanas on human behaviour, both in health and in disease. Yoga has been adopted by the psychiatrists also as a very soothing and helpful relaxation technique.

The incidence of mental diseases is increasing at an alarming rate in the whole world. Modern life with its tensions and complexities, the high speed and cut-throat competition, all give rise to a vast multitude of mental ailments—major or minor. As pathogenic germs attack a weak body, in a similar way when the mind becomes weak, it falls prey to various tensions and anxieties, which in turn may lead to serious mental diseases. Modern man has a weak ego, that is why he lacks the required immunity towards these disease producing factors. Technological advancement has turned man into a machine—a robot. Actually in cybernatic terms man is treated like a machine—he must perform like a machine—not like a man. Precision and speed are the aims—not quality and creativity. Man is fast loosing his essential human qualities like joy satisfaction laughter patience and self-control.

Even worse is the modern philosophy of materialism of going on amassing material wealth—which can bring no satisfaction in life. 'Living for the pleasures of life', 'satisfying one's senses to the full' are thought to be the best because it is believed that 'the control or the deprivation of senses leads to mental disorders'. Such philosophies containing half truths, do more harm than good, for these lead to utmost desolution and depression. The "man at the top" is lonely and frustrated in most of the cases.

In India, thankfully, the incidence of mental diseases is still less in proportion to our population. The large masses of Indian people are still patient and satisfied with their lot. They do not run after material wealth and are resigned to their fate. These simple people may be living a depraved life under poverty line, still they are more contented. They do not run after pleasure only, they are not part of the rat race rampant in modern society. They are called either primitive or non-civilized by the so called educated classes steeped in modern values. May be they are less civilize if civilization means adopting the current values and life styles. But actually they are more contented and lead a more mentally healthy life, with less tension and anxiety. They are sticking to the age old path shown by our ancient sages "simple living high thinking".

Moreover, it is a recognized fact that mental diseases are far more serious than physical diseases. In physical diseases, the patient suffers the pain and all its consequences, whereas in the case of mental diseases, the patient, his family members, his neighbours and the community at large—have to suffer the consequences of his acts. Take for example the case of a psychopathic killer a sex—maniac, an alcoholic, a pyromanic. They make the life of the people near them unbearable. Similarly a paranoid dominating father can have a life long negative effect on his family specially on young children.

In the light of the above facts, one is bound to think of a remedy which can relieve this mental agony. The answer lies in Psychotherapy. The name is new, but the science itself is as old as mankind. As soon as man become conscious about his mental problems, he tried to find a solution for them and thus psychotherapy was born. Psychotherapy means trying to solve psychological problems by psychological methods. Let us see what psychotherapy is.

Psychotherapy

The modern psychotherapist is a doctor with a special attitude to most of the organic and mental ailments, which modern medicine still has to grapple with. He holds, these ailments are, basically the result of false mental attitudes and ideas. A patient's life, he believes, is a result of such false attunement to reality, inhibited to an unbearable degree in the free unfolding of its very essence.

Psychology speaks of drives, a psychic apparatus, a mind of a person, consciousness, ego. Nevertheless, even Freud was forced to admit that his theory of drives was 'the mythology of psycho-analysis'. Other theories also give just as little information about man or his mind. Western Psychology tells us nothing about the subjectivity of the subject, the personality of the person and his consciousness in a manner that would actually enable us to understand the connexion between these, the environment and our real selves.

A Western therapist finds it difficult to deal with patients who do not come to him with clearly defined neurotic symptoms, but who suffer 'only' from a diffused meaninglessness, vacuity and ennui of their lives, or who are reduced to dispair by the question—"why is there being?"

Ancient Indian science of man is far in advance of the comparatively new modern psychology which is scarcely a century old. India's finest minds—the rishis, have for more than four millennia, continuously contemplated the fundamental nature of man and of his world. They have given to these problems much more time and energy than western science has devoted to investigating the external physical phenomena of universe. In old Indian texts religion philosophy metaphysics all are one, a large whole. Indian philosophy is not anchored in magic or mystique, it is not full of archaic and primitive conceptions. It has given the highest philosophy of Advait (Absolute monism). It has given the concept of 'Shoonyta' or the great void, shoonyta is not negative, it is a void which is more 'filled' than all the plentitudes of the universe.

In India the philosophical systems deal with two problems: (1) The endless sufferings of mankind and (2) Man's powerful longing for release from suffering and for happiness—ways to salvation. If philosophy is a prescription against human suffering, then all such philosophy is in reality psychotherapy.

Indian thought understood man as an essentially luminating Atman—being, belonging directly to Brahman or Supreme being.

Then Indian therapies are "elucidation therapies". In reality the Eastern and Western therapies are so close to each other that their point of contact becomes visible at once. Remember Freud, who discovered that the criterion setting his psycho-analytic method apart from all other medical therapies is the simultaneous occurrence of an illuminating insight into the hidden nature of a neurotic disturbance and of therapeutic liberation from his suffering. "Where Id was, let Ego be." Since Fraud all the Western therapies—whatever the name—have been endeavouring to make the patients themselves look into their unveiled nature, to make them transparent to themselves. The Western psycho-therapeutic methods need urgent improvement of their capacity to illuminate the inner self. They have to see the light and the light-giving source, which Indian systems can provide.

Indian thinking has vastness, it is liberal-enough to include the whole universe in it. Western thinking is ego-based, hence narrow. There is always a possibility of human growth and maturity in Indian thought, to find an unpurturbed and unpurturbable inner peace, which is lacking in Western systems.

One major difference in Western psychotherapy and its Indian counterpart is self-purification—the inner insight of Indian sages, not found even in the most rigorous training of the therapiests of the west. The Indian Guru gives initiation only to those who pass his strict tests and then trains him, to become not a mechanical therapist only—but a seer—who cures, advises tries to improve and mould human being on the whole.

Then, there is the question of liberation from one's ownself—truly freeing from the inner evil dark aggressive and destructive animal drives. The Western systems, after Freud, make the patients conscious of these forces and to control them. But in the East, this dark evil is conquered by just the opposite-pure love. There is no hate, no desire, only Vairagya renunciation. Vairagya, here does not mean bodily withdrawal or running away. It means renouncing all self-seeking attachment to things or to people. Samadhi or 'Nirvana' is the ultimate of self-detachment.

All present there is widespread frustration and unrest. In this age of turmoil, all thinkers educationists, psychologists, sociologists and philosophers are trying to minimize human misery and to attain better mental health, happiness and higher states of consicousness. Here our ancient systems can show new light. For Indian psychotherapy has many points of merit:—

- Indian psychotherapy can be applied to almost all types of psychic disorders of functional nature—from very acute chronic disorders—to milder cases of behavioural maladjustments.
- Indian psychotherapy provides mental health and hygiene programmes for the improvement of normal personalities.
- Indian psycho-therapeutic systems are philanthropic in nature. Rich and poor can all be benefited by them without any fees. Patients and their family do make offerings according to their capacity.
- The scope of Indian psychotherapy is in fact large. It believes in the continuity of behaviour from abnormal to normal and from normal to super-normal.
- Atharva Veda claims that 'not only human behaviour but even physical and cosmic events can be controlled by psychogenic practices'.
- Indian systems cure the whole personality, not just the symptoms. It cures psyche, nerves and the body with its multifarious techniques and approaches.
- Its methods can treat patients of all ages, religions, male-female, rural-urban, literate-illiterate, poor and rich equally.
- Indian psycho-therapeutic systems have evolved from Indian culture and Indian tradition. They appeal to Indian psyche, in a way in which Western or foreign methods can never appeal. (Edipus and Electra complexes are not a part of our psyche. As Surya and Jayarama (1964) have remarked, "The Indian psycho-therapist of today is a product of Western training. He has learnt his lesson of psychological treatment and therapy in the language and style which is altogether alien to his own birth place and its environment. The words of the foreign language are scattered and irrelevant for his comprehension. They cannot act as a medium of communication, cannot comprehend the whole being of person in his past, present and future. The Indian psychotherapist cannot make any

contribution to the theory of Psychotherapy. We have become a bad copy of Western theory and practice we tend to burden our patients with technical terminology of a foreign language." Surya and Jayarama further make clear the difference between the mental patients in the East and the West. "The Indian patient seeks the succour and support of his family patriarch." It is not just the transference, it goes much deeper to familial roots. Pande says, "Modern psychotherapy is a Western institution, a product of foreign culture and foreign soil. If psychotherapy and mental health movement has to survive in India, it will have to be rooted in Indian soil".—Pande, 1968.

Dhairyam also emphasizes the same idea. "To flourish in India, psychotherapy will have to be rooted in the culture and spiritual tradition of India." —Dhairyam, 1961.

Thus Indian psychotherapy is already turning to Indian culture and Indian traditions. It has come up in three ways—

- From the special demands and expectations of Indian patients.
- From a realistic evaluation of Western psychotherapy and its glaring differences from Indian background.
- From a renaissance or reawakening among Indian public.

New Indian psychotherapy after 60s shows three trends—

- New leaning towards the eternal classic Geeta.
- Sanction to guru-shishya parampara in therapeutic situation.
- Finding new paradigms for the Indian masses, about three-fourths of which are still illiterate or semi-literate.

Leaning Towards Shrimad Bhagwat Geeta

The founder of the All India Institute of Mental Health, Bangalore (now NIMHANS) the late Shri M.V. Govindaswami had a famous saying—"Mahabharata is a great text book of psychopathology and Geeta a great treatise on psychotherapy." Under the able guidance of Shri Govindaswami many researchers tried to study Geeta to explore new patterns for Indian psychotherapy. Shri Satyananda (1972) says about Geeta—".....Geeta relieves man of his sense of guilt regarding the world, it solves his conflicts. It gives him strength and moral courage, and the insight to look within and understand oneself."

Geeta is a living psychology. It has to be moulded in modern terms. It shows many ways of self-improvement.

The Basic Pattern of Guru-shishya Relationship

The advocates of guru-shishya relationship in therapeutic situation are Dhairyam, Carstus and Neki. According to the therapists the relationship most acceptable to Indian patients in therapy is the traditional guru-shishya relationship. According to Neki (1973), this relation is automatic and is not bound by any worldly relations. (as in Western psycho therapy it is considered to be a transfer of the attitude towards parents). Neki (1978) himself experimented on this aspect. He has this to say, "The dilemma before the Indian therapist is whether he should reform the individual (his patient) or his environment. The Guru is above this, he is liberated from the bondages of this world. He himself is an epitome of culture ad tradition. He teaches the patient, not only self-expression but self-control. He teaches the path of Geeta—"Follow the path of your Dharma (duty) fearlessly." The Guru is very actively participating in the whole process. He takes the whole burden of decision upon himself and gives insight to the sheshya (patient). But this also is true that the duty and the responsibility of the Guru is much above that of a mere therapist. He is a friend, philosopher and guide in the real sense.

New Paradigms for Indian Masses

A swiss psychotherapist Dr. E.M. Hock wrote a book Psychotherapy for the illiterate in 1964. Dr. Hock worked for years in India away from the westernized cities in the distant areas of Kashmir. She has been well-versed in Indian cultural traditions and customs. According to her any paradigm for the masses of India has to be rooted in Indian traditions.

So Indian psychotherapy is already finding new paths for itself. This book is a small attempt to introduce to the new and blooming psychologists and psycho-therapists with our own systems, which are ancient and ingrained in our own soil and culture. Only three main systems have been discussed viz., Atharvanic psychotherapy, Ayurveda and Yoga. This covers the whole ancient Hindu field. These are ancient, but still very alive and effective, specially Yoga and Ayurveda. These two incorporate the basics of Atharva veda.

In the beginning a glimpse of Western systems and Indian systems is presented and afterwards the comparisons are given wherever relevant. The reader is here reminded that it is an attempt at introduction only. For further details the researcher will have to move over to the basic texts. A detailed Bibliography is provided for this purpose.

The aim has not been to criticize or downgrade any system but to point out the positive aspects of all the systems. This coming together of Eastern and Western systems may show a new path to the world of Psychotherapy.

One

An Overview of Therapies

Perfect health is a myth. You can seldom find a man whose body is in perfect health. Some sort of major or minor ailment is always lurking behind. In the similar way, a perfectly healthy mind is also a myth. Modern studies in mental health problems clearly indicate that it is almost impossible to find a man or a woman with a perfectly healthy mind. Some abnormality, some disorder or defect is always present. Since there is more knowledge available about physiology than about psychology, the physical diseases get easily and quickly detected, than the mental ones. Mental abnormalities come to light only when they have acquired serious form and have become almost incurable. For this reason it becomes essential to detect and tackle mental diseases from the very initial stage. Or better still, adopt a life style which does not allow these mental problems to come up at all. This is where the Indian system of mental health and therapy can help. If properly understood and researched it can spread new hope for the suffering humanity. It can lead to a more healthy and wholesome life style and a unique and novel method for diagnosis and cure of mental ailments.

It is a vastly recognised fact that mental diseases are far more serious and have more far-reaching effects than physical ones. In physical diseases, say cancer or T.B., the patient suffers all the pain and its consequences, of course near and dear ones are also affected, but not in a serious way. Whereas in the case of mental diseases, the patient may suffer, but his family members, the neighbours and the community at large, have also to suffer the consequences of his perversions. Take the example of a psychopathic killer or a sexmaniac or pervert. They make the life of people around them, unbearable. Similarly a paranoid dominating father can have a long lasting negative effect on his wife and children, specially the young ones.

Another major problem with mental diseases is that these are often genetically caused and transmitted. A vast amount of research in Genetics has already taken place, but they have as yet not found out the real culprit—that is, which RNA factor causes these diseases or deficiencies. Genetically caused mental disorders are mental deficiency cerebral palsy, epilepsy, schizophrenia, etc. These are much more dangerous and harmful than the killer physical diseases like cancer. They may lie dorment for two three or four generations and then suddenly surface in the next generation. These genetic effects are said to last for as long as seven generations.

Upto the present, the close of twentieth century, there is no cure for genetically caused mental diseases like cerebral palsy or schizophrenia in its various forms. But psychiatry, a branch of medical sciences, treats many of these with chemotherapy.

The major therapies available to the Western therapist are as follows:—

- Bio-medical Therapies
  - (i) Electro convulsive therapy ECT.
  - (ii) Psychosurgery.
  - (iii) Chemotherapy.
- Psychodynamic Therapies
  - (i) Freud's classical psychoanalysis.
  - (ii) Neo-Freudians.
  - (iii) Others like Jung Adler Erickson etc.
- Behaviour Therapies
  - (i) Based on classical conditioning of Pavlov.
  - (ii) Instrumental conditioning of Skinner.
  - (iii) Modelling.
- Humanistic Existential Therapies
  - (i) Client centered therapy of Carl Rogers.
  - (ii) Gestalt therapies.
  - (iii) Existential therapies and TA.
- Cognitive Therapies
  - (i) Rational Emotive therapy of Ellis.
  - (ii) Cognitive therapy of Beck.
  - (iii) Self-instructional therapy of MEICHENBAUM.
  - (iv) Reality therapy of William Glasser.

Biomedical therapies come under the field of Psychiatry. The three main techniques used in Psychiatry are electric shock or electro-convulsive therapy, Neurosurgery and Chemotherapy.

Electro-convulsive or electric shock therapy as it is more popularly known, is a very old method. There is a description of a Unani medical man under the Roman empire. This medical man who was a surgeon used to tie a special type of fish on the temple of the patient which produced convulsions in the patient. This treatment was used for the cases of severe headache. Then there is the mention of another physician, in England in 1781. He was a court-physician of King George the third. By chance this court-physician administered a larger do larger dose than required, of camphor, to a patient of camphor than required, to a patient. The patient started shivering. Later on, this physician, Oliver found that this chance treatment brought about an improvement in the patient, both physically and mentally.

From 1930 to 1950 ECT was used extensively. It was given in most mental hospitals for depression and melancholia. In this treatment some electrodes are placed at the temples of the patient. An electric current of 70 to 160 volts is then applied to the brain for one second or half second. The patient experiences a severe shock, body is convulsed and he loses consciousness. The body of the patient is at first tense, rigid and later on becomes lipid. This total process takes only one minute or even less. Then the patient becomes unconscious. After sometime (this time differs from patient to patient) he wakes up but cannot remember anything. In the beginning of this therapy, i.e., 30s and 40s, these shocks were given for weeks and months continuously. But now the physicians have become wary of the after-effects. Nowadays a patient is given at the most ten shocks and these are given after a gap of 20 or 3 days.

ECT is clearly effective in certain cases such as deep depression and melancholia. But it is being used either in very serious cases or when other milder treatments show no results. Previously electric shocks were given in the cases of schizophrenia also, but now it is found that these are not very effective. In cases of manic-depressive psychoses only in depressive phase shocks are given and they help in reducing this phase. Nearly 90 per cent cases of manic depressive psychosis improved with this treatment.

Most of the specialists agree that electric shock is effective in cases of involutional melancholia also. But how exactly it works is not yet clearly known. According to some it effects the brain cells, for others it works on the limbic system of CNS. Still others believe it to be just a psychological or superficial effect, which works only because the patient thinks it is working on him. A case from a hospital in England was cited by Friedberg (1976). He mentions that for two years the shocks were given to the patients and they were getting well also, when after two years it was discovered that the machine had not been working and there were no shocks at all. After this, an experiment was conducted by Lambourn and Gill (1978). In this experiment a group of melancholic patients were made to go through all the processes associated with ECT, but only half of them were given actual shock. It was found that there was no difference in the rate of recovery and other effects in both the groups. This experiment clearly shows that improvements are the result of a psychological effect. Nowadays the use of ECT has decreased, because of its negative after effects. A special harmful effect is seen on memory. At first the immediate memory of the patient becomes dull. The patient remains as if in a lost sort of state. Later on sometimes even the long-term memory is damaged, and there is no new memory. The other negative after-effects are vertigo and loss of appetite. Some specialists are of the opinion that in ECT brain tissues suffer a permanant damage. Famous author Earnest Hemmingway went through electric shocks twice. He described the experience of shock as very painful "My head, my memory which were my assets were destroyed". After just one month of taking ECT second time, Hemmingway committed suicide.

Due to the reports of harmful after effects, the use of ECT has considerably decreased since 1950. Now it is being used in difficult and rare cases only and that also after much delibration. Still some greedy unscrupulous psychiatrists go on using it because of personal profit only. The experimenters and physicians in 80s and 90s are trying to find ways and means by which the beneficial effects of ECT may be increased and the harmful effects may be minimized. All in all, ECT is still a very powerful technique in the hands of the psychiatrist.

Psychosurgery

As the name implies, it is surgery which is performed to help in some psychological problem. It may be done on any part of the Central Nervous System either brain or the Spinal Cord. Surgery is used as a last resort in cases where all other methods have failed. The importance of Psychosurgery in treatment of mental diseases increased in 1930-40 when new techniques of surgery were discovered. Now, of course, the latest techniques are in use. But it is still considered 'the last resort'.

Psychosurgery can be of many types. We shall take up some only.

Prefrontal Lobotomy

This is the oldest techniques. In this the connections between the frontal lobe and the rest of the brain are severed. This is done on very aggressive and not controllable cases of mania. This shows result in transformed behaviour of the patient. He becomes quiet and sociable. But it has its negative points. Sometimes after the operation the patient becomes indifferent, unenergetic, devoid of feelings. They are called human vegetation or even the living corpse. They can do nothing. Due to these drastic effects the use of lobotomy has become rare since 1950.

Surgery of the Limbic System

It was started around 1940. Today laser beams, ultra-sound technique help the surgeon to reach the exact spot where trouble lies. This exact location helps in considerably reducing the damage to surrounding brain tissues. New studies indicate that in acute melancholia, obsessive-compulsive psychoses and anxiety cases, this technique can be very helpful. But one thing should be clear that this also is the last resort, to be used only when all other methods have failed.

Chemotherapy

When the treatment is done with medicines or chemicals, it is known as chemotherapy. This method is being used most extensively now. There are various reasons for this:—

- Chemicals or medicines are easily available.

- The intake is easier, the patient just swallows the pill.
- There is more knowledge about chemicals due to advertisements.
- Many tranquilizers and anti-depressant drugs are available in the market even without prescription.
- Sleeping pills, etc., have become a part of daily medicines for some. Tea or coffee are stimulants.

Chemotherapy helps in many types of mental problems. These are most effective in emotional problems, in manic depressive disorder in its cyclic form and some behavioural disorders. Many types of anti-psychotic drugs are found helpful. The market is flooded with anxiety reducers and tension relieving drugs, because these are the demands of modern age.

There are some pre-conditions for the use of chemotherapy—

- The drugs are habit-forming, so there should be drug-holidays, so that the habits are not formed.
- The effects of drugs on human beings should be pre-determined and their antidotes found, so that there is no problem afterwards.
- Sale of harmful drugs should be checked. They should not be sold without medical prescription, not even sleeping pills.
- Self-medication is to be avoided at all costs.

The latest example of chemotherapy is the use of thorazine in the treatment of Schizophrenia. A Swedish psychiatrist Dr. Arvid Carlsson (1967) suggested the use of Thorazine, which according to Carlsson, works as resister of Dopamine. Dopamine is a bio-chemical transmitter which transmits messages in the brain. During twenty years millions of Schizophrenic patients were administered Thorazine. Soon the harmful effects started showing, only 40 per cent showed limited improvement 30 per cent had to repeat the treatment and 30 per cent were declared as treatment-resistant cases. Out of the 40 per cent showing limited improvement had one or more of these effects, physical disability-dragging, lack of feelings, listlessness-throwing hands and feet, social alienation etc.

Due to these ill-effects SANDOZ, a pharmaceutical company of Switzerland introduced a new drug named Clozapine, in 1980. The main characteristic of Clozapine is that it does not have negative after-effects, the company claims. Clozapine helps in reducing schizophrenic symptoms, specially inactivity. But it is very expensive as the patient has to be constantly under the care of the medical team, frequent blood tests are required.

So it can be expected that a dreadful mental disease like Schizophrenia can be controlled by chemotherapy, and the after-effects may also be controlled later on.

Psychodynamic Therapies

This is the oldest therapy and is still prevalent. Modern Psychotherapy originates with the great SIGMUND FREUD. Freud discovered the unconscious, analyzed the dreams and invented, rather re-invented 'sex'. His talking out method revolutionized the whole concept of psychotherapy.

The history of modern psychotherapy begins with Freud and his psychoanalysis. Freud was a medical man. During the year 1895 he was trying to treat cases of Hysteria along with Bleuler in Vienna. Here he chanced upon a case which is now famous in psychoanalytic circles as the case of "Miss Anna O". From this case Freud found that the source of hysteria lies in the emotional resistence of the patient. By the talking out method, this emotional barrier or resistence is removed, old experiences are lived again, this acts as a cathartic process, which releases the long repressed emotions, the emotional block vanishes and thus the symptoms of disease also vanish. This was the little seed, which became, with time a mighty tree of psychoanalysis, which is flourishing even today.

Freud was a trained medical man, who was more interested in treating the cases of hysteria and other mental diseases. He had a flourishing practice in Vienna. In 1938 the Nazis burnt his library and he had to flee to London to save .his life. In 1939 he died of cheek cancer. Most of his writings, case-records, dairies etc. were burnt down, only those writings which had already escaped to England and America are now available.

What is Freud's Psychoanalysis?

Volume after volume are being written or had been written about psychoanalysis. Here we can just give a glance into the whole vast and deep theory.

There are three forms of psychoanalysis—

- It is a complete theory of personality development.
- It is a total and comprehensive philosophy about human nature.
- It is a tested and tried method of psychotherapy.

The momentous historical contributions of Psychoanalysis are—

- It gave the concept of 'unconscious' and made unconscious processes the basis of all human behaviour.
- The foundations of all adult life are laid down during infancy, which are impossible or near impossible to change later in life.
- This theory helps in understanding mental life of man and how this understanding can lead to elimination of mental disorders.
- Psychoanalysis for the first time emphasized the inner dynamics of man—how internal conflicts and anxieties lead man to develop various mechanisms of defense.
- Psychoanalysis tries to reach the inner most recesses of the human unconscious.
- The main techniques of psychoanalysis are free association, dream analysis, transference process and slips of everyday life.

Personality Theory According to Freud

Freud gave a three tiered theory of personality structure. These are named as Id, Ego and Superego. These are not the separate galleries of a mansion, rather these are the intertwined, inter-acting processes of a total whole. Personality is a totality comprising of these three internal systems. Of these Id is the biological component, Ego is the psychological 'I' and Super-ego is the socio-cultural aspect.

ID— ID literally means 'it'. It is named 'it' because it is so primitive and secondly man does not want to recognize it as his own, within himself that is why 'it'. Id has been likened to the molten lava within a volcano where primitive wishes and desires are present in their original form. Our society builds up a crust on the mouth of the volcano to repress these wishes and desires. They may he dormant but they never die and come up in the form of dreams, slips of pen and tongue, babblings of the mentally ill people etc.

The only principle governing ID is hedonism or seeking pleasure. It wants immediate gratification of its needs, without any other consideration. It has been likened to a spoilt brat who always wants his own wishes fulfilled. It never grows up, never changes. It is the reservoir of all mental energies, emotional, creative tendencies flow from it. It comprises 7/8th of total mind. It is unconscious no one knows that one has such a thing within himself. Before Freud, no one thought such a thing existed, but Freud, on the basis of his clinical studies, proved it beyond all doubt.

Ego— It is the core of personality or that aspect of personality which is put up for facing the society. It is the doer, the administrator, which controls and regulates behavior. While ID was always there, Ego develops gradually from the age of two or two and half years. It forms the core of personality. It has to face three masters, the Id with its perpetual demand for gratification of its needs, the Superego with its strict norms and the external world, the society with its controls.

Ego is conscious, its basic function is to establish harmony between the inner needs and outside demands. Its main principle is reality, which means it has to fulfill and curb according to the reality it faces. It is always conscious of outside reality. Its force or instrument is the intellectual faculty.

Superego— This is actually an extension of the Ego, which is built on the basis of socio-cultural norms. This demands that the ego act on the basis of justice morality, ideas of good and bad, right or wrong. This is concerned more with moral ideals than with reality. It is neither hedonistic like Id, nor realistic like Ego. It demands total adherence to the ideals. The moral preachings of parents and teachers are integrated into it. Superego controls the blind demands of the Id and leads realistic Ego to idealism. It is the inner norm or judge which dispenses justice in the form of praise and blame. The rewards it gives are self-praise, self-importance, self-esteem, and the punishment is in the form of guilt feelings and a sense of inferiority.

This three tier theory of structure of personality is generally accepted now in general psychology also.

Psychoanalysis on Human Nature

The view of human life, as presented by Freud and others is deterministic, pessimistic, mechanical and reductionist. According to this view, man is moved by non-rational tendencies, represented by unconscious. It is deterministic in the sense that according to Freud the basic structure or foundation of personality is laid in first five years of life and it is impossible to change it later. It is the first stage of psycho-sexual development of the libido. The total mental energy or libido is limited and it is divided between Id, Ego and Superego, thus more energy to one means less energy to the other. Freud reduced all human behaviour to certain basic tendencies or instincts. There are two basic instincts : the Eros-love and Thanotos-destruction. Love and hate-creating and destroying are the two sides of the same coin.

The greatest contribution of Freud to mankind has been his discovery of the unconscious. Human thinking has never been the same since Freud happened. Freud proved the existence of the unconscious by his innumerable studies. The following are given as proofs of unconscious:—

- The first and the foremost dreams are the evidence of unconscious, where the repressed wishes and desires come up in symbolic forms.
- The small slips of pen and tongue in daily life and minor ommissions in behaviour.
- Post-hypnotic suggestions.
- Material obtained from free association.
- Material obtained from projective techniques.

Therapy According to Freud

All mental disorders and problems are caused by unconscious wishes desires and conflicts. Freud compared human mind to an iceberg, the major portion of which lies buried under the ocean. In the human mind only one-eighth is conscious while seven of eight parts are buried in the unconscious. The conscious part of the mind does not know about the existence of the unconscious. This unconscious consists of the primitive wishes and desires. Here lie buried all the traumatic experiences of the individual, for example, no one remembers his own birth. It is a traumatic experience for the infant and is buried underground. Then all the repressed wishes and desires find place in the unconscious. All these experiences which are beyond the consciousness are also beyond its control.

So the therapeutic process in psychoanalysis consists in bringing the unconscious material upto the conscious level. When these unconscious wishes and desires become conscious, it is possible to control and select them. Treatment means making manifest all the hidden meanings of the repressed material, for these repressed wishes are the barriers in the way of mental health.

The Concept of Anxiety in Psychoanalysis

According to Psychoanalysis anxiety is a state of mental tension. Tension serves two purposes, first is activity-arousal or initiating an activity so that, as a result of this activity, tension is removed; secondly, it serves as a warning signal. Anxiety warns the Ego that if it does not act now, the crisis will be accelerated, and the Ego will be drowned. Then the Ego tries various rational intellectual ways and means to control anxiety, if it fails in conscious intellectual methods, then the Ego employs some unrealistic, non-rational methods. These unconscious methods are known as defense mechanisms or mechanisms of Ego-defense.

Anxiety is of three types according to psychoanalysis—

Real Anxiety— When it comes from some external source and is in proportion to the source.

Abnormal Anxiety— Here the source of anxiety lies within, it is that the repressed primitive unwanted and undesirable tendencies may show up, and one may be reprimanded from outside (society etc.) due to them.

Moral Anxiety— It arises from the Superego. The Ego is always apprehensive that it may not go against the moral code of conduct laid down by oneself.

Defense Mechanisms

As we have seen above, whenever Ego is in danger and is not able to overcome that danger with rational ways and means, it often employs irrational childish ways and means to overcome the danger. The purpose of these means is to provide timely relief.

These means help the Ego in facing the danger. These are not necessarily maladaptive. They may have adjustment value, only if these are not the means of escaping reality. All defense mechanisms have two characteristics:—

(i) They deny or distort reality.
(ii) They work on the unconscious level.

Which defense mechanisms a person employs, depends on two main factors—one, his level of mental development and two, the degree or intensity of anxiety faced.

So Freud's doctrine is one of tension-reduction and a state of harmony within, which is gained with the help of the defense mechanism. Some of the main defense mechanisms are:—

Denial— Just deny, don't accept as real, whatever is threatening, burying one's head in the sand during sand-storm like an ostrich.

Projection— One projects outside, on to the others, whatever is non-acceptable or undesirable in one self.

Fixation— It means the person is fixed at some particular stage of his psycho-sexual development. Development means that the individual seeks to become self dependent. But in fixation his development is fixated at a certain stage, he cannot get out of this fixation and is permanently dependent on parents or others. He does not want to be independent, he wants to be near his mother or father, for ever.

Regression— Literally regression means 'going back'. When some problematic or traumatic situation arises, the person goes one step lower on the developmental ladder.

Rationalisation— When the 'ego' is hurt or belittled in his own eyes, it tries to find good reasons or excuses for the lapse. It is a sort of self deception, for example, cursing fate for failure.

Sublimation— It is the best and civilized way of finding outlets for primitive repressed tendencies, for example, channellizing aggressiveness in competitive sports, or infantile attachment to mother to goddess worship.

Displacement— If one has some strong feelings for others but cannot express them due to fear or social sanctions he gives vent to these feelings by letting it out on others.

Repression— Just bury all undesirable, anxiety producing

feelings in the deep ocean of unconscious. To Freud repression is the basic defense mechanism.

Reaction-formation— Doing just the opposite of what is really inside—sweet talk for those you hate or the child who really hates the new sibling shows extra affection for him.

These are in short some of the more important mechanisms of Ego defense. There are many more, which can be detected.

Development of Personality: According to Freudian Theory

The developmental viewpoint is the main contribution of Freud and Psychoanalysis. Freud takes development in the sense of psycho-sexual stages. There are three stages in psycho-sexual development of a person, according to the seat of sexual pleasure. These are known as oral stage, anal stage and phallic stage. All these three stages are covered upto the age of five. After that there is childhood or pre-puberty stage. This is called the latent stage, where all previous development lies sleeping and is given a stability. Then again comes the stage of upheaval, known as puberty or adolescence.

Modern therapists as a whole accept this scheme of development laid down by Freud, because it is through a knowledge of these stages that one can know tendencies, normality and abnormality requirements, personal and social processes, their dysfunctions etc. An obstruction or barrier at any stage means defective and abnormal adjustment at later stages. It is during these stages that healthy or disordered behaviour patterns are formed.

According to Freudian viewpoint three main areas of social and personal development are fully laid down in first five years of a person's life. These three areas are:—

(i) Love and trust—interpersonal exchange of both.
(ii) Facing and coping with negative tendencies.
(iii) A positive acceptance of sexual feelings in oneself.

Aims of Psychoanalytic Therapy

According to Freud himself, the aim of psychoanalysis is 'helping the individual in gaining self-knowledge' so that he may have better self-control. In the words of Freud—"Where Id was, let Ego be." In general terms it means that in place of uncontrolled repressed tendencies, the overt, controlled, socially acceptable, Ego tendencies develop.

In short, aims of Psychoanalytic therapy are as follows—

- Leading the person towards greater psychological maturity.
- Controlling primitive tendencies, consequently better self-control.
- Seeking harmony between biogenic needs and social reality.
- In seeking this harmony there is a conflict between pleasure and reality—one has to weigh and compromise.
- Trying to find indications of abnormality in infantile experiences.
- Eliminating anxiety, the most prominent symptom of abnormality.
- Increasing ego-strength, decreasing pressure from repressed desires, so that the patient may find mental strength to improve himself.
- Increasing insight so that the patient may understand his inner needs and regulate them.

According to Freud Psychoanalytic therapy may end in two ways:—

1. When the patient gets rid of the symptoms and is free of his inner conflicts and emotional blockings.
2. When the analyst decides that all the repressed material has come out in the conscious, the inner blocks have vanished and the symptoms of the disease will not recur.

The actual procedure of psychoanalysis comprises the following—

Free Association, is also known as 'the talking out method'.

Dream analysis

According to Freud, during sleep the conscious mind relaxes. The censor is less careful. The inner material repressed wishes and desires, which are denied access during waking hours can come up. Thus, dreams prove to be very helpful in giving information about unconscious material. Freud called dreams "The Royal road to unconscious." But even in dreams the primitive repressed wishes and desires cannot surface in their original form. They have to take a disguised symbolic form. Dreams are not clear and it is difficult to trace 'latent content' from "the manifest content". The symbols occuring in dreams are mostly universal, that is, they are common to all mankind everywhere, some are socio-cultural. Symbols also occur in myths and legends, art, poetry, etc. Dreams reveal long standing emotional problems, as well as current conflicts.

Transference— This is a very prominent process in psycho-analysis. Transference here means that during the process of therapy serious and strong acute feelings emerge for the therapist. The feelings may be positive or negative—love or hostility. According to Freud these are the basic attitudes of the child towards his parents or grand parents which are now transferred towards the therapist. Now therapist can understand and change them into positive attitudes.

Interpretation— This is the basic technique in Psycho-analysis. Modern therapists call it re-learning or re-training. This process runs along free association or dream analysis. Here interpretation means giving "a conscious meaning to the unconscious material". The therapist has fragments of 'told' material, from these scattered fragments he has to reach the unsaid or hidden material. This type of interpretation gives the patient awareness about his own self and he can make improvements, treatment and change of behaviour now becomes possible. But what is to be interpreted?

- The resistences in the patient, by which he tries to keep the hidden material repressed.
- His needs and conflicts, his personal dynamics.
- The process of transference, with a view to resolving it.
- A constant search and interpretation, so that change is made possible.

Interpretation, at any level, should be deep and wide-ranging. It should come at the appropriate time at the time the dream is narrated, not two months after the dream. Another thing to remember is that the patient must have attained the understanding and maturity to understand this interpretation. If this type of preparedness is not there, interpretation can do more harm than good.

Psychoanalysis after Freud

Freud had many students and co-workers. Some of them started to rebel even in his life time. The first ones to part ways were Alder, Jung and Otto Rank etc. Later Horney, Fromm, Sullivan also separated. The basic difference was on the following points:—

- They were all against the over-emphasis on sexuality and biological basis.
- They did not accept a mechanical and deterministic view of human life.
- They put more emphasis on socio-cultural and interpersonal factors.
- They do not accept a man as just a biological machine, they regard man as a social being.
- They all agree on the basic tenets given by Freud and work within the framework of psychoanalysis. There are differences among themselves, but they are collectively known as neo-Freudians.

Main Points of Difference and Similarity between Psychoanalytic theory of Freud and Indian Psycho-therapy. Indian psychotherapy here means Ayurvedic system of psychotherapy.

Differences

The Basic Concepts— Freud lays emphasis of the biological nature of man, his instinctual needs and desires while the Indian system although not denying lower instincts, emphasises higher or spiritual nature of man.

Sexuality— Sexuality is the central theme of Freud's theory around which the whole mental life revolves. The Indian viewpoint does not deny sexuality, it just accepts it as a basic need and as a part of human nature.

Unconscious— Freud invented unconscious. It is unique to him. Indian system does not have any idea about unconscious.

Psycho-sexual Development of Personality— This concept also is an original one in Freud and is not found in Indian system.

The Structure of Personality— Freud suggested a three tiered structure of personality in Id, Ego and Superego. Indian system does not present any such structure of personality.

The techniques of dream analysis and free association are not found in Indian system although transference is found in a very different context, as we shall see later chapters........

Similarities in Both the Systems

- Both the systems lay emphasis on the need to increase the ego strength of the patient.
- Aim of therapy according to both is an acceptance of oneself in totality, with all positive and negative points.
- Both accept the importance of insight which means looking within' and understand one's own nature. With increased insight there is better control over oneself, which means gradual inprovement in mental functioning. Means for this insight are different in both.
- Both stress the need for emotional stability in maintaining mental health, as also of getting rid of inner conflicts.
- Both systems give prime importance to harmony in mental life for Freud between conscious and unconscious and for the Indian system, inside and outside and sides or aspects of mental life.

Carl Jung

Jung was Freud's favourite and was named as a successor after him. But he parted ways with Freud in his life time, which pained Freud a lot. Jung had a very long life-term of work, which established him as a renowned psycho-analyst. He takes the basic tenets of Freudian theory but disagrees with him on several important points. The points of departure are the following—

About Human Nature

Unlike Freud, Jung regards human life as purposive is Human life not as purposive. Human life is not just biological or sexual development as is envisaged by Freud. To Jung all human life and development has a purpose. Human life is not a string of interrelated events. It has goals and moves towards those goals. Thus, Jung gave a positive optimistic and creative view of human life. The ultimate aim of human life is self-realization. The present is not governed determined by past only, it is also governed by the future.

About Unconscious

Jung described two levels of unconscious. One, personal unconscious, which is a person's own wishes and desires his own experiences, specially those experiences which were painful to the ego and hence, were buried under the conscious level. These are emotional and instinctual tendencies on a primitive level. This level is the same as Freud described the unconscious. The other level, according to Jung, is the collective or racial unconscious. This is the original concept given by Jung. To him this racial unconscious contains the memories of the whole mankind. These are always being transmitted from one generation to the other. The main collective memories are stored there in the form of archetypes. Archetypes are actually signs or symbols found in all humans. These universal symbols recur in dreams, in myths, arts and culture. They contain the wealth of generations of human intelligence and help in further advancement of mankind. The child, the mother, the wise old man are some of the common symbols or universal archetypes found in all religious myths and art, also in dreams.

Persona

Persona is the outward social mask taken by the Ego. The persona is determined by the role the person has to play in his social life. This is a sort of outer social covering of the Ego. Under this covering the ego strives for social adjustment and finding social approval.

Duality Within Personality— Anima the inner woman, Animus, the inner man. According to Jung every person has a man and a woman within him. If he is a man outside, a woman lies there in his subconscious mind, similarly if she is a woman, there is a man hidden in her mind. Here man and woman of course mean mental qualities or tendencies. The whole personality is an integration of these two. This is something like the concept of Ardhanarishwar in Indian myths.

The Flow or Direction of Mental Energy

Introvert, extrovert, if the mental energies are directed within oneself, then the person is said to be an introvert, if these are directed towards the world outside, he is said to be an extrovert. This duality was first presented by Jung and is now accepted in general personality theory.

Four Basic Mental Processes

These basic mental processes are common to all human beings, but there is predominance of one process in every one. These basic mental processes are—

Rational— these people follow logic, are objective and unbaised.

Emotional— emphasize their own emotions, not reason or logic.

Sensorial— have acute sensibilities.

Insightful— take in the whole, the gist the inside of things.

Jung laid stress on the creative abilities of man. The aim of therapy according to him, is taking the patient towards self-realization. Thus, the theory of Jung is positive, creative and elavating, not deterministic or mechanical.

There are many similarities in Jung's theory and Indian system of psychotherapy. The main point is in laying more emphasis on positive creative side of human life. Second is a concept of human life as purposive, not merely biological. Then both the systems emphasize self realization as the goal of therapy. His use of symbols and archetypes are also found in Indian system, as we shall see in later chapters. Other neo-Freudians need not be discussed in detail at this stage. They will be discussed at relevant points.

Two Ramifications of Psychoanalysis

After Freud and the rebels there emerged two prominent branches of Psychoanalysis.

Ego-psychologists

They also take up Freudian analysis as their take-off point, but are against the over-emphasis on sex and instinctual nature of man. They emphasize the role of Ego in human behaviour. According to them Ego is not just a poor sandwich between the Id and the environment. It also performs other normal mental functions such as perception memory, thinking, which are tension-free. Ego performs the adjustive functions adjustment of human values and social life. According to them Ego has to play a positive role. It has to adopt to explore and conquer his world. It does not merely run away from pan, it strives for higher aims also. According to Ego-psychologists, the purpose of therapy is to explore the channels to regulate and control behaviour, and to understand the many unconscious forces which influence human behaviour.

Erik Erikson (1964) is a very important psychologist among the post-Freudian Ego-psychologists. He mainly discussed the stages of development of human personality. According to Erikson Ego is known to develop between two poles—one how he feels himself and two how others feel about him. If one know oneself he develops a sense of association and assimilation. It also gives continuity to the stages of development how, future emerges from the past. In the stages of development each stage is closely linked with the other.

According to Erikson there are eight (8) stages of human development, three during first five years of life and five in later years. Each stage here denotes the development of some specific mental trait. For example, the first stage which is equivalent to Freud's oral stage, is the stage of trust, the crisis being that of trust and mistrust. If the infant at this stage feels himself wanted and loved, they develop the positive side or trust. The second stage Erikson called the autonomy stage. The child wants to be independent he wants to dominate and control his environment. This gives him a sense of adequacy and self-dependance. It may be a period of rebellion also. At this time the child should be given independence and also support, let him experiment, they should learn interdependence in a healthy way.

The third stage, parallel to Freud's phallic stage, is called the stage of 'initiative'. The main conflict here is initiative or guilt complex. Here the child learns primary skills, identity with gender-role, moral standards and discipline of primary tendencies. All these 3 stages are gone through in first five years of life. The five stages after this are:—

1. Latent stage (5-11 yrs) Industry Vs. Inferiority
2. Adolescence (12-18 yrs) Identity Vs. Role
3. Early youth (19-24 yrs) Intimacy Vs. Loneliness
4. Youth (25-40 yrs) Production Vs. Stability
5. Adult age (40 onwards) Ego organisation Vs. Depression.

It is not possible to go into the details of all these stages. Erikson called them the stages of psycho-social development of man. He discussed these stages in detail in his book *Childhood and Society* (1964). Erikson had his own system of therapy also, based on these stages.

Psychoanalytically Oriented Psychotherapy

This is the third form of classical psychoanalysis. It was meant to make the process of therapy brief and more effective. The propounders of this form were Alexander and French (1964) of the Chicago school. They accept the basic premises, but depart from it in many details. In this process there is no coach (for patients to relax) no free association, no dream analysis. This a brief therapy. It has also been used in crisis intervention by Caplan (1964), Sifneos (1971). In place of structuring the total personality, they seek brief and focussed solutions to acute immediate problems. Modern psychoanalytic therapy is no longer 'the coach' and the long drawn out procedure. It now has sleek and compact techniques, far removed from classical Freudian therapy.

This therapy is quite close to Indian system in the emphasis on ego functions and positive role in striving for higher aims of life. They both recommend a control and regulation of behaviour for better adjustment to the outside world. They also believe that psycho-social and cultural factors play a greater role in human life than biological factors.

Behaviour Therapy

This is a recent therapy of American origin. It emerged out of the behaviour theory of Watson (1924). Behaviour therapy is, "The use of experimentally established principles of learning for the purpose of changing unadaptive behaviour. Unadaptive habits are weakned and eliminated, adaptive habits are initiated and strengthened."

—*Wolpe, 1969*

This therapy has also been called (behaviour modification) and (behaviour intervention). This is concerned with outward behaviour and has nothing to do with interval conditions, personal feelings or unconscious factors. Two forms of behaviour therapy are in use— (1) Pavlov's classical method (2) Skinner's instrumental method.

The word 'behaviour therapy' was first used by Lindzey and Skinner in connection with changing of abnormal behaviour. This therapy gained popularity during 50s. From 1950 to 1980, it gained immense popularity, so much so that behaviour modification techniques became a necessary addition to all types of modern psychological clinics. It has the sanction of modern psychotherapists. Its basic techniques are—conditioning, deconditioning, reconditioning and reciprocal inhibition therapy.

Behaviouristic View about Human Nature

This a wholly scientific objective theory. Its basic assumption is that behaviour is systematic and by well-planned experimentally controlled methods, the laws determining behaviour can be ascertained. This method is based on direct objective data. It has no philosophical notions about human nature. Human behaviour is determined by socio-cultural factors. Behaviour is learned with the help of biological equipment and environmental forces. Man here becomes a 'response machine'. But the modern behaviour therapy is neither mechanical nor is it deterministic. They accept the choice, the decision, the growth of the patient. Thus, behaviour therapy branched into two:—

1. Classical behaviour therapy of Watson which is mechanical and deterministic.
2. More liberal behaviour therapy of Skinner & Co.

The behaviour therapy rests on the principle that all behaviour is learnt, unadaptive or abnormal behaviour is also learnt, and so it can be 'un-learned', new better adaptive behaviour can be learnt. This is a process of learning per se by which new reactions are learnt.

The therapist in behaviour therapy acts (1) as a teacher, (2) as a director (3) as an expert. He controls and manipulates to change other's (patient's) behaviour. He acts as a reinforcer, gives rewards for desirable and punishment for undesirable behaviour. He also acts as a role-model for the patients. (Here we can find a similarity with Indian system) Knowingly or unknowingly the patient adopts the values beliefs attitudes and behaviour of the therapist.

Methods and Techniques of Behaviour Therapy

The most important contributions of behaviour therapy are providing to the clinician objective and experimentally tested methods and techniques, which can go on improving. Thus, trial and error is used for improvements in these techniques. This is a self correcting system where techniques can be used, their outcome evaluated. Some of the main techniques are—

Systematic Desensitization

This is used for removing abnormal anxiety. The patient gradually learns to be de-sensitized to a difficult anxiety producing situation. Wolpe (1958) used it for associating pleasant experiences with phobias or anxiety producing situations. Relaxation techniques form the part of desensitization. Other techniques are implosive therapy and flooding which consist in flooding the patient with anxiety situations so that he may be deconditioned from them. Assertive training is another technique which is much in vogue in modern management circles. It seeks to improve inter-personal relations and asserting ones ownself. It can make vast difference in behaviour. It is learnt in a play way situation. Aversion technique is used mostly in cases of drug or alcohol addiction. It is very prevalent and popular. There are many other techniques life positive reinforcement, extinction, modelling, response shaping etc. which can be used according to the nature of the problems.

Behaviour therapy can be useful for a wider population where patients are poor and illiterate. It has widened the circle of psychotherapy and intervention among the masses on one side and serious psychotic patients, autistic patients and mentally deficient children and adults, on the other hand.

The critics of behaviour therapy call it a mere outer or superficial treatment which removes the symptoms, but does not reach the root cause of the disease. The roots of mental problems lie deep in the unconscious, if these are not destroyed, only symptoms are treated, then they surface again in the form of other symptoms. The behaviour therapist reply to this charge. Rachman (1967) and Wolpe (1969) did a follow-up study of the cases treated by them. They did not find the symptoms returning even in a single case. According to Rachman there are clinical and experimental evidences to show the permanent effect of this therapy. It is very successful in chronic cases of neurosis, phobia and other behaviour disorders such as stammering, enuresis, alcoholism, drug addiction, tense states etc. Rachman emphasised the fact that even when the root cause of the disorder was not known either to the therapist or the patient complete recovery and removal of symptoms was possible.

The second criticism of behaviour therapy comes from the existentialists. According to humanist existentialists, behaviour therapy can be successful in cases where higher levels of intelligence are not required. It can reach only the working level, it cannot solve the problems of those who seek 'the meaning of life' or the person who is going thru identity crisis or is suffering from a feeling of inadequacy. Behaviour therapy can give temporary relief in acute symptoms, but it cannot help a person reach his own creative heights. It cannot give self-satisfaction or self-realization.

In the end it can be said that behaviour therapy is simple clear efficient and scientific. It is progressing on the basis of experimental work. It saves much time and energy. With all its drawbacks and limitations, it has helped in mitigating sufferings of mankind to some extent. Its techniques are checked and rechecked experimentally. It is a successful method.

Humanistic Existential Psychotherapy

Since the beginning of the twentieth century there have been two opposite poles in the field of psychotherapy. One is the European trend (started by Freud) which accepts internal unconscious tendencies to be the main source of human behaviour. On the opposite pole is American tendency to emphasize external environmental factors which give rise to behaviour. Psychological counselling and therapy are also divided in these two poles. During 1950s some prominent psychologists protested against this polarization. Maslow for example, said, "there is a need, for a third force between these two poles." They wanted a more 'human' psychology. For this group of thinkers 'man is not only a response machine. He is a total being, with aims and purposes of his own. Man is not a puppet driven by unconscious tendencies, nor is he a raw material to be moulded by environmental forces. He has a will, a giving and taking pleasure, a potentiality to evolve. Self-realization is the ultimate goal of man, certain internal and external factors might have blocked the way to natural progress. The job of the therapist lies in removing these barriers to progress and help the patient proceed on his natural path. This process involves active participation and co-operation of the patient also.'

In a way this also leads upto the existential philosophy. It presents a positive optimistic view of human life. That is why it became so popular. It is also a reaction against too much of science and technology. Modern science and technology are 'dehumanising' the man. He feels insufficient, insecure and a victim of various tensions and conflicts. This is a viewpoint, a value, in Psychology.

The main premises of humanistic-existential viewpoint are—

Holism— that man is a total whole, and should be taken in totality.

Phenomenology— the perceptual personal experience of man is more important than the apparent behaviour.

Insightful, extra sensory experiences are given more importance than empirical facts.

Man's uniqueness or individuality is given a central place.

Historical or environmental factors are not so important as the values, aims and aspirations for future are.

There should be no mechanisation or atomisation of human virtues such as value, creativity, choice and self-realisation.

Man is pre-action as well as reaction. On the one hand man adapts to the environmental demands and on the other hand he has positive aims and aspirations. Uptil now, the negative side of human nature has been emphasized such as disorders maladaptations diseases etc. Now the emphasis should shift to positive values.

Man is free by nature, he has conscious and super conscious of super conscious.

Man has lost meaning in life, he is suffering from loneliness, and alienation a sort of existential void. There is an existentia existential crisis resulting in neurosis.

Humanist-existential therapy is a sort of encounter in which one communicates with another being. Both accept the sovereignty of each other and in the process man finds the meaning of his life, he is not only 'being' but 'becoming'.

The techniques of therapy differ vastly. Rollo May (1953, 58, 61) developed some specific techniques, which include the gradual awakening of self-consciousness, self-dependence, self-decision, the conscious effort to keep one's uniqueness and individuality and above all, seeking a meaning of life by the individual himself. Man is always seeking self-realization or completeness within himself.

What is Self-realization?

Abraham Maslow (1968, 1970) presented a positive view of life. According to him only the negative aspects, like abnormality, disorders, diseases were being emphasized. These negative aspects result in negative behaviour patterns. Now there should be more emphasis on the positive side. *Self-realization is a positive goal of human life.* Maslow described in detail the characteristics of self-realized people. They can face the uncertainties of life and can also take risks. They accept themselves and others. They are full of life energy and creativity. They are loners and are self-dependent and self-satisfied. They are capable of deep relationships and have tender caring attitude. They are also humourous and love joys of life. Mostly they are free of internal conflicts and make major decisions of life themselves. They go on evolving progressively.

The Humanistic existential approach has been criticized as a viewpoint, a philosophy of life. It is not a therapy and does not offer any therapeutic techniques as such.

Readers will note that this approach comes nearest to the Indian approach to mental diseases and their treatment.

Other Methods and Techniques of Psychotherapy

Logotherapy

Vienna born Victor Frankl propounded this method. Frankl had to spend three painful years of his life in the Nazi concentration camps, run by Hitler and his men during Second World War. Frankl's parents, brother and wife were killed during their stay in these camps. He somehow came out alive although he had to undergo all sorts of extreme mental and physical hardships. During this period of intense pain he tried to seek the meaning or value of life. He named his method LOGOTHERAPY (LOGOS = meaning) Actually it is a form of existentialism. This is a very simple and clear method. Therapy consists in giving deeper meanings to life and solving problems of life with new meanings to love-hate, life-death etc. According to Frankl the basic purpose of life is to find "meaning of life". This seeking of meaning of life goes deeper than the search for power, for liberation, for tension reduction. If man is unsuccessful in finding the meaning of life, he is faced with an 'existential void' and meaninglessness in life. Frankl likes to call it 'an existential vacuum'. This feeling is intensified and spreads during the difficult or stressful times. It may be or may not be accompanied by madness.

According to Frankl mental illnesses of a physical nature came within the scope of clinical psychology, but deeper problems and spiritual aspects come under Logotherapy. The problem of moral conflicts also falls under Logotherapy. In therapy the patient has to find his meaning of life for himself. This meaning is different for each individual, his uniqueness, his destiny, his heritage all come together to give a new meaning to his life. The most important factor is short span of life. If life was eternal there was no end to it, then it would not have been necessary to find any meaning to it. Then there would be no question of decisions or responsibility.

Therapeutic processes in Logotherapy consist in changing the meanings and attitudes. The patients are encouraged to grasp the meanings and responsibilities, so that they themselves change their beliefs and actions. The past and its problems are not at all important, emphasis is on present problems and future behaviour. Another thing special to this method is that the abnormal symptoms are neither removed nor eliminated, instead the attitude and viewpoint of the patient towards these problems is changed.

Frankl discussed two specific techniques of Logotherapy. One for removing phobia or phobic behaviour and contra-thought. For phobic behaviour, there is paradoxical intention, which means the patient is asked to think of the object or situation of his phobia—this is done in a very pleasant and light atmosphere. And then the patient is encouraged to laught at it "Oh ! I was afraid of this !" and thus gradually the patient overcomes his phobia. In contradictory thinking, the object of compulsion is associated with positive and pleasant wish or experience.

In short Frankl's method is one of understanding the problems of existence and facing them directly. The patient is lead towards expanded consciousness and greater responsibility. This method is neither complete nor very clear, but touches the problems of life which no other system touched.

Frankl seems to be quite close to Indian thought in two ways. Firstly, we must remember what Lord Krishna, in Bhagvatgeeta, preached to Arjuna in the battle field of Kurukshetra. He explained the meaning of life and responsibility. This is what the therapist in Frankl's system tries to do—to explain the meaning of life and of man's responsibility in life. Secondly, the modern Indian philosopher, J. Krishnamurti also talks of expanding and evolving human consciousness. This expanding of consciousness is seen as the solution of all philosophical and spiritual problems of man. This is what Frankl also says.

Gestalt Therapy

This therapy also started in Europe as a result of phenomenology and existential philosophy. The name of the propounder of this system is Frederick S. Perls. He was born in Germany and trained in medicine and psychoanalysis. When Hitler came to power in Germany Perls migrated to South Africa. Here he started practising psycho therapy and here the basic concepts emerged, which were later known as Gestalt therapy. His basic tenets are presented in his book *Ego Hunger and Aggression* (1946). It was published in England in 1947, and in USA in 1969, he wrote many more books, including an autobiography called *In and Out of the Garbage Pail* (1969).

In 1946 Perls migrated to USA, where he started many

institutions of Gestalt therapy. The end came in Vancouver in 1970. He was a forceful dramatic impressive personality, due to which the number of his followers went on increasing. The followers included general public as well as professional colleagues. The followers carried on Perl's work after him.

Gestalt therapy started as individual therapy but as it evolved, it came closer to group therapy, second special feature is that it was carried on, on normal people who were seeking solutions to their problems. It was only in later years that Perls turned towards clinics and mental patients. In this way this system works with individuals, groups and encountergroups as also in personality development groups.

The Basic Concepts of Gestalt Therapy

Perls's Gastalt therapy was born in Germany and was profoundly influenced by the Gestalt psychologists Wertheimer, Koffka, Kohler, Lewin and specially Goldstein. The Gestalt theory emphasizes Organization and relatedness, which is in contrast with reductionism of Wundt-Tichner and of mechanical behaviourism of Watson. Perls applied this theory to human life, integrating the various aspects dynamic, affective, cognitive and social in one whole and then understanding it as a total unity. Here Perls took the Holistic viewpoint of Goldstein. He stressed the adaption of the individual to his environment by organising the activities of its various organs. Perls took the help of dynamic psychoanalysis and gave new interpretations to its basic concepts. He extensively used human motives and defense mechanisms. But he differed from psychoanalysis in emphasizing the present. Here he was near existential philosophy. The centre of attraction and action to Perls lay in the field of present experiences. Perls regarded himself and his Gestalt therapy as one of three main existential viewpoints, the other two being 1. Frankl's Logotherapy and 2. Binswenger's existential analysis.

The Main Tenets of Gestalt Therapy

Man has innate capacity to evolve. This capacity or development comes with insight or a meaningful synthesis with one's environment.

To fulfill one's needs, new and meaningful needs, one must have a positive and creative interaction with his environment.

By expanding and evolving the consciousness, one can know the internal imbalances, and the efforts to remove these imbalances can be initiated.

'Biological self-regulation' is the basic mechanism in all living things.

The Aims of Gestalt Therapy

- To reestablish this self-regulatory mechanism, so that his inner energies may be aroused and he can find perfection.
- Being conscious is itself therapeutic—you are aware of your needs and also that these are to be fulfilled.
- The Gestalt therapist helps his client in becoming what he/she really is, it goes behind the games he plays and removes the outer coverings of defense.
- Therapy is the process of blossoming of potentialities, opening up and expressing feelings and emotions.
- Leading a man to his original state is the basic motive.
- Evolution, be it in life or in therapy, comes from immediate awareness. It has a preparedness to accept responsibilities.

The three main points of Gestalt therapy are:—

1. Consciousness,
2. Here and now,
3. Responsibility for actions.

Perls himself emphasized "Now". The past has gone, future has not yet arrived so live this moment now is here.

Now = Experience+consciousness+reality (Perls 1970).

So a Gestalt therapist removes the barriers in the way of self-awareness, directs immediate experience. He creates an awareness about the present in the patient by questions like what, why, when, how, for what, how it happened etc. He does not interfere in the talk of the patient, but side by side goes on creating new awareness.

Gestalt therapy has two main techniques— (1) Rules and (2) Role playing. Perls believed in gradual widening of the consciousness. "Lose your mind, and come to your senses." In role playing the patient himself plays the parts which are within himself.

Thus, he can get rid of all the guilt and shame accumulated in his mind.

All in all Gestalt therapy is valuable. It is brief and is more suitable for the groups, thus can reach a larger number of patients. It lays stress on experience. It is more suited for the problems of modern life. The complexities of life and technology today have dried up the sources of all human feeling. It seeks to rekindle these sources of feeling. Its emphasis on here and now seems to be near to the mood of modern times. Its awareness techniques are found to be very useful and are being used by other therapists also. Its practice leads to beneficial behavioural changes.

Transactional Analysis of Eric Berne

This is a newly developed technique. It is in the form of a contract into which the subject enters. Its emphasis is on rational intelligent behaviour of man. Eric Berne gave a new technique of psychotherapy in 1961, 1968, known as TA or Transactional Analysis. Transactions are the inner states where one person, his ego, plays the role of a child, an adult and the parents. Then these inner transactions are analysed.

TA presents a non-deterministic view. A person can choose, decide and can alter his own decisions. A man writes his own life script—his own internal relationships, the teachings of parents. If these states have a balanced adjustment to the environment, the situation is said to be "OK". And if the subject does not feel good and comfortable, it is said to be "non OK". Games are the roles people play in their lives, that is the role of the child (C) of adult (A) of parents (P).

In TA therapy stress is laid on developing an independent outlook and life style in the individual, which will have awareness enthusiasm and depth. In groups, persons make contracts and follow them and act on them. The person himself analyses his actions or transactions that is why it is known as transactional analysis. 'Strokes' or affectionate slapping is recognised as important in human relationships. Not only man, animals also enjoy patting. Strokes may be physical or just mental. These affectionate strokes are necessary for healthy mental development.

In recent years TA has become very popular being the most

famous technique after 1970. Its terms like strokes, encounters, 'I'm OK You'r OK' contract, life script etc., are very popular currently. It has a tendency to become just intellectual exercise. It sometimes gives over-stress on terms like OK etc.

Cognitive Therapies

The cognitive concept gained currency in psychology during 1960 and after. The concept was adopted in clinical field also, and many therapies employing cognition as base, came into existence. These therapies were diverse, some being near behaviour therapies, and others closer to Gestalt viewpoint. But the central formula underlying these therapies was one and that is : Maladaptive behaviour is the result of maladaptive thoughts, beliefs and perceptions, so for treating them it is essential to change these thoughts, beliefs and perceptions. It is actually a plan for relearning. It is called cognitive restructuring also. It is nearer to behaviouristic therapy, because here the patient is encouraged to change his irrational thoughts. There are three main techniques in cognitive therapies:—

- Rational emotive therapy—Ellis RET
- Beck's cognitive therapy.
- Meichenbaum's self instructional training.

The field of cognitive therapy is expanding due to its popularity and applicability to modern day problems. It is more useful in problems where the anxiety level is high or where low self control make a person's coping ability very weak.

Reality Therapy—RT

Reality therapy was given by William Glaser (1965, 1969, 72, 73). It is more popular among school counsellors, teachers and rehabilitation social workers. It raises some basic questions such as 'what is reality ?'

The centre of reality therapy is modern behaviour. The role of the therapist here is like a teacher's role. He presents a model and prepares the patients to face the reality, so that they may satisfy their needs without harming others. The essence of reality therapy is to recognize individual responsibility and this is mental health.

According to Glaser reality therapy takes very different theories and techniques from other traditional therapies. It consists in creating a "success identity". Glaser's therapy gained popularity because it was direct, easy and useful. It is a technique of behaviour modification. According to Glaser a patient is not only problem-ridden diseased person. He is a person with innumerable potentialities. The potentialities are to be evolved. A person has to understand himself and take responsibilities.

Glaser recognizes one need and that is the need for one's identity. One can have a success identity or a failure identity. Every one has a developmental force within, which means basically every one needs and wants development. Ultimately man is creator of himself he becomes what he wants to become.

Modern Developments

Modern techniques take two specific forms:—

Relaxation Training

Bio-feedback

Relaxation training is really popular these days. It is used to lessen the tensions of everyday life. It relieves all bodily aches and pains and also reduces mental tension. Pleasant experiences and pleasant memories are encouraged. Tranquilizing methods are used. Yoga is gaining popularity as a relaxation technique these days.

In bio-feedback, the patient learns to change his own biological processes such as heart rate, temperature etc. Under this even involuntary processes are brought under conscious control. The patient sees his own physical processes on the monitor and tries to control them. This can be a very important technique if proper training is given.

By this short and sketchy description of the Western techniques of psychotherapy, one can easily conclude that east is east and west is west. That is the ancient philosophical deep seated techniques have very little in common with the intervention techniques of today. The behavioural intervention techniques are simple but mechanical and superficial. The psychotherapies in Indian system are more deep-rooted. They do not present any common point except that both aim for a better mental health for the man.

Two

A Glimpse of Indian Psychotherapy

At the very outset let it be understood here only a brief overview of the system is being presented, to give a total view at a glance. Later on all this will be taken on separately. This overview becomes necessary, so that, even at the risk of repetition, a total perspective is retained.

Here one may also refer to the glaring differences between the Western and Indian systems. Apart from being centuries away in time dimension, there are dissimilarities in other fields also. In Western psychotherapy there are more or less definite distinct theories and each have their own specific therapies. The Indian psychotherapies are in the form of large general philosophical doctrines. You have to dive and fish them out of the vast ocean of philosophic literature, for example, of Vedas. The therapies here are hidden in the aphorisms or sutras, and most of them are in general terms with possibility of varied interpretations. There are no specific or distinct theories and connected therapies here.

Moreover the Indian system is an ancient system, perhaps the oldest in the world, whereas the Western theories and therapies are of quite recent origin, the oldest-psychoanalysis-being just over a hundred years old. The wisdom of Indian system is ingrained in a complex old language Sanskrit, which although scientifically perfect, is an out-of-use language. This makes the Indian system far away from the main stream of modern life. So while going through these systems, it will be better to keep these important points in mind, before jumping to judgements.

Here some of the Indian systems will be presented in brief and in chronological order as far as possible. The three main systems are Atharva veda, Ayurveda Charak, Sushruta, Vagabhatta, and Yoga.

The Vedic Times

The source of Indian psychotherapy can be traced back to the Vedic times. Veda means knowing or knowledge. There are four vedas—Regveda, Yajurveda, Samveda and Atharvaveda. According to the Indian belief Vedas originated from Brahma, the creator himself. No one knows the exact time or age of the creation of the Vedas. Some put it to 9 centuries BC and others of 4 century BC. The general consensus seems to be on 6-7 centuries BC. From the Creator, they were passed on in a long and continuous verbal tradition to the Rishis or sages. There appears to be a long chain of Guru-shishyas or the Rishis and their disciples, one handing down the wealth of wisdom to the other in verbal form. All this rich material was in the form of hearing and remembering for several generations that is why Vedas are also called Shruti or 'heard'.

The oldest available documents written on Bhoj patras are all later representations. In all these documents the author sages state that 'they are just the narrators or commentators of the wisdom of "such and such a Rishi, who got it from his Guru......" Not a single author in a single document says that he himself is giving this information or he has found 'this' thing.

Atharva Veda

Atharva veda contains the earliest known account in the world, of mental illnesses and their remedies. There is again controversy regarding the age of Atharva veda. According to some scholars it is the last one of the four Vedas, but according to others, it is a contemporary to Samveda. Max Muller says that the Vedas are about 4000 years old and Atharva Veda is the last in origin. Lok Manya Tilak dates Vedas from 10,000 BC.

The original name of Atharva Veda was Atharva Acngirash. It consists of the names of two Rishis—Atharva (Bhrigu) and Angiras. Later on it was shortened to more convenient Atharva Veda only. It is also known as the Amrita Veda, because it seeks to promote and sustain life through medicine. Atharva Veda is known to contain Bhaishajya or medicine, besides other Shakhas or Charanas. In all Atharva Veda contains 9 schools or shakhas—all of these are not available in written form. Only two of its shakhas are now available, others having been lost during all the elapsing 6-7 centuries.

The two available Shakhas are SHAUNAK AND PAIPPLAD. PAIPPLAD was discovered by a European Von Roth in 1875 in Kashmir.

There are 20 Kandas or divisions in Atharva Veda. Then there are subdivisions of these Kandas or books known as ANUVAKS. All of this is in verse, in SUKTAS or MANTRAS. According to Satavalekar, there are 573 Suktas and 5127 mantras in all, in Atharva Veda.

The approach of Atharva Veda is practical and psychological. It provides solutions to everyday needs and problems. It seeks to know individual self-psyche—and attain power in the world. The scope of Atharva Veda is very wide and is dealt under broad headings. Satavalekar holds that by the Atharva Veda, we get knowledge of the soul. According to him, the Atharva veda is specially related to Atma and Mana (psyche). It shows the ways and means to do everything, such as removal of illness, victory in war, through energy of Mana (psyche).

The Atharva-veda is full of philosophy and psychology. In fact, its central theme is Mana. The highest peak of Indian Philosophy—the Vedanta—originated from the Atharva veda. It states that : "There is enormous psychic energy in the universe, which is named as Brahma. Individual psyche, when united with Brahma, becomes itself full of energy. This energy can be acquired by anyone by the practices given in Atharva-veda."

Atharva Veda is psychological in nature and approach. It has suggested the practical application of psychic energy over matter. Atharva Veda covers many subjects. It aims at the welfare of humanity. It tries to help man to live a full life of one hundred years and attain Brahma (The supreme energy). As it deals with human life, the subject of abnormal behaviour and therapeutics comes under its scope. But the material is all scattered in a mixed up form. To collect, to classify and to explain it, is no easy job. Still scholars like Shende, Karambelkar, Arsh, Whitney, Max Muller, Satavalekar, R.G. Shastri etc. have all tried to do it to the best. We shall try to analyse this matter and see what Atharva Veda has to offer by way of treatment of mental diseases, always keeping in mind that the material is some thousands of years old.

Ayurveda

As stated earlier, Ayurveda forms a part or section of Atharva Veda, so the fundamental ideas of Atharva Veda are naturally incorporated in Ayurveda.

Ayurveda is the science of life (Ayu=life + veda = science). It has been regarded as an Upaveda by Sushruta, Vagabhatta and Mahabharata. Brahmavaivarta Purana states that Brahma created the Ayurveda as the fifth veda. It is generally admitted that the Ayurveda is a Vedanga, Upveda or Upang of the Atharva Veda.

There seems to be a long history behind the origin of Ayurveda, on which there is agreement among scholars upto a point and then there are differences afterwards. As stated above Brahma, the Creator is said to have created Ayurveda. Brahma taught it to Daksha Prajapati, who in turn, imparted it to the Ashwini Kumar twins. From them it was learnt by Indra. Upto this point there is agreement about the origin. Indra was approached by Bhardwaj Muni with a request to learn Ayurveda. Bhardwaj was the first mortal to learn it from Indra. Then Bhardwaj Muni taught it to a few deserving disciples. One of these disciples was Atreya Punarvasu. Then Atreya Punarvasu taught it to six of his disciples. Thus through these Rishis the knowledge of Ayurveda was spreading all over India.

At about 7th century AD an All Aryavrata Ayurveda Congress was held somewhere in Himalayas. Here it was decided to write and preserve the teachings of Atreya. Several texts were prepared accordingly. Out of these texts, the one prepared by Agnivesha was held to be the best by the assembled Rishis. So Agnivesha's text became the standard text for Ayurveda at that time.

As time went by several commentaries of Agnivesha were also written. At present three exponents of Ayurveda are regarded as unrivalled in their respective fields. These are : Charak in therapeutics, Sushruta in surgery and Vagabhatta in general principles of medicine. The three Samhitas in their names—Charak Samhita, Sushruta Samhita and Ashtanga Sangraha are famous by the name BRIHADATRAYI or 'the three great ones' in Ayurvedic parlance.

Ayurveda presents a holistic, patient-oriented approach. It is not disease oriented study or diagnosis based on symptoms.

It studies the patient in body and mind. It also gives a life-style adopted to maintain good health. Ayurveda is the knowledge of life. It emphasizes the need to keep a healthy mind, body and soul. It is also environment-friendly, in that, it lays stress on the need to live in constant harmony with nature. It included herbs and other natural processes in its therapy like Panchkarma, or sun-bath.

According to Ayurveda each individual has a specific Prakriti or Canstitution. It suggests a Ritucharya, acting according to seasons and Dinacharya best way of adopting a daily routine of life which help in leading a normal healthy life. As a whole the stress is laid on prevention, but methods to diagnose and cure the diseases were also given.

As said earlier, the Gura-Shishya paramparas of verbal communication later crystallized in Samhitas or texts. The best known Samhitas are Charak Samhita, Sushruta Samhita, Vagabhatta's Ashtanga Hridaya, and Sharangdhara Samhita. Somewhere in the fourteenth century, due to various socio-political reasons, the system stopped growing and fossilized. Successive Muslim and British occupation of the country did everything to undermine its growth. It lived on, only because it had become a part of every man's life. Indian people's very way of life was governed by Ayurvedic rules in one way or other. For example, Hindu diet, cooking methods, condiments or seasonings have been borrowed from Ayurveda.

The major drawback to Ayurveda has been the language. All the main texts or Samhitas are written in Sanskrit, which is a complex and non-use language, which makes it less accessible to the general public. Then all the information is packed into cryptic stanzas. Someone has compared Samhitas to "zipped" computer file, where everything lies under the 'zip'. If translated and interpreted, they would become unzipped, occupying phenomenal memory and space.

Another problem comes from the small Sanskrit stanzas—sutras or axioms. These are open to different interpretations because of the nature of the language. For example, the word 'rasa' in Sanskrit can have 13 different meanings depending on the context in which it is used, it means 'sap' juice, body fluid, the primordiale tissue etc. So there are more than one interpretations to the same sutra.

One more point leading to loss of popularity was the difficulty in preparing the prescription of a Vaidya. It requires special skills, specially the medicines which are slow to prepare such as Kadhas, Asavas seem cumbersome and entirely out of place today.

In conclusion we can say that Ayurveda gives a formula for healthy living. Mind is given immense importance in Ayurveda in the origin of diseases. Ayurveda incorporates the mind and soul as part of human organisation, and suggests ways and means to keep the mind healthy and tension-free.

As cited earlier there are three main Ayurvedic Samhitas viz. Charak Samhita, Sushruta Samhita and Ashtang Samgraha.

Charak Samhita

Charak Samhita is in the form of question-answer method. The questions are asked by the disciple Agnivesh and are answered by the teacher Atreya, in the Himalayas. In the beginning and at the end of each chapter, there is usually said, "as explained by Atreya, compiled by Agnivesh and redacted by Charak, and Drudbal, the matter is given here." So the author of Charak Samhita is not Charak himself but a long chain of Rishi before him. He is only one of the interpreters of this his ancient learning Ayurveda. This Samhita was the seed sown by Atreya, watered by Agnivesh and nurtured by Charak, and became popular as Charak Samhita.

The first text of Ayurveda available at present is by Drudbal in the 9th century AD. In this it has been repeated many times that this is an ancient work being restored and reconstructed by him, i.e., Drudbal.

The scope of Charak Samhita is very vast. It gives detailed discussions of all sorts of mental and physical diseases, their etiology, diagnosis, prognosis and treatment. Not only that, it touches topics, like cosmology metaphysics, ethics, philosophy even physio-chemistry. It discusses all the eight branches of Ayurveda, including Bhootvidya psycho-pathology or psychotherapy. It will be discussed in detail in a later chapter.

Charak Samhita is the first scientific documentation of Indian medicine after Atharva-veda. The general approach in it is psychosomatic. The Sutra 11/46-47 clearly proves that Bhoot-vidya or psychotherapy was a separate specialized branch of medicine practised by specialists in those days.

According to Charak, Bhoot-vidya is one of the eight branches of Ayurveda. It means that branch which deals with morbid psychic functions and disorders. A wrong idea has generally been formed from it that 'super' or 'evil' spirits cause mental abnormality as and when they enter the human body. But a careful perusal of the Samhita clearly shows that according to Charak, real cause of mental disease is not different spirits but the behaviour of the individual itself. The past deeds give rise to abnormal behaviour or symptoms. The word Bhoot here means something remembered from the past and not evil spirits. Charak has given a detailed description of nosology, general etiology and diagnosis of mental diseases which we shall discuss in a later chapter.

Sushruta Samhita

Sushruta himself was a renowned surgeon and his Samhita deals mainly with surgery. It is a sort of compliment to Charak Samhita which deals with medicine. The origin of Sushruta Samhita also is Atharva Veda, and it comes upto Indra. From Indra Atreya and Dhanvantari took Ayurvedic learning. Then Dhanvantari imparted the knowledge to his disciples, chief among them being Sushruta. Sushruta Samhita is also in the form of questions and answers — questions by Sushruta, answers by Dhanvantri.

About the time of Sushruta, there seems to be no agreement. According to Gulab Kunverba Society of Gujrat, he was a contemporary of Charak. To A.D. Shastri, Sushruta was the son of Vishwamitra and his time was 2000 BC.

Sushruta Samhita is a redacted treatise, named after Sushruta but given by Nagarjuna. It presents a surgical approach. It has 120 chapters divided into 5 groups—one of the groups being Bhoot vidya or psychotherapy. Sushruta Samhita is great as far as surgery is concerned. It discusses Grah diseases of children and adults separately. It gives Mantras and ritualistic therapy also. In the field of psychotherapy Sushruta is richer than Charak. Surgery is the special field of Sushruta and his surgical methods are being followed even now. Sushruta Samhita has been translated into several Indian and foreign languages.

Ashtanga Sangraha of Vagabhatta

Of the three great treatises of Ayurveda—the Brihadtryi—Ashtanga Sangraha of Vagabhatta was last to appear. Its time is placed as that of Gupta Empire, as 6th century AD. Ashtanga Sangraha was attributed to Vagabhatta, who was the son of Singh Bhatt and belonged to Sindhu Pradesh. Vagabhatta composed two Samhitas—'Ashtanga Sangraha' and 'Ashtanga Hridaya', the latter being an abridged edition of the former.

Vagabhatta also traces the origin of Ayurveda to Atharva Veda and regards it as an Upveda of Atherva Veda. Vagabhatta has actually combined the teachings of all past masters like Charak, Sushruta and others in Ashtanga Sangraha. Vagabhatta was himself a Buddhist, so some of the vidyas of Buddhists also entered Ashtanga Sangraha.

Ashtanga Sangraha, as the name denotes, is the combination of all the eight Angas or branches of Ayurveda including Grah Chikitsa or treatment of mental disorders. Vagabhatta included the Aparajita Vidya of the Buddhists along with tantras and mantras in therapy. These are not found in Charak, Sushruta or Atharva Veda. The mantras and the Tantra therapies have been discussed in detail. All types of major and mild mental abnormalities like Bhoot Grahs, unmad (insanity) and apsmar are given with etiology, diagnosis symptoms etc.

The therapies discussed are Dravya and Adravya meaning materialistic and non-materialistic means. Of these Adravya are mental as Upvas, mantra, santwana, dan, tap, shocks, sleep, prayashchita etc. Vagabhatta prescribes the correction of intellect, patience and knowledge of one's own self as the best therapies to cure mental disorders. So the use of psychogenic ways for therapeutic purposes means psychotherapy for Vagabhatta.

In conclusion, one can say that Ashtanga Sangraha of Vagabhatta is a combination of the prevalent Brahministic trend of Atharva Veda, the newly risen Buddhistic trend and all the trends of psychotherapy present at that time, combining all the good points of others, Vagabhatta has also contributed his own ideas to psychotherapy.

Yoga

No other Indian system has gained as much popularity and scientific acclaim as Yoga in modern world. It has been used as a relaxation technique and exercise by the therapists world over. But yoga is much more than that.

The word Yoga itself has 80 meanings in 'Hindi Vishwakosh'. Yoga literally means to unite—connection or union. It comes from the root 'Yuj'=to join. So in general Yoga means any method by which something apart and desired is united with or achieved. In this broad sense it can take any number of meanings.

Yoga, specifically is one of the six man systems of Indian philosophy. It refers to the system propounded by Maharishi Patanjali. With time the word iained many more meanings. But the main and universally accepted meaning of Yoga is as a system of self-culture, and realization of individual union with the Supreme self (Atma with Paramatma).

In general Yoga denotes the tenets of Patanjali's "Yoga Sutra". Yoga Sutra was actually the first documentary approach and this system is known as Raja Yoga. It refers to the method of mind while Hatha Yoga refers to the method of body. There are other Yogic methods also, such as Karma Yoga, Gyan Yoga, Laya Yoga etc.

The approach of Yoga is psychic. It advocates Chitta-vrittinirodh or restricting the fluctuations of mind—mental control. The doctrine of Yoga assumes that the mind can be made to function at higher levels by proper training which is given by Yoga.

Yoga also owes its origin to Vedic times. The practices of Yoga in some form or other, and the mention of Yoga are found in all the Vedas, the Upanishads. This is called the Puratana Yoga or older ancient Yoga. The credit for presenting Yoga as an indepedent school of metaphysics goes to Patanjali. Patanjali has rightly been called 'the father of Yoga.' Patanjali's influence was so great on Indian thought and culture that two of the anti-theistic schools—Jains and Bouddhas also accepted Yoga as an absolute way to individual emancipation or Moksha.

Yoga has been rejuvinated in the 20th century. It has been called "scientific and based on actual experiments." Foreign scholars like Geraldine Coster, Max Muller, Flagg Moore, Havall and Hans Jacobs and more recently an American therapist who took the name Swami Ajaya, have highly acclaimed it. Among Indians, the prominant names are Shri Aurobindo, Swami Shivananda, Swami Vivekananda etc.

Many researchers and scholars have compared Yoga with other Western systems of psychotherapy. They all found that Yoga far excelled in effectivity than any other method of psycho-therapy. It is a well-known fact that psychological problems weaken the Ego, causing damage to ego-strength. The Ego becomes too weak and unable to cope with reality. Yoga seeks to train the Ego by psycho-physiological methods and thus gradually increases the patient's ego-strength or Atma-bal. Pranayama and other such exercises give energy to the nerves. The ego goes on gaining strength, control of senses and the ability to cope with reality. Yoga thus has a triple action, it treats body, nerves and psyche, so that it is able to control the disorders in less time and with more efficiency.

Yoga has been found to have similarities with some Western systems of psychotherapy, specially psychoanalysis. But all in all, Yoga is a far advanced and complete theory and a much more efficient practice. It is useful for all times places cultures and people. Yoga leads not only from abnormality to normality, but from normality to super-normality.

We have just had a glimpse of the major psychotherapies of India, namely—Atharva Veda, Ayurveda and Yoga. Each of these have their own techniques and practices, still there is a uniformity of approach. These are all spiritually oriented. They believe in one-ness of body-mind and soul.

The approach of Atharva-veda is purely psychogenic. It believes in omnipotence of psyche. Only sometimes it is psychosomatic. Whenever the use of medicines is suggested, a mantra or some other mental accompaniment is always there. Medicine is never administered alone.

Ayurveda of course inherted its approach from Atharva Veda, as the former is a branch of the latter or an Upveda of Atharva Veda. But during the passage of time, its concepts changed from the original ones. Just imagine the Atharvan Bhaishajyas or practitioners, living in calm and peaceful Ashramas in the forests, themselves ideals of moral behaviour, with Siddhis, tapa, tyaga and self-control. They applied their techniques of therapy on the patients only when they had attained Siddhis themselves. These Siddhis were psychic energy gained by oneself and then transferred to others for the purposes of healing. For the later Ayurvedic practitioners or Vaidyas this type of ideal behaviour was not possible. Thus, the approach changed, now they relied more on medicines and other psychosomatic means. Even in the field of psychic disorders, the approach of later Ayurveda was psychosomatic or somatogenic.

The approach of Yoga is strictly psychogenic, but at times also psychosomatic. Patanjali in his Yoga Sutra, has given a practical shape to the psychogenic approach of the Vedas in the form of Yogic exercises and Sadhnas. In later Yogic practices, specially in Tantra Yoga physical and cosmic energy is also used along with psychic energy. The mantras of Tantra Yoga are based on psycho-physical energy of psyche and cosmos, in contrast to the mantras of Atharva veda, which are based on psychic energy.

Three

The Vedas

The Vedas are the ancient wisdom of India. The traditional Hindu view regards the Vedas as the source of all knowledge. These are supposed to have existed as long as mankind itself. And these are not created by man (अपौरुषेय). According to Hindu belief the Vedas came from the mouth of the Creator—Brahma himself. Then this tradition was carried on by the ancient seers—the Rishis from one generation of guru-shishyas to another in verbal form. These were chanted and are mostly in lyrical form. The Vedas have been called Shruti (श्रुति) also, as these were learnt through hearing. That is why no written commentaries or any other records are found in early times.

Another reason for not having early written commentaries was that the Vedas were considered as a source and storehouse of all knowledge and wisdom. Confining them to writing will mean limiting them to a beginning and an end. It was a definite belief that they were अनादि-अनन्त with no beginning and no end. अनन्ता वैवेदाः. Since the knowledge of Vedas has a divine source, it can have no beginning and no end. How can then it be limited into a commentary or an interpretation by a mere mortal being?

The Time of Vedas

Vedas have been accepted worldwide as the oldest books of human culture. But there is controversy about their actual time. The Western and Indian scholars differ considerably in fixing the correct time and age of Vedas. According to Western scholars the time is:—

Max Muller-McDonald-Keith	1400 BC
Hague-Whitney-Wilson-Griffiths	2000 BC
Jacobi	4000 BC

According to Indian scholars—

Lokmanya Tilak	6000 BC
Pavagi (on the basis of geological evidence)	240,000 BC
Pt. Dinanath Shastri (on the basis of astronomy placing of Nakshatras)	300,000 BC

The common consensus seems to be that the Vedas are more than four thousand years old but their written records are found only from 1500 BC. Second agreement is on the fact that these are not the work of any one single human mind. They contain the thoughts and visions of a number of ancient seers or rishis.

The Relevance of Vedas

Vedas provide the first in the world and finest solution to human problems. They contain the knowledge of this world as well as the other world, of physical objects as well as spiritual issues, the knowledge of ascendence of man as well as his decadence अभ्युदय एवं निःश्रेयस. Swami Dayananda said that, "Vedas contain truths of science as well as truths of religion. Dayanand has rather understated than over stated the depth and range of Vedic wisdom."

Mrs. Wheeler Wittox of America—An Indologist has this to say—It (India) is the land of the great Vedas, the most remarkable works containing, not only religious ideas for a perfect life but also facts, which science has since proved true. Electricity, radium, electrons, Airships all seem to be known to the seers who found the Vedas.

Shri Narayan Bhavanirao Pavani—In Vedic India says, "Vedas are the fountain head of knowledge, the prime source of inspiration, nay the grand repository of Divine wisdom and even eternal truths." Pavani further says, "The Vedas contain many things not yet known to anybody, as they form a mine of inexhaustible literary—wealth, that has still remained unexplored."

"Vedas are treatises on exact science." Panyam Narayan Gaur. Vedas give allegoric descriptions of geology and other natural phenomena. Vedas give two forms of knowledge or vidya: *Para vidya* पराविद्या, that knowledge which can lead to the knowing of divine—the god and the ways which lead to him. *Apara vidya* अपराविद्या, the knowledge of this world. Knowing the physical world and then converting it into action and behaviour.

Apara vidya is Head learning. Apara is the flower while Para is soul wisdom. Para is the ruit. The combining of Para and Apara vidya leads to Abhyudaya (अभ्युदय) and Nihshreyas (निःश्रेयस). Abhyudaya is all the things comforts which can be obtained in this world by physical outward means. Nihshreyas is the knowledge of God ब्रह्मज्ञान the way to God. Apara is known by direct evidence and inference and whatever cannot be reached by direct observation or inference is Para vidya. It is Veda.

The Meaning of Veda

According to Panini, the great grammarian, Veda comes from the root vid (विद्) meaning to have authority to profit or gain or to think. Combining all these meanthings. We get all the three characteristics of the Brahma or Vedas as given in Shruti, सत्–Authority or generation of life, आनन्द–Profit or gain, चित्–To think or sustain life.

This is the wider meaning of the word 'Veda'. But practically Vedas mean the specific sacred texts, the instruments for attaining this worldly and other worldly knowledge. These texts are the collections of mantras, each with a specific subject-matter, although there is some overlapping of matter. The four Vedas are—

Rig Veda (ऋग्)— Is considered to be the oldest. It contains mantras of prayers to Vedic Gods Indra, Agni, Savita etc.

Yajur Veda (यजुर)— It is mostly in prose form. It gives the methods and correct procedure of performing the Yajyas of different sorts, for different purposes, such as gaining victory over the enemy, अश्वमेध begetting a son पुत्रयेष्टी.

Sam Veda (साम)— Is mostly in singable lyrical form. It deals with ways to fight and to ward off the forces that disturb 'Yajya'. It also gives ways to appease the various Vedic gods.

Atharva Veda (अथर्व)— Is the only Veda which contains worldly problems and their solutions such as, how to live a long and healthy life, medicines for snake-bite, and other common ailments, fighting common and chronic diseases, ways and means to defeat and eliminate the enemy etc.

Rishis are the seers, persons with special abilities, who can see the hidden truth of this world—who saw and understood Vedas and imparted the knowledge to their able shishyas. Rishis were also called Mantra drishta मन्त्रद्रष्टा (Remember Rishis are not 'creators' but only seers of mantras) Vedas are also known as 'Shruti', because all the knowledge of Vedas was communicated by reciting and hearing. Vedic Richas were heard and retained in mind as there was no writing material and printing technology some four or five thousand years ago. The Atharvans prayed for a long-lasting and large memory to retain all the wisdom it is gaining (A.V.1/2-3).

Branches of Vedas

It is believed (on the basis of evidence present in other ancient treatises) that the Vedas had one thousand one hundred and thirty one (1131) branches in all. Of these, only ten are available at present—

Rig Veda— (1) Shakal.

Yajur Veda— (2) Kanv (3) Taittiriya (4) Madhandini and (5) Maittrayani.

Sam Veda— (6) Jaimini (7) Ranayini (8) Kauthuma.

Atharva Veda— (9) Shaunak (10) Pippalad.

In 1963 the Shankaracharya of Kanchi Kamakotipeetham, Shri Chandrashekharananda Saraswati, established a Veda Sanrakshan Nidhi, a trust for the preservation and protection of Vedas. Here electronic devices are being used to preserve the original form of the Vedas. The original mantras are being recorded. It also aims at preparing Vedic scholars.

The Divisions of Vedas

Each Veda is divided into 10 kandas or sections, but this division is not according to the subject-matter.

Every Veda has four parts. Samhita, Brahman, Arnayaka and Upanishad.

Samhita— The original collection of mantras is known as Samhitas. They have been divided into Shakhas or Charanas. Pt. Satyavrata Samshrami says, "It seems that in ancient Vedic charanas or schools, for sake of convenience of the study the whole lot of mantras were divided into sections known as the samhitas."

Brahmanas— Are the books of commentaries, giving interpretations of the mantras. Each Veda has its own specific

Brahmana. Some have more than one Brahmana also. The Brahmana of Atharva veda is known as Gopatha Brahmana.

Arnayakas— Are a sort of supplementary books. These lay down the rules and rituals for those Aryans who have attained a mature age and have retired to the forests.

Upanishads— Give philosophic analysis of the Veda Mantras. These are considered most important part of the Vedas as these contain the real Vedic philosophy.

Veda Samhitas are in Mantra-sutra or concise axiomatic form. To understand, these have to be expanded and interpreted. Brahmanas give these interpretations and also give the rules and procedures for interpretations. Vedas are not created by men. But the commentaries the Brahmanas etc. were created by various Rishis such as Yogyavalakya, who is said to have authored *Shatapatha Brahmana*. Here also, the thoughts are given in Yagyavalakya-Maitreyi dialogue form. But these have been recorded by some anonymous shishya.

Shakhas or Charanas of Vedas — पठान्तरे पृथग्भूता वेदशाखा

The original mantra—Samhitas are the same, but these may have been sung or recited in different ways—and these different ways of recitation came to be known as Charanas or Shakhas. These are not the branches of the Vedas but the styles of recitations of the original mantra Samhitas. In Shakhas or Charanas the original text of Samhita मूल पाठ may or may not be changed or improved but the name of the originator of this type of recitation is joined with the Samhita, for example the Patha of Rig-veda by Shakal is known as Shakalya Shakha. The recitation by Atreya came to be called Atreyi etc.

Vedas have been called by various other names. Some of these are—

Mantra मन्त्र-मननान्मत्रो वेद — Vedas are known as mantras because one meditates or thinks over them.

Chhanda छन्द — The literal meaning is 'to cover' Chhandas are alliterations, these Chhandas organise and give shape to the thoughts of the original poets. That is why the Vedas came to be known as Chhandas also. There is a story in Shatapatha Brahmana, which says that when the devas became afraid of death, they covered themselves with Vedas—so Vedas came to be called Chhandas or covering.

Nigama— Vedas are known as Nigama also, as these are the instruments for getting real knowledge.

Shruti— Shruti means what is heard. Vedas are called Shruti because they are heard, recited and committed to memory.

The four Vedas represent different branches of knowledge—

Rig Veda ऋग्— Represents knowledge, wisdom. It deals with theorems and experiments. It is the basis. It is in poetry form.

Yajur Veda यजुर— Is Yagya Pradhan यज्ञ प्रधान. The process of preparing reagents and apparatus is recorded in the Yajurveda. It is karma or action. It is mostly prose.

Sam Veda साम— Is devotion or उपासना. It sings the praises of Vedic gods. It is lyrical and is mostly sung very melodiously. The first singable lyrical literature in the world.

Atharva Veda अर्थव— Deals with science of life. Whatever knowledge is contained in the first three Vedas, is supplemented in Atharva-veda. It deals with the divine but also with problems of this world such as the diseases which trouble man or how to conquer the enemy. It is in a mixed prose poetry form.

ब्रह्मानिःश्वसितं वेद चतुष्ट यम्

The four Vedas have been uttered—breathed out by Brahma the creator. The four Vedas provide three types of Vidyas—

आधि भौतिक— Pertaining to this physical world, such as how the kings should rule, how to administer justice etc.

आधि दैविक— Pertaining to the devas—which deva is of what kind and nature and how to appease him.

आध्यात्मिक— Pertaining to the soul, spiritual knowledge—the relation of man with god—atma and paramatma. The Vedic literature says that the Vedas are— अनादि — without beginning, अनन्त —without end, नित्य — eternal.

Vedas include philosophy and metaphysics and also the sciences like geology and astronomy. Ayurveda, the science of healing, is also a part of Atharvaveda.

Vedic literature includes—Mantra-samhitas, Shakhas, Brahmana, Arnayakas, Upanishads, Vedang and Upang, Upveda, Shrouta (श्रौत) and Guhyasutra. There are six upangs of Vedas-Mimansa-Jaimini, Vaisheshik-Kanada, Nyaya-Gautam, Sakhya-Kapil, Yoga-Patanjali, Vedanta-Vyas.

These contain all the six schools of Indian metaphysics or philosophy.

Brahmanas— These are specific interpretations of Veda Samhita. Each Veda has its own Brahmana, as given below—

Veda	*Brahmana*
Rig	Aitreya
Yajur	Shatpath
Sam	Sam
Atharva	Gopatha

Upanishads— These are interpretations of Veda mantras. There are ten Upanishads viz., Isha, Ken, Katha, Prashna, Mundak, Mandookya, Taittiriya, Aitreya, Chhandogya and Vrihadarnayak.

The other branches or angas (अंग) will not be very relevant here.

Vedic Science

Vedas are repositories of deep wisdom. These are the treatises on science at an advanced level, not for the beginners. Here are only Sutras—axioms which give only hints—not the details. One has to expand and interpret them to get the pearls of wisdom contained there. Secondly, the subject matter is not given at one place for one particular subject. If one fact is in second chapter, the other connected with it will be found in ninth. It is a great difficulty for the researchers. Another problem is also very important—the one of language. Sanskrit in itself is a complex language, Vedic Sanskrit is even more so. Even if one masters the language, the problem arises of real and authentic meanings. One Sanskrit word carries so many meanings — for example the word 'Rasa' रस has at least 16 sixteen meanings according to Sanskrit Kosha which one is correct and relevant at some place? Even the authorities differ on such interpretations and that is how भुत-विद्या. Psychiatry came to be associated with witchcraft.

The basis of Vedic Science is Prana or energy. This energy is omnipresent and more ethereal than the energy or electricity described by science today. Sense-organs cannot grasp or perceive this energy or Prana. It is something which leaves the body when a man is dead. This energy changes form—it may take a solid form when it becomes apparent. Prana lives within one self as well as out in the world. In man it is represented in body mind and soul. Vedas seek health and well being of human beings which unites body, mind and soul into one single whole.

Medical Science in Vedas

Vedas divide medicine into four broad divisions—

(1) Human (मानवी)— Pertaining to men-medicines made by men.

(2) Divine (दैवी)— Pertaining to superhuman powers.

(3) Rakshasi (राक्षसी)— Pertaining to evil powers who are out to harm others.

(4) Tantrik (तांत्रिक)— This is found in Atharva Veda only. Later on Buddhists took it up and changed it into Aparajita vidya, which is mysterious. In Atharva Veda it includes Mani-Bandhan or tying of charms. Those charms may be made of herbs, some stones—precious or semi-precious or barks of trees—all these are harmless and there is nothing mysterious about them. Secondly, it includes हस्त स्पर्श touch by hand somewhat like Reiki. And lastly it also includes will power or Sankalapa.

Atharva Veda

Atharva Veda is the last Veda to come. It is more worldly than the other three vedas. It presents a beautiful harmony between this world and the other world, reality and spirituality. The Atharvanas or Atharvedic rishis, when they pondered on matters relating to spirituality, went into poetic form. But sometimes, when they discussed the matters relating to this world, they use prose also. The 15th and 16th kandas are mainly in prose.

Atharva veda forms the basis for all the Indian systems of medicine. Ayurveda came from Atharva Veda. Charak, Sushruta, Vagabhatta all cite Atharva Veda as their source.

Atharvanic science of healing—Chikitsa Vigyan—has eight branches, called Atharvediya Ashtanga. These branches are—Sharir Rachna शरीर रचना — Anatomy, Kriya Sharir क्रिया शरीर — Physiology, Bhashaj भेषज — Pharmacy, Rogotpatti रोगोत्पत्ति — Origin or source of diseases, Rog vinishchaya रोगविनिश्चय — Determining the disease, Nidan निदान — Diagnosis, Upchar Khand उपचार खंड — Treatment, Bhoot-vidya भूत-विद्या — Psychiatry.

Bhoota-vidya forms the 6th Khanda or branch. It is solely concerned with mental diseases and mentions several type of mental maladies such as उन्माद (insanity). Apasmar (epilepsy), Khshipta rog (a kind of mental infliction), Dhanurvat (a kind of convulsive disease).

The Upachar Khand of Atharva veda, the section on treatment of disease, mentions eight types of therapies or treatments. These are as follows:—

Pani-sparsh पाणि-स्पर्श	—	Touching by hand. Some what like Reiki.
Surya Kiran सूर्य किरण	—	Solar therapy by rays of sun.
Pavanopchar पवनोपचार	—	Treatment by wind or air.
Pavakopchar पावकोपचार	—	Treatment by fire.
Jalopchar जलोपचार	—	Treatment by water. Hydro-therapy.
Mantropchar मन्त्रोपचार	—	Treatment by Mantras.
Havanopchar हवनोपचार	—	Treatment by Havana.
Ashwasana आश्वासन	—	Assurance, a verbal method of treatment.

The second chapter of sixth Khanda gives Manas rog chikitsa (मानस रोग चिकित्सा) or treatment of the disease of the mind. This treatment of mental disease by mental methods is known as psychotherapy in modern world. The origin of mental diseases is said to be Pragyapradh प्रज्ञापराध or crimes of conscience. Dushswapna is given as one of the many mental diseases. Other minor mental disorders mentioned are Krodh (anger), Moth (attachment), Shok-vishad (depression), Irshya-dwesha (jealousy).

Unmad is called a disturbed state of mind caused by papa (sin), jwara (fever), krimi (small insects) etc. There is prayer to Agni Devta, "O Jataveda, please destroy these specific krimis (insects) which are causing me pain." Thus treatment suggested for unmad (insanity) in Atharva veda is prayer. The counsellor suggests—"May the Agni Devta give you peace." Medicines, mostly herbal and man made are suggested for unmad and other mental ailments, like jatamansi, ajashrangi, guggul, pippli, brahmi booti etc. Bhoots and pishachas (evil spirits) are also said to cause mental problems as these destroy the Vivek (विवेक) the sense of balance and judgement. More of this will be given in next two chapters.

Vedas, thus present a beautiful picture of harmony between this world and the other world, of reality and spirituality.

Samskaras

Atharva Veda in Grahya Sutra gives all the Samskaras of Hindus. These Samskaras are meant to refine human nature, to make it cultured. This is actually acculturation or socialization of man. By means of Samskaras the raw nature of man is changed and refined into a cultured Aryan nature. Samskaras are sixteen in number. They start from the time of conception known as Garbhadhan (गर्भाधान), Punsawan (पुंसवन), then giving him an identity—a name, a family name (कुल) and gotra (गोत्र) by which he will be known. A person thus initiated in his early childhood can never face an 'identity crisis' known to the modern world. Anna prashana (first feeding of cereals), Vidyarambha (starting formal education), Yogyopveet (starting of the first that is Brahmacharya Ashram). The Hindu Samskaras continue even after death in Shraddha and Pind-dan.

Atharva Veda, thus, presents a full of life picture of Vedic people. It is vast in its canvas and scope. It shows the early Aryans as simple devotees, nature worshippers, performing Yogyas and appeasing Gods. But Atharva Veda gives their more human and natural aspects as well. As greedy for more wealth, more comforts, as those who believe in demons, who are fearful, hateful and revengeful, who can become the victims of sexual pleasures and play tricks to entice cold maidens. They are also shown to perform ill, harmful rites (ghor घोर) to conquer their enemies. They wish to be free of physical and mental ailments. On the whole they are human and peace-loving people.

The next two chapters will deal with the methods of treatment for mental ailments given in Atharva Veda.

Four

Atharva Veda-I

Atharva Veda contains the earliest recorded account in the world, of mental illnesses and their remedies.

Atharva Veda also is the source of all Indian systems of medicine and psychotherapy. That is why we have to go into the depth and see what is really there in Atharva Veda.

The Vedas

The Vedas are ancient sources of knowledge. All our traditional wisdom about metaphysics philosophy, psychology, astronomy, astrology, science, mathematics, literature, grammar, ethics, sociology, civics and administration, medicine or for that matter any branch of learning, is found in Vedas, in nut-shell or Sutra and Sukta form. That is why, in India, the origin of all types of knowledge is traced back to the Vedas.

The exact date or age of the Vedas has not yet been established. According to Hindu belief, the Vedas came right from the mouth of Brahma, the creator, himself. These are not of human origin and, as such, have no beginning (anadi) and no end (anant). But, now, scholars agree that Vedas are of human origin, though, not of one single author, but a long chain of generations of rishis and their shishyas (disciples).

There is no agreement about the date of their origin also. While Lok Manya Bal Gangadhar Tilak puts the origin of Vedas to be at least ten thousand years before Christ, Max Muller puts it at four thousand years BC. One other German Scholar Dr. Jacobi also puts the time to be four thousand years before Christ. Some scholars, on the basis of astronomical calculations, put the date of Rig-veda to be at least 5500 BC. One of these scholars is Pandit Shankar Balkrishna Dixit. Even European scholars now accept the time of Vedas to be between 6-4 thousand years BC.

The Vedas have been going on in a verbal form from one Guru to his shishyas. To facilitate this verbal memory they have been mostly in the concise form of Sutras or mantras. They are also poetical and singable, so that shishyas learnt by singing them. The language is Sanskrit in early form. The language of the early Vedas is distinctly different from the later ones, in that the later rigours of grammatical rules had not appeared then.

All the Vedas contain mantras, which are poetic expressions of Vedic wisdom in very concise form. This mantra-sukta technique became necessary because all the material was to be learnt by heart and retained. Only sometimes prose is also found.

Vedas are four in number—Rig Veda, Yajur Veda, Sam Veda and Atharva Veda. Although the subject-matter in them is different, there is some amount of overlapping also.

Rig Veda— is considered to be the oldest. It mostly contains prayers to the Gods—which are nature or natural things, sun, moon, wind, sky, earth, water, akash, mountains, rivers etc. The highest is sun or Savitri and Agni or fire and Indra.

Yajur Veda— is mostly in prose form. It deals with Yajya in all its forms and the correct and proper procedures to perform Yajya.

Sam Veda— is in a lyrical singable form. It contains Stuti or prayer of devas of nature. It also deals with ways to fight all the objects or elements which in any way disturb yajya, and also ways to appease Vedic gods.

Atharva Veda— contains vedic stutis, yajya. But also deals with more worldly knowledge like how to cure diseases, to eliminate the effect of poison, live a long and healthy life, medicines (Bheshaj), ways and means to eliminate the enemy, fight common and chronic diseases which trouble common man, etc.

Each Veda is divided into 10 Kandas or sections. Each Veda has four parts—Samhita, Brahmana, Arnayaka and the Upanishad. Samhitas are collections of mantras of different Shakhas. Brahmanas give an interpretation of these mantras. Aranayakas give the rituals for the Arya-jan, who have attained a mature age and have retired-vanprasthis. Upanishads provide a deep and philosophical analysis of the ved-mantras. Upanishads are thus, considered to be the most important part of the Vedas.

Dr. Vachaspati Gairola says, "The large heritage of vedic knowledge which is available to us today is not the work of any one rishi, or one group, one ashrama, one mind, one time. This is a long tradition of centuries, of many groups of rishis, many charanas or shakhas, many ashramas, and many minds."

Atharva Veda

Atharva Veda occupies a unique position among the four Vedas. Firstly, because the other three Vedas deal with matters of other world, the gods, the nature and supernatural, while Atharva Veda is more worldly. It seeks to solve the problems of this world and its common people. It deals with topics like leading a long and healthy life, to avoid sorrow, to ward off illness, to vanquish or win over the enemy, etc.

Secondly, and more importantly for students of psychology, the central theme of Atharva Veda is Mana or mind. In all the processes of life, Atharva Veda puts in the contribution of Mana, to complete these processes, such as in the performing of yajya or helping the king in performing his kingly peaceful and helpful duties. Thus the Atharva Veda samhitas contain the knowledge of the other world, the Brahma, as well as of this world.

Thirdly, Atharva veda contains what is now known as Ayurveda, and Ayurveda is actually regarded as a sub-section or Upveda of Atharva Veda. The seeds of medicine and surgery are found scattered in the Atharva Veda and all the later masters of Indian medicine like Charak, regard Atharva Veda as their basic source.

Atharva Veda contains the first ever record in history, of mental diseases like unmad, apasmar etc.

The Origin

The name Atharva itself is very old. It occurs in Rig Veda. The worshippers of fire (agni-poojaks) were known as Atharvanas. Later, purohits or priests were known by the name atharvanas.

Gopatha Brahmana gives a tale about the origin of rishi Atharva. When Brahma, who is self-created, was doing severe penances Tapasya, a stream of sweat flowed down from the pores of his body, due to the harsh nature of the tapa. This stream later divided into two branches. One branch was roasted due to heat, and was named Bhrigu—the roasted one. He also got the name Atharva because of his simple and non-violent nature. The second stream carried the rasa fluid, from the ang or organs of Brahma, so the rishi who was born from ang+rasa was named Angirasa. Later Brahma himself was merged in these two streams. These two rishis Atharva (Bhrigu) and Angirasa gave birth to one hundred and twenty (120) sons, all of those were rishis and were perfect in mantras. The large amount of mantras, they composed came to be known as Atharva Angirasa Veda or only Atharva Veda.

This tale of Gopatha Brahmana seems to be symbolic and points to the two branches of Atharva Veda. Bloomfield says, "It is quite possible that Atharvanas and Angirasas were separate lines of priests (rishis) and these two jointly composed Atharva Veda. In fact in most of the literature, the term Atharvana has been used for the good auspicious rights and rituals, such as Bhaishajya, Paushtikarma etc. While Angirasa came to be applied to those mantras and rituals which are bad or impure, violent and destructive. In other words, Atharvana means those parts of this veda—the Atharvanic Karmakand, which are holy, pure peaceful and wholesome. And Angirasa is that part which is impure which conveys a tendency to hit or attack, which is Ghor (घोर) or more terrorizing. In Kaushik sutra also Angirasa comes under those Kalpas which aim at aggression or destroying the enemy."

Actually the name Atharva-Angirasa, describes the two-fold subject-matter of this Veda, one benevolent and the other malevolent. Atharva Veda has been called by many other names also. In Atharva Veda itself (10/2/30-32) it has been called Brahma veda, because it describes and expands the nature of Brahma or universal energy. It deals with Brahma and shows the ways to attain Brahma with the use of its mantras.

Atharva Veda is also known as Bhaishaj-veda because it contains an ample number of mantras carrying the knowledge of medicine or therapeutics. The name Amrita-veda is also used for Atharva Veda because it incorporates Ayurveda, which is the nector 'Amrita' of life and gives secrets of a long and happy life.

However, the original name of this Veda was Atharva Angirasa Veda which referred to the two sections of this Veda. The one Atharvana meaning those mantras which are good pure auspicious and convey well-being, while Angirasa came to be the name given to those mantras which are impure, not good, which seek to harm others, for example Maran, mohan or uchchatan mantras. Atharva Veda thus contains mantras which are supposed to bring happiness and prosperity, as well as the mantras which can be used as the instruments against the enemies.

The name Atharva derives from the Sanskrit root 'tharva', which conveys cunningness and aggressiveness. Atharva denotes one who is without cunningness and aggressiveness. One who is simple and peaceful is known as Atharva. Later an Atharvans were a kind of priests those who worshipped Agni or Agni-poojak.

The Branches or Shakhas of Atharva Veda — "नवधा ऽऽथर्वणो वेदः" There are nine shakhas or branches of Atharva veda—

(1) PIPPALAD, (2) STAUD or TAUD, (3) MAUD, (4) SHAUNKIYA, (5) JAJAL, (6) JALAD, (7) BRAHMAVAD, (8) DEVA DARSHIN and (9) CHARAN VAIDYA.

PIPPALAD is named after a great sage. The oniy copy of this Samhita was found in Kashmir by Von Roth in 1875. It was in Sharda lipi or original script of Kashmir. The authenticity of this particular copy is a matter of controversy. The great Veda scholar Whitney has based his works on this copy.

Another branch available now is Shaunikiya. Pandit Ramakrishna Shastri's Hindi rendering of Atharva Veda is based on this. All the other Shakhas have been wiped out with time or are still waiting to be discovered. We come to know about all the Shakhas of Atharva Veda by references in (1) PANINI Mahabhashya, (2) CHARANA VYUHAS, (3) PURANAS and (4) The Sayan commentary on Atharva Veda. The last one, SAYAN'S commentary is considered most authentic. The combination of PIPPALAD and SHAUNKIYA Shakhas is now known as Atharva veda. Shankar Pandurang Pandit edited its Bombay edition entitled, "Atharva veda Samhita with the commentary of Sayanacharya"—1895-8-4 vols. Sayanacharya in his commentary adopts readings from the PIPPLAD Shakha mostly.

MAUD, TAUD, JAJAL, JALAD, BRAHMAVAD and DEVADARSHIN are there in name only. CHARANVAIDYA which is supposed to be the largest, is not available as yet.

The Scope of Atharva Veda

This Veda consists of 6026 mantras. Of these 1768 are of Atharva rishi, 967 of Brahma rishi, 670 of Bhrigavangirasa and the rest of other rishis. Atharva Veda has 20 Kandas or chapters, 731 Suktas and 5987 mantras according to Pandit Baldeva Shastri. Shankar Pandurang Pandit gives the number of Kandas as twenty and Anuvaks (books) as 111 (one hundred eleven). The Suktas are 573 according to Satavalekar and 598 according to Whitney. Upto Kand 14 there is agreement. Satavalakar and Whitney differ about the number of Suktas and Paryasuktas in Kand 15 and 16. The total number of mantras are 5127 according to Satavalakar and 5038 according to Whitney.

There is a diversity in the topics discussed in Kandas, so the matter cannot be classified according to subject-matter.

The Subject-matter of Atharva Veda

Atharva Veda is mainly concerned with well-being of humanity. Atharva, here seems to mean 'one who wants peace and stability by following non-violence and non-cunningness. This word also conveys special abilities and special capacities to work towards its aims.'

Pandit Bhagwat Sharma Upadhyay, in Hindi Vishwakosh, says, "The stress in Atharva Veda is not so much on the use of Karma Kanda or the rituals, as on doing right or wrong, high or low, do-s and don'ts, popular beliefs, and tendencies of life. From this point of view, the importance of Atharva Veda is much more, for the historian, than of the other three vedas. The first references to puranas, history, gathas etc. are found here. This Veda also points to many such traditions which are not only older than Cig-Veda, but really go back to very very old times."

Atharva Veda presents a detailed description of the life style of a very early stage of human society, which has just entered the agricultural stage. The importance of animal wealth cows, oxen, horses is much more. New kingdoms are being established. Men want to live happy healthy lives upto one hundred years. They want to conquer the enemies, to ward off painful chronic diseases like TB (Yakshma) to ward off evil spirits from the newly born infants and their mothers, and also to woo shy ladies.

The human practices depicted in Atharva veda are of special interest to cultural Anthropologists. The Atharvana age is unique for its magical beliefs— Jadu tona, one which saves the person from the jadu of others, and the other, called 'black magic', which means attacking the enemy with a wish to harm, maran, to attract, mohan, and to take away from Uchchatan. Atharva Veda seems to be a meeting place of two cultures, one the higher Liryan Culture of well-wishing, well-being, thinking of Atma and Brahma and the other lower culture prevailing in the general public or comman man. This common man is afraid of evil spirits, of enemies, of painful diseases and seeks a redress from them. This other aspect of human society is not represented in the other three Veda which present only lofty ideals and deva worship, prayers and Yajyas.

Sciences in Atharva Veda

Atharva Veda presents a high level of sciences, not in the present sense of experimentation and technology but the basic ideas. It contains Ayurveda which is a very advanced science of health and diseases. It will be discussed in the later chapter. Atharva Veda deals with diseases both mental and physical, their symptoms, diagnosis and prevention also. The main physical diseases are various types of fever, pain in the heart and the joints, TB or Yakshma, tumours Vrin (वृण) etc. Then it gives methods of surgery in urinary problems, in cases of difficult child-birth etc. It suggests treatment of tumours by hydro-therapy (जल-चिकित्सा) Various herbal therapies are suggested for poison and also for shake-bite. Of a special interest today is the description of small creatures difficult to see with the eyes-called (कृमि) which enter the body and cause various diseases of eyes, nose, teeth. We know them as bacteria today. According to Atharva Veda these creatures can be destroyed by the rays of the sun and by fire. The words used for these invisible and disease-causing creatures are rakshas and pishach (रक्षस् पिशाच). Some herbs and medicines are mentioned, which can destroy these Krimis.

Atharva Veda also know various types of poisons and also suggests many herbs and medicines which can counteract poisons. One verse gives the wonder formula "Poison is the cure for poison". (विषस्य विषमौषधम् 7/88/1) Of special interest to our topic is Kand 16 which contains mantras to ward off the evil dreams (dush swapnas.) Kand 17, which has mantras of prayer for upliftment and the Kand 19 which contains bhaishajya sutras.

Therapies in Atharva Veda

Atharva Veda suggests various methods for treatment of diseases as also the methods for conserving energy in the body, uplifting mental powers and penances for all the wrong doings committed knowingly or unknowingly. Of main interest are the following sections of Atharva Veda—

Bhaishijiyani (भैषज्याणि) are concerned with various types of diseases, their symptoms as well as medicines for treatment. The physical diseases mentioned are : various types of fevers, TB, pains, tumours. The detailed descriptions of the symptoms are given. Mental diseases like unmad, apasmar are also described. Bhaishijiyani includes the basic principles of Ayurveda. In this we find the idea of three gunas (गुण) of body vata, pitta and kapha (वात, पित्त, कफ) and three gunas of mind viz., sattva, rajas and tamas. It gives in details body parts and their structures and functions—not of course as the physiology of today, but quite accurate. It even mentions veins and arteries.

Many medicines are mentioned which can overcome diseases and death. Four types of medicines are given— vanaspati or herbs the leaves, flowers, fruits barks and roots of plants, vanaspatya those obtained from smaller plants, veerudh obtained by other means, and aushadhi—man made, chemicals etc. Then aushadhis are of four classes—

Atharvani (अर्थवाणी)— those used for creating peace energy health पुष्टिकरणी.

Angirasi (आंगीरसी)— those used for bad purposes as maran mohan uchchatan.

Daivi (दैवी)— those chemical mixtures which can make man अजर अमर.

Manushyaja (मनुष्यज)— all medicines prepared by man the ordinary medicines.

There were special rituals for preparing the medicines, mantras for digging up the roots, for picking flowers and leaves, for grinding and preparing aushadhis. Atharva Veda mentions

289 aushadhis, these are scattered in the whole Samhita. Uptil now there have been no attempts to list them in any authentic way.

Ayushyani (आयुष्याणि)— These are mantras in Atharva Veda, giving prayers for a long and healthy life—living upto one hundred Sharats शरदंशतम् and saving oneself from diseases, keeping off death. It gives some measures like mani bandhan मणिबन्धन and mekhala bandhan—tying of a waist band, to protect oneself from evil influences. It is here in Atharva Veda that we find the mention to lying of the Raksha-sutra in the wrist of right hand for males (left for females) for a long life. This tying of Raksha-sutra (कलावा) is still a part of all religious functions for all Hindus. It is supposed to bring the benediction of the gods and to ward off all evil influences.

Paushtikani (पौष्टिकणि)— These suktas pray for showering of blessings of gods for a healthy robust life. Health here is both body and mind. Various means such as milk and ghee of cow are mentioned as health giving.

Prayashchitani (प्रायश्चितानि)— These include penances for untoward or unwanted unsocial behaviour, such as lapses of character or anti-religious acts, all sins committed knowingly or unknowingly, other types of ommissions and commissions in social life. These also include mantras for mental errors, for bad dreams, for ill omens. These show that man at that early age, feared the after effects of his own acts, the ill omens etc. and tried to ward them off by various means, one of which was by doing self-inflicted penances or prayashchit.

Insanity (उन्माद) and Other Mental Diseases— These are not given under a separate caption as पौष्टकाणि etc. These are scattered among other material.

Insanity was supposed to be caused by pretabadha प्रेतबाधा. For the well-being of thus affected person, there was prayer, to ward off the rakshas and grahi (रक्षस-ग्रही) the charm was made with 10 types of holy woods (2/9/1) and tied to the patient.

For the treatment of mental diseases the ways suggested are—magic, tona-totka, maran mohan uchchatan mantras etc. These are the forerunners of later tantrik procedures. It is because of this sort of rituals and witchcraft that some western scholars formed a wrong notion, that Indian System of psychotherapy consisted of black-magic tona-totka only. On a deeper study it becomes clear that the real system was not this. Only when a malady had no other treatment, these means were resorted to.

The rituals (अभिचार) mentioned in Atharva Veda are no magic actually. These are means to some ends. These arouse emotions and the aroused emotions create desirable effects on the patient. They lead to positive and life-supporting feelings in themselves and others, and thus create a psychological atmosphere of peace and well-being. They raise the morale, so much so that the patient can attack the enemy or terrorize the enemy. These rituals, in this modern scientific age, force us to think and judge them as a means to prepare man to face all problems of life with hope and without fear. In this sense the various rituals are like a dynamo giving emotional energy, rather creating emotional energy, in the whole system of man's life. For this reason, rituals become essential for life and well being. These rituals are found in every living healthy society in some form or other. They touch the lowest strata to society and become essential to life. Every religion has its own rituals, these rituals prepare us and arouse us to perform the daily routine of life.

Another point is, as Winternitz points out, that the Gandharvas and Apsaras, occuring here and there as causing agents of mental problems, "may be the symbols of an individuals wishes and desires. " Similarly rakshasas causing mental diseases may also be symbolic.

The Importance of Atharva Veda—Specially to Psychology

Of the four Vedas, the Rig Veda seeks to increase knowledge, the Yajur Veda throws light on right type of deeds and duties the Samveda inspires to worship the Ideal Being and the Atharva Veda shows the way to know the individual psyche or self and also to attain power in the world. R.C. Sharma says, "The Rig Veda, the Yajur Veda, the Samveda, bless us for the other world, but the Atharva Veda blesses us for the other as well as for this world."

Atharva Veda is also known as the Brahma Veda or Atma Veda. According to Max Muller, "Brahma meant originally force, will, wish and the propulsive power of creation. Atma means breath or spirit or self. Brahma itself is but self." Atharva Veda deals with both Brahma and Atma, it is more comprehensive than other Vedas.

According to Satavalekar, "Atharva Veda is specially related to Atma (soul) and Mana (psyche)". Satavalekar is of the view that by the Atharva Veda, we get knowledge of the soul and the ways to attain the energy of the soul (atma-bal), that is why it is known as Atma veda also. The Atharva Veda shows the ways and means to do everything, for example curing illness, victory in war, defeat of enemies through the energy of Mana (psyche).

As far as the sociological aspect is concerned, Atharva Veda relates to the common folks, not the higher intellectual class. It narrates the fears and apprehensions of the general public and not the upper crust of society. The character, the behaviour and the life style of common people are described in details. Those who fear the disease, death, and the enemies, those who want to woo ladies and those who believe in rakshas and pishachs as entering the human body and these other worldly creatures as the causes of diseases. They perform Yajyas for the welfare of all and also of themselves. They also resort to rituals to harm the enemies. In Kaushika sutra many such mantras are given for harming, for killing etc.

The basic approach of Atharva Veda is mental or psychological. Medicines are prescribed but are always accompanied by the mantras or mental content. Even for preparing the medicines digging, grinding, pounding of herbs for medicines, separate mantras are provided.

Atharva Veda abounds in practical advice. It seeks to provide solutions to everyday needs and problems of the common man like snake-bite or pains of joints or fevers. The advices are for the attainment of Brahma, i.e. higher plains, then how to achieve atma-bal (ego-strength) and at lower levels, how to vanquish the enemy or ward off invisible creatures like rakshas or pishach.

The approach of Atharva Veda is also integrative in the sense that it treats body, mind and soul as an integrated total entity. The means which strengthen the body also strengthen the mind. For example, the Paushtikani sutras pray for "the showering of blessings for a robust (पुष्ट) healthy body and mind" so that one may live upto a hundred sharats (जवेत शरद: शतं) free of diseases and death.

Henry Lefever says, "whereas the Rig vedic poets loved to dwell upon the wonders and beauties of nature and the greatness of the gods who created and upheld the natural world, those of the Atharva Veda tend to dwell more upon the psychological qualities necessary in the sacrificer."

Thus, on the whole, the approach of Atharva Veda is psychological, practical and integrative.

Abnormal Behaviour in Atharva Veda

Before starting any discussion about abnormal behaviour in Atharva Veda, some points have to be kept in mind—

Atharva Veda deals with many subjects, and therapeutics is only one of the many subjects dealt with. There are so many other subjects and there is no uniformity of matter. The suktas lie scattered throughout the Samhitas. The researcher has to wade through to find relevant material. It is not like modern books, where you open a book and find all the material connected with the subject under one chapter heading.

Secondly, the scope of subjects covered is very vast—so some subjects are touched only briefly. Abnormal behaviour and its treatment is one of the many subjects. Its treatment is so brief that at times only hints are given. For explanation and elaboration of the subject one has to go to the other sources of information. Sayanacharya's commentary is very useful in this way.

The aim of Atharva Veda, as declared, is the welfare of humanity. It helps men to live a rich and full life upto hundred years and then attain Brahma. Thus rules and regulations are given to live a full healthy life, and in this context come the diseases and the ways to ward off the diseases. Therapies both mental and herbal are suggested. It is in this context that therapeutics comes under the scope of Atharva Veda.

The approach and treatment to matter, thousands of years back, is of course different. To make it more intelligible it has to be put in modern terms as far as possible. Modern terms and concepts are to be fitted there, without distorting the original matter.

Once you dive into the depths of Atharva Veda, you find

gems of wisdom lying scattered there. You, quite simply, cannot ignore or underestimate the wisdom of those sages, who lived in jungles and meditated to find this wisdom, some four or five thousand years ago.

Though the reference to rakshas and pichachs are found in Atharva Veda, these seem to be more symbolic terms. For example, the tiniest creatures Krimi (कृमि) are given the name raksha's, so the term rakshas in Atharva Veda seems to symbolize all evil and undesirable elements.

The Basic Concepts— Atharva Veda contains some basic concepts which were taken up by Ayurveda and are prevalent even today among the practising vaidyas. These concepts are—

The Gunas— According to Atharva Veda the human body is composed of three basic gunas or elements, viz., vata (wind), pitta (bile) and kapha (phlegm) Atharva Veda XVIII/2/29 and 33. From the birth these three elements are present in every human body in a certain balanced way. This equilibrium of elements has to be maintained throughout life. So, the equilibrium of these gunas or elements means normalcy—no disease or disorder, while any disturbance or disequilibrium of these gunas causes abnormal condition or disease.

Normality and Abnormality— As pointed out above, normal means a balance or equilibrium of gunas. Abnormality is a matter of increase or decrease of these gunas, which causes disturbance or disease.

Therapy— Therapy here means restoring the equilibrium of the gunas with the help of medicines.

Mental Health and Mental Disease— Like body, the mental structure also constitutes three elements gunas or urittis or the characteristics. These are called sattva (true, pure), rajas (erotic), tamas (the black, the low). These are the gunas or vrittis of the mind or manas, and are present in all human beings, since birth. These vrittis are also found in a state of equilibrium. As soon as their equilibrium is disturbed, mental disorders emerge. Of these three vrittis, sattva is pure and true. It never gets corrupted, Freud's Rajas denotes sensual pleasures, enjoyment. In Freud's terms it means Eros (काम). Tamas literally means blackness. It is the lowest tendency of evil, of destruction—Thanatos in Freudian terms. Although sattva is pure, true, but having only sattva-vritti is also not normal. Rajas and tamas may increase or decrease in degrees. In both the ways, when there is an excess or when there is a lack of these two vrittis the person becomes abnormal. Normality means having all the three vrittis in a balanced manner. A normal person must have rajas and tamas vrittis in him, but they should be balanced in the total personality. For example, krodh anger, is a tamasik vritti, but a normal person must possess a certain degree of anger; to fight against injustice, to assert one's rights.

According to Atharva Veda (VIII/2/1, 9, 12) the doshas or corruption or disturbances of rajas and tamas gives rise to mental diseases, hence these doshas have to be discouraged.

On physical level the human body is made up of three elements viz vata, pitta, kapha, which must be in a certain balanced state for physical health and well-being. Similarly on the mental level, the human personality has sattva, rajas and tamas vrittis, which also must be in a balanced state for mental health and well being.

Every person has the physical gunas and mental vrittis, but their degrees and combinations are different for each one, and this different combination gives the unique quality or individuality to a person. G. W. Allport in his famous trait theory also puts forward a similar view. According to Allport the traits are the same for all individuals, but their combinations are different and this difference imparts uniqueness to personality.

The gunas and vrittis are found in a balanced state in the normal persons, but when the balance is disturbed, abnormality eusues. Either excess or lack of a guna or vritti causes abnormality. In his famous book *Psycho-dynamics of Abnormal Behaviour* Brown also puts forward a similar view. According to Brown, "The chief tenet of modern psycho-pathology is that abnormal psychological phenomena are simple exaggerations (i.e. over-developments or underdevelopments) or disguised, that is perverted developments, of normal psychological phenomena."

—Brown, J.F., 1940

Abnormal Behaviour in Atharva Veda

Atharva Veda treats mental behaviour in very broad terms. Many behaviour abnormalities are given in detail. The therapies have also been discussed. Let us have a look at these—

The first kanda, in the seventh sukta, two types of diseases are given, one, adhi—arising out of the body due to wrong diet etc. Second, vyadhi—arising out of shapa or curse or ill-will. The cure for vyadhi is given as mental peace and relaxation. We can compare the modern techniques of relaxation for tension reduction.

Mana is always active always working. The best use of this active state can be by attaining self development and general welfare of people, by keeping mana engaged in meditation. The mana may also suffer from imaginary fears. To ward off these fears (भय) mantras and rituals are used.

The rishis of Atharva Veda, specially the seventh sukta, know that we have to remove pain and disease, common man wants relief from pain and anything which can alleviate suffering and pain can be used as a medicine-aushadh. That is why these rishis did not hesitate in giving place to such rituals in the holy Vedas praying to agni to destroy rakshas's etc.

The first kanda 15th sukta is for pushtikarma (पौष्टिकर्म) or such activities which help in gaining health and long life.

The second kand is concerned with bheshaj (medicine) deerghayu prapti (attaining long life) shap mochan (liberation from curse) etc. It also discusses kama shakti or sex drive 2nd 15/ 1-4 give पौष्टिकर्म.

The third kanda deals with kings, kingdom, army as also with shanti (peace) and paushtikarma. It is interesting to note that it contains part of *vastu* also. The third kanda deals with soumanasya or goodwill for all.

The fourth kanda deals with many subjects including bheshaja chikitsa, rit-yagya and atma-vidya or how to make mana strong (in modern terms it means ego strength).

The fifth kanda deals with many samskaras and the punsawan samskara (पुंसवन संस्कार) is one of them. It is performed during the pregnancy itself, to sow the seeds of good samskaras at the prenatal stage, in the citizens to come.

The sixth kanda contains dushswapna nasha, or how to eliminate bad dreams, soumanasya or wishing for well-being, mekhla bandhan or tying of waist-band for protection. It also deals with irshya or irshyalu i.e., jealousy and jealous persons and gives methods to cure one of jealousy (6/18/1-3).

In its reference to bheshajaya, the sixth kand suggests which medicines to take from earth, from rivers and from ocean. It also mentions papavashan or controlling sins as also arishtkhshayanam (पापवशान/अरिष्टक्षयणाम्) or removing badness and ill-will. (6/29/1-3).

The positive aspects of the sixth kanda are also interesting. One is suggesting means for a long life dirghayu-prapti. Then it prays to varchas-jyoti—"to let the divine light enter into us" that is the person or persons who are praying. Then there is praspar chittaiki karana (परस्पर चित्त ऐकीकरण) which means people who are of similar hearts (attitudes) to have a conjugation or come together for the welfare (सममनस्क).

The sixth kanda deals with bad dreams in some details. It states that, "may we be saved from dushswapnas, which arise from anrit (अनृत) or untruthful behaviour" (6/45/3). Then the dream is described as neither living nor dead (i.e. neither conscious nor unconscious) and as creating wonderful images. 'We send these bad dreams to our enemies (6/46/3)' (प्र॰ 13 अनु॰ 5 सं॰ 57).

Dushswapnas are said to be immortal as they never die, but recur in some form or other.

Soumanasya-keeping the mind at peace and well wishing—occurs at many places. It also means keeping harmony in body and mind, and having a balanced mind.

Medhavardhanam is a sort of prayer, "may high intelligence come to us or may our intelligence increase."

Of special interest to the subject-matter of this book is 6th kand 111S which deals with उन्मत्ततामोचन or getting relief from insanity. It describes in detail the behaviour of a patient suffering from unmad, how he blurbs (बरबराना) crying (विलाप). It may be due to devansat or rakshaspari—or due to paps (पाप) sins committed by the patient. It asks the patient to be quiet. It also says that Apsaras, who cause dushswapnas, may make you well again.

112 similarly gives a wish or prayer : may you be free of the binding (पाश) of the Pichachi पिशाची.

113 gives ways of removal of bad deeds (पापनाशन) "O bad deeds go into the rays of the sun, or the smoke coming from the fire, or go to the fog". 113/3 says, : "Ishwara purifies the papas—in the five sense organs (ज्ञानेन्द्रिय) in five organs of action (कर्मन्द्रिय), mana and buddhi (मन+बुद्धि) in all the twelve places. Still if they (papas) reside

in you, wise people will remove your pain with the use of mantras." Unmochan उन्मोचन is being relieved from papas or sins.

6/139 deals with soubhagya vardhan or creating or enhancing good luck.

The seventh kand deals with soul and its upliftment. Here many goddesses are also named like Aditi Poosha etc.

The eighth kand gives ways on how to get a long life, and destroying enemies and other subjects.

The ninth kand deals with variety of subject like madhuvidya eroticism, welcoming visitors, removing TB (yakshma) etc.

The tenth kanda is concerned with pollution of actions or the Angirashi techniques of sending back ominous objects or kritya कृत्या. It deals with Brahma prakashan emergence of Brahma the divine light, and gaining victory over enemies, (note the divergence in the subjects.)

This kanda gives manibandhan (मणिबन्धन). It is a defence method to ward off evil (like charm or तावीज). Manibandhan is also supposed to help in gaining ojas and manliness वीर्य पुरुषत्व अविनाश, चक्षु प्रकाश. Then there is Satgyan and ritgyan which mean a good knowledge. The ancient rishis ask the question—"who is the basis of this world— सर्वाधार who created akash prithvi this this. . . . . ." and then answer, "The Lord", there are mainly praises of the lord. The gods mentioned are Indra, Vishnu mainly.

This description is given to let the reader have a real taste of what is there in Atharva veda and the style in which it is presented.

The Classification of Abnormalities in Atharva Veda

The abnormalities given in Atharva Veda can be classified in many ways. P. Arsh has classified the mental diseases discussed in Atharva Veda into two broad categories, the first is that of severe disturbances like unmad, and the second are the defects of mental processes, such as krodh (anger) moh (attachment) shok (depression) dushswapna or (bad dreams).

A more logical classification is given by Dr. H.G. Singh (1977). Dr. Singh considers it more feasible to classify the mental disorders given in Atharva Veda in three categories, viz., (1) severe disorders, (2) mild ailments and (3) the methods of personality improvement, integration and health (पौष्टिकानि).

The category 1—severe disorders— ranges diseases which are far removed from normality like unmad.—This includes all the diseases known as psychoses and neuroses in modern terms. It includes Grahi or (hysteria), apasmar (epilepsy), manaspap (schizophrenia), bhaya (phobia), pap bhawna (guilt and inferiority feelings).

The category 2—mild ailments— are deviations of normal mental processes and can be called neuroses in modern terms. They exist in normal behaviour, though in abnormal in larger degrees than normal, for example krodh. These may also be character defects like moh or eroticism or emotional outbursts.

Shafer and Lazarus have classified functional mental disorders into three categories—"psychoses, neuroses and disorders of less serious nature." About the last or mild disorders, they say : "The number of personality and behaviour disorders of less serious nature than psychoses or neuroses, are of definite interest to clinical psychology. Child delinquency, maladjustment, marital, scholistic and occupational difficulties and many types of failures in inter-personal relationships may require and respond to some form of psycho-therapy. More recently there has developed a wide spread tendency to extend the psycho-therapy to the mild, chronic and acute neuroses as well as to the incipient cases of emotional disturbance." Shaffer and Lazarus, 1952 Atharva Veda more than four thousand years ago, had realized this necessity and dealt in detail with milder ailments of the mind, behaviour and character.

The last category of this classification by Singh deals with the positive means to improve personality and mental health. These have been given in Paustikarni suktas and some other suktas like samansayani. These are concerned with improvement in memory and learning, Atma-bal or energizing the ago, and integration and harmony within the person. This is a special unique feature of Atharva Veda and all other Indian systems to give more importance to the positive side them to the negative side or disorders and diseases.

As seen from the above discussion Atharva Veda aims at synthesis. This synthesis is of body and mind, of various aspects of the mind, and of the psyche and cosmic energy Atma and Parmatma or Brahma.

The following Table 4.1 presents the classification of mental abnormalities as dealt in the Atharva Veda.

TABLE 4.1.
CLASSIFICATION OF ABNORMALITIES DEALT IN THE ATHARVA VEDA

Severe Disorders	*Mild Ailments*	*Personality Improvement*
1. Unmad (insanity)	1. Krodh (anger, aggression)	1. Medha vardhan (memory and learning improvement)
2. Graha (siezure or hysteria)	2. Irsha (jealousy)	2. Paushtikarni (energising the ego) Atma-bal
3. Apasmar (epilepsy)	3. Moh (attachment)	3. Samansayani (integration and harmony)
4. Bhaya (phobia)	4. Dushswapna (evil dreams)	
5. Manaspap or schizophrenia	5. Shrap (curse or compulsive evil suggestion)	
	From— Dr. H.G. Singh, 1977	
6. Pap bhawna (guilt and inferiority)		

Symptoms, Diagnosis and Etiology of Abnormal Behaviour in Atharva Veda

The symptoms of diseases are given as well as the methods of diagnosing mental diseases. But all these are scattered in the Suktas of different Kandas of Atharva Veda and it is very difficult to bring together under one heading, the material given here and there. Secondly, it has to be admitted that Atharva Veda is not good at the description of symptoms and diagnosis of diseases, though it is very good in giving the therapeutic processes.

The approach of Atharva Veda is therapeutic in nature. It is not diagnostically oriented. Symptoms and diagnosis have been neglected by the sage-authors of Atharva Veda. At least the two Shakhas, Pipplad and Shaunak which are available at present, deal with symptoms and diagnosis of mental diseases in a very sketchy way, while they are very rich in therapy. It may be that the shakhas which are not available, might contain symptoms and diagnosis in more detail.

Now we start with abnormalities and improvement programmes one by one and shall come to therapies in a later section.

Severe Disorders

Main disorders mentioned are six in number:—

Unmad— Unmad is a general name given to insanity. It is given in AV VI/3/1-4. Various Indian and foreign authors have commented on these viz., Whitney, Max Muller, R. G. Shastri, R. C. Sharma, Satavalekar, P. Arsh, Shende and Griffith. The authors give different names to the malody discussed in the Sukta as "unmad", "mania", "muktika adhikari" etc. But "unmad" or insanity are most used names and seem appropriate.

The Symptoms Given— Incoherent and irrelevant talk, generally nuisance and often violent, has to be kept in chains sometimes, mind out of order disturbed, unquiet, excited, crying loudly etc. These symptoms seem to match the description of insanity and psychosis in modern psycho-pathology.

Causes or Etiology— Atharva Veda gives two types of causes for this disease—(a) Devansat or the sin against the gods,

(b) Rakshaspari or caused or influenced by the demons.

Devansat— a sin against gods is a symbolic term and makes a general assertion. According to P. Arsh the correct explanation for this term is—"overthrowing the authority of devas—the gentle, ideal learned and honoured people, they may be gods, gurus, parents, society, culture. It means neglecting sattva vritti, i.e., all the acts comprising goodness and misusing the fine senses make one insane." P. Arsh. The same opinion is expressed by Satavalekar also.

So in Atharva Veda, some four thousand years back, we find the fact, scientifically established by Freud in the recent past, i.e. 20th century.

In psychoanalysis similar term representing the authority of parents, gods, gurus, society etc. is superego. It also represents whatever is known as sattva guna all gentle and good. In insanity this superego is overthrown negating sattva guna. Scebelon in Atharva Veda. Some four thousand years back we find the fact scientifically established by Freud in the recent past, i.e., 20th century. It is that insanity is caused by the wrath of the Gods or overthrowing the authority of the super-ego.

Rakshaspari or caused by demons. It has been misunderstood as caused by 'demons entering a human being and leading him/her to wrong ways. The word 'demon' Rakshas here is symbolic. It means coming under the influence of rajas or tamas evil and badness. Insanity is caused by an over activity or an increase in rajas and tamas. It is not caused by outside factors. It is a functional disease caused by internal factors.'

Here again we find a similarity in psychoanalysis. Freud gave the term Id—"A reservoir of both life and death instincts"—According to Freud Id acts on a pleasure and pain principle. So we can safely conclude that rakshaspari of the Atharva Veda can be taken as a name for the forces of Id as given by Freud. The man is under the influence of demon, i.e., his own inner instinctual desires. According to Brown, in the psychotic or insane personality." The ego allies itself with the Id and supports the demands of Id, denying reality. The Id drives breakthrough in a disguised and socially unacceptable form, super-ego may disappear. Brown 1940.

The therapy for unmad in Atharva Veda VI-3 has been explained by Max Muller, Shende, Shastri, Sharma and Arsh. Therapies are Agni and havana chikitsa, aushadh, divya and manas chikitsa, adesh or suggestion, prayashchit and utarna transference. These therapies will be discussed in the next chapter.

Grahi— Hysteria—an attack of seizure. Atharva veda describes this disease in many ways in II/10/628, II/9/1, VIII/2/12, XII/3/18 and VI/113/1-3 VI/112/2 etc. Max Muller has explained these as a demon or as a fit of seizure, an attack of disease, as a misfortune etc. The disease is personified as a female demon 'grahi' a disease which catches hold of a person and alters his personality. It means that the person's ego—his consciousness—is shadowed and suppressed by the disease. The patient becomes helpless—Griffith translates the term 'grab' as seizure, Whitney and Karambelkar also use the term fit and seizure and call it a disease like epilepsy.

Shende thinks that grahi brings convulsions and seizes the joints so grahi is a disease of fit, convulsions and seizure. Satavalekar enumerates several kinds of grah's, most common are raksh, rakshas, pishach, gandharva and apsara. Their symptoms are mentioned in AV IV/37/1-12. There is a difference of opinion and confusion over the interpretations of these mantras. Sayanacharya and following him, Whitney think that the grahs as named are the supernatural spirits which attack human beings. Arsh and R. G. Shastri consider them to be the symbolic names for germs of diseases. Satavalekar considers them as kinds of mental diseases, named unmad. In the 11th mantra, the symptoms given as behaving like a dog and monkey are symptoms of a patient suffering from unmad.

AV II/2/1-5 gandharva and apsara occur as causing this disease. Satavalekar interprets gandharva as Atma and apsara as energies of atma. Winternitz on the other hand holds that the gandharvas or apsaras "may be the symbols of an individual's wishes and desires", which may be the causing agents of mental problems.

The words 'gandharva' and 'apsara' have occured in Atharva Veda in various ways, as high being as divine beings of attractive kind who only attack lovely women for their pleasure. They are also said to combine the pishachs as lower beings and attack human beings, they have to be driven out by plant-medicines.

Apsaras are supposed to be the wives of gandharvas. They are worshipped at the time of marriage, they bestow luck on people but also bewild the mind of man (AV II/2/5). They are beautiful divine dancers. They like gambling and delude the mind 3 of men.

Among all other characteristics of gandharvas and apsaras the most outstanding ones are their eroticism and sexuality. B. D. Vedalankar, while interpreting AV XII/1/50, explains gandharva as 'vilasi purush' (erotic type of man) and apsara as vilasini stri (erotic type of women). R.G. Shastri is of the opinion that these words—gandharva and apsara are used symbolically in the Atharva Veda.

The words gandharva and apsara have been used variously in Atharva Veda, but four meanings are more common. Firstly that these are not common physical beings nor microscopic germs. They represent psychic phenomena-urges of the mind. They are constituents of the mind. Secondly that they are erotic or sexual in nature urging for union with a person of opposite sex. Thirdly these words symbolize many of the material and non-material symptoms of the diseases such as dancing, loving fragrance etc. Fourthly they cause mental abnormality or disease. Thus we can conclude that in Atharva Veda gandharva and apsara symbolize psychic symptom-formation, caused by sex frustration among male and female both.

When there is hyper function of sexual urge aroused in a male or female then he/she gets more and more emotionally crazed and entangled in the love object. If this emotion is not discharged in reality then suppression and frustration lead to severe symptom formation, which in turn may take the form of attack by gandharva/apsara which are the symbols of object cathexis, grah or complexes. Grah can be used for a complex. Commenting on AV II/2/5 Max Muller says, "primarily the madness which gandharva/apsara can cause, and which are called upon to remove, is in accordance with the general character of these divinities, the madness of love........"

The descriptions of hysteric fit and seizure by Freud as well as Brown come very near to the mental disease described as gandharva and apsara grahs in Atharva Veda. The patient is in the grip of heterosexual urge, it does not leave him and overpowers him at the time of fit, which is like a compulsion (grah) from which the patient cannot get relief. At the time of fit, its own love object, symbolic gandharva/apsara, which is a part of his own psychic personality, passionately seduces it. It is self-hypotism-self-eroticism and so is hysteria.

According to renowned western authorities like Max Muller, Whitney, Griffith etc. symbolism and personification have always played a very great role in the Atharva Veda. T. V. Kapali Shastri says, "we have seen that symbolism is the key to unlock the secrets of the veda." —1951.

Now it can be concluded that the grahs named as gandharva and apsara are actually the names of functional/mental disorders caused by the frustration of the sexual urge. It is known as hysteria in western terms. In the same way raksh, rakshas and pishach are the symbolic names of mental diseases of compulsive and functional nature. The symbols have a correspondance with the nature of the symptoms of the diseases.

The therapies suggested for this type of mental disorder in Atharva Veda are aushadh chikitsa (medicines), manibandhan (tying of special charms) havan, adesh (suggestion) transference and prayashchita. They will be dealt in more detail in the next chapter.

Apasmar (Epilepsy—the Convulsive Disease)

The description of this disease is found in AV VIII/1/3, 4, 6, 7, 16, 18-21, XIX/36/6 and II/4/2. AV VIII/1/16, is the special sukta describing the disease. The disease is explained by Max Muller as— "The demon that tears out the tongue." This demon is named as 'Jambh'. Whitney also calls it the demon Jambh and explains it as convulsions or lock jaw. Sayanacharya and following him Sharma (R.C.) think that Jambh is a demon of fatal mental disease. Bloomfield, Whitney and Shende also interpret Jambh as convulsions or lock-jaw. Karambelkar calls Jambh "a demon of convulsions."

Arsh, explaining AV II/4/2 says, "Jambh is a mental disease of destruction which catches hold of the joints." Satavaletar gives the meaning of Jambh as teeth mouth and jaws (literally jamming up of these or lock-jaw).

Actually **AV** VIII/1/16, gives the name of the disease as Jambh, which seems to be a psychic disorder in which there are convulsions and also jamming of teeth and jaws. Jambh the demon is a personification of the disease.

Readers must have noted that in grahi (hysteria) also there are convulsions. But there are definite symptoms to distinguish between grahi and apasmar. These features are described by Max Muller as, "during the convulsions patient lies down, inattentive and cut off from this world, mind (consciousness) disappears (becomes unconscious). Only men and youth are thus attacked and women weep for these men." Max Muller (1964). So the three outstanding symptoms of apasmar are—(1) Convulsions and lock-jaw, (2) makes unconscious and (3) tears the tongue of the patient.

Modern psychiatry gives in detail the symptoms of epilepsy as given above. Dawson W.S. gives the symptoms as— consciousness is lost, 75 per cent cases begin before the age of twenty, tongue is bitten (tearing off) and the joints become stiff.

Dawson distinguishes between hysterial fit and epilepsy on many points— (1) Epilepsy is more common in males, while hysteria is not. (2) In epilepsy tongue is always bitten, not so in hysteria. (3) The loss of consciousness is complete and sudden in epilepsy, but is gradual in hysteria.

The most remarkable symptom according to AV VIII/1/16, is the closing of the jaw and tearing of the tongue. And in modern psychiatry also this is the only outstanding symptom of epilepsy which distinguishes it from all other convulsions. One more similarity is found, explaining AV VIII/1/16 Max Muller says, "darkness falls", while Brown and Drake R.M. say that conciousness is 'clouded'—these terms "darkness" and "clouded" are similar terms. So the symptoms mentioned in AV VIII/1/16 are specifically those of epileptic convulsions. This disorder or epilepsy is personified in demon Jambh who 'tears the tongue out' or 'jaws cut the tongue'.

Another feature is the hereditory nature of epilepsy, given both in Atharva Veda and modern psycho-pathology. Sayan **AV** II/8/1 considers apasmar as a kshetrya (hereditory) disease coming through parents. Shende also endorses this view as well as Bloomfield who translated it as hereditory disease.

The therapies given are the use of Jangid tree product in the form of amulet AV II/4/2 and medicine, havan chikitsa and mantra therapy.

Bhaya (Phobia)

Atharva Veda gives various rituals in shanti-karm which help in driving out fears of many kinds. These fears are named as—bhaya (fear) of bhuchal (earthquake, storm), agni (pyrophobia), yama (death), varuni (hydro phobia), vayu (air), enemy and persecution etc. AV II/15, IX VI/40 and XIX 14, 15 are for driving out fear in general AV VII/32/3 is meant to drive out the fear of germs (krimi) which cause diseases (pathophobia) Mantras are for individual and group use. According to R.C. Sharma, sukta IV/10 should be used to remove hydrophobia and IV/25 to remove airphobia. AV VI/112 is meant for removing the fear of enemy and persecution (thanatophobia). The use of jangid mani is suggested for hydrophobia and darbh mani to cure thanatophobia. Besides manis, other therapies suggested for fears are manibandhan (tying of charms) suggestion, autosuggestion, prayer, havana and kavach (amulet).

According to Atharva Veda bhaya is caused by an increase in rajas vritti or love for one's own self and the tamas vritti getting weak. Strong tamas can fight fears, but when it gets weak, fears overcome man. Thus according to Atharva Veda bhaya or phobia is caused by internal factors and is a functional disease.

Manaspap— AV VI/45 gives three mantras for this disease. There is a difference of opinion among scholars on the interpretation of these mantras. Whitney has given a literal meaning to it as 'mind-evil'. Max Muller and Karambelkar opine that it is for expiation of delinquency. R.C. Sharma and Satavalekar hold that it is meant for evil dreams. None of these seems to be correct.

No doubt it refers to the abnormality to mind or sin to mind. The symptoms enumerated in Atharva Veda are— (1) the patients hear voices not coming from any physical source outside, but arising from his own mind. The voices are unpleasant, their words are of persecutory nature, (2) the patient shows apathy. His mind is not in family or in business, (3) the patient has a split personality, (4) he prays for protection. Modern psycho-pathology describes the symptoms of schizophrenia paranoid type in a similar way. The major symptoms of this disease are— (1) the splitting of personality, (2) schizoid nature, that is apathy towards family, business and other social demands, (3) vivid auditory hallucinations of obscure words and (4) delusions of persecution. So the disease given in AV VI/45 is evidently the disease known in modern psycho-pathology as schizophrania paranoid type. It is caused by an increase in rajas and tamas both. Tamas increases so much that it becomes self-destructive.

In the three mantras, the remedies suggested are auto-suggestion, confession, havan, transference and prayer.

Pap-bhawana (Sin, guild and inferiority feeling)— Pap-bhawana is mentioned in Atharva Veda at several places. Without going in details, it will be better to summarize these.

AV III/31/1-11 explain 'pap' and 'punya' where 'pap' means adopting the behaviour destructive to one's own self and others and 'punya' means leading a life constructive to one's own self and society. Henry Lefever, in his book *The Vedic Idea of Sin* has elaborated on this and considers Atharvedic conception of sin as psychological. In modern dynamic psychology 'pap' corresponds to the behaviour—'overthrowing the authority of super-ego, which results in sin guilt and inferiority feeling'. So psychologically 'pap' means a feeling of guilt and inferiority in the ego, affecting the activities of the ego and leading to abnormal behaviour.

The word 'pap' is used in Atharva veda in three senses—sin, guilt and inferiority feeling. When somebody is affected by 'pap' it appears psychologically in 'pap-grah' (inferiority complex) and physiologically in the form of different diseases, calamities and distress. AV VI/113/1-3 explains that the misuse of sense organs gives rise to 'pap' in mind, which creates rheumatic diseases which are cured by correct knowledge (सद्ज्ञान) . In Atharva Veda 'pap' is caused in two ways—by one's own misdeeds and inflicted from outside. Many misdeeds of one's own are enumerated and inflicted from outside are also given in large number mainly those which come from family such as debt, or from society.

When 'pap' is removed the behaviour of the ego becomes normal and as a result one gets prosperity success and knowledge.

Karambelkar says, "In both Rigveda and Atharva Veda the conception of 'pap' is assimilated with the idea of disease. As a disease confers a taint upon the patient so a 'pap' does. So both the disease and the sin were thought to be external and fit to be banished by means of spell." Modern psycho-pathology also considers guilt or inferiority feeling as a pathological symptom of mental disease. It is directly related to feeling process. It is a purely functional disorder.

Atharva Veda gives both individual and group therapies for 'pap'. These are the means of release from the sin. Lefever also gives means of releases from sin, as prayer etc. The means suggested for 'pap bhawana' in Atharva Veda are as follows — (1) Prayer and sacrifice to different gods, (2) auto-suggestion, (3) suggestion by the priest, (4) prayashchita-tapa and confession, (5) hydro-therapy bathing and sprinkling water, (6) expiatory rites, (7) medicine from apamarg plant, (8) mani (amulet) of varun tree and (9) transference.

Mild Ailments— Manas pap and pap-bhawana are treated

differently in Atharva Veda as these are different types of mental disorders. As seen earlier, these are not actually diseases, but disorders of normal behaviour. These are less severe in nature but are abnormal. In normal behaviour these are controlled. Arsh calls them

Krodh (anger or rage).

—*Manasik dosh*

Mention of krodh occurs in AV VI/42/1-3 and VI/43/1-3. It shows that anger is expressed in the grinding of jaws and teeth and tensing the nerves of the face. It destroys commonness and friendship. It is a functional disorder caused by increase in tamas. Sattwa is covered by tamas. Its action is towards outer reality.

Atharva veda suggests four ways to avert krodh—(1) by suggestion, (2) by minute thinking, insight and sweet voices, (3) by forceful suppression by a priest, a therapist or any other person and also by (4) appeasement, cold drinks, such as darbh grass (खस) which cools off the mind.

Irsha (Jealousy)— It is described in AV VI/18/1-3, VIII/45, 46, 47 and VII/74/3. Some commentators like Whitney call it a disease, while others like Arsh, call it a mansik dosh and rog. Satavalekar also calls it a dosha of mind. It is a functional disorder caused by the increase in tamas. It is likened to a fire which burns and destroys the energies of mind and body. This idea of fire is carried in the Hindi and dialects also as jalna (जलना) . In irsha the cognitive process of mind is affected, it becomes inactive.

Atharva Veda suggests therapies to cure irsha. These are (1) suggestion by a priest with rites, (2) the use of certain medicines like samundraphal (usually found near seas), (3) minute thinking and insight and (4) sweet voices sweet talk.

Moh (Eroticism) or Kama (Sex)— In Atharva veda mantras, kama and moh occur in a variety of ways. Kama is personified as a primordial creative power. It resides and works in every male and female. It is natural and necessary for the creation and survival of life. It is regarded as pious. Similarly Freud and many other Western thinkers emphasize the importance of sex. In Indian thought kama is regarded as normal, so long as it is within the limits of society, time and place. But when out of limits it becomes abnormal.

The abnormality of moh or kama is described in AV III/21/4, III/25/6, III/139/1-5, VI/130/1-4, VI/131/1-3 and VI/132. We can summarize these ideas as follows—

The abnormality of moh is of two types—one is its hyper function, which has to be brought down to normal function and the other is its hypo function or low function which must be increased or lifted to make it normal. Both extremes are caused by the rise and fall of rajas vritti. Brown in his *Psycho Dynamics of Abnormal Behaviour* also describes them as the anomalies of the sexual function.

AV III/21/4 deals with hyper function of moh, according to Satavalekar and Whitney, to cool or lower down its degree, the means suggested are—prayer to kama, havan in agni, because kama is like agni. So this mantra or prayer is a sort of sankalp or auto-suggestion. AV VI/30-132 suktas are meant for cooling the burning fire of sex in man. The idea of Max Muller is just the opposite. He considers these suktas to be a means to arouse kama in men and women. The mantras of III/25/1-6 and VI/139/1-5 are in the form of prayer to arouse love or kama. The use of a medicine prepared by *sahasrapami (menoeeheCeea)* a plant, is also suggested.

Dushswapna (Evil dreams)—This has been discussed at many places in many suktas. B.D. Vedalankar in his famous book *Vedic Swapna Vigyan* discussed the Atharva Vedic concepts of dreams in full detail. Atharva Veda describes dreams as one of the three states of mind in a being— (1) Jagrat (waking), (2) Swapna (dream) and (3) Sushupti (half waking half-sleeping). According to Vedalankar, in Atharva Veda, dreams are classified as normal dreams and morbid or evil dreams (*ogMrnJehve*). The normal dream is good and promotes harmony in personality, while the evil dreams create evil thought processes, they increase rajas and tamas. These are grahi or catch hold of the mind as corruptions. The evil dream is considered to be mental disease worthy of psychic treatment by a therapist—AV XVI/7/7-8, Arsh says that evil dream is definitely a mental disease and gives its etiology and therapy. Shende says evil dream in Atharva Veda is a condition of sin of mind—it may lead to calamity and death. It requires pacification. Satavalekar says that kand XVI in Atharva Veda calls evil dreams a *vyadhi*. It is caused by both rajas and tamas not finding outlet in the waking life. The causes or etiology of dushswapan as given in Atharva Veda are:—

(1) *Grahi*—or the different mental complexes.
(2) *Nritti* or the tamasik vritti destructive images within.
(3) *Abhuti* or the unfulfilled wishes produce them as a way to wish fulfillment.
(4) *Nirbhuti* or the loss of precious things or prestigious positions in life and trying to regain them in dreams.
(5) *Parabhooti* or defeat from a rival or enemy revengeful dreams against rivals or enemies.
(6) *Devjamiyon*—all sorts of constructive or destructive drives. In Pipplad shakha XIII/24/5, 6, II some more causes of evil dreams are given. Evil dreams are symbolically called the sons of—
    (1) *Varun*—i.e. fear and sin cause evil dreams.
    (2) *Sam*—i.e., sleep itself.
    (3) *Gandharva and apasaras*—i.e., the sex urges.

Here, compare Freud's theory of dreams that says—dreams are wish-fulfillment of sexual nature. These include free play of suppressed urges both constructive and destructive in nature also fear and anxiety.

B.D. Vedalankar has discussed the devices suggested in Atharva Veda to drive away evil dreams. These devices or therapies are:—

(1) By increasing sankalpa shakti or psychic energy-will-in oneself.
(2) Suggestion and auto suggestion since dreams are natural and they must come, replace evil dreams with good or auspicious dreams.
(3) By prayers to gods specially Brahma and Kama.
(4) By prayer or suggestion to transfer evil dreams to enemies.
(5) By jal or hydrotherapy.
(6) By medicines prepared from the apamarg plant.
(7) By therapies in mental hospitals AV XVI/7/7, 8.

B.D. Vedalankar has proved that there were mental hospitals of special types in the Vedic times where evil dreams were treated by the therapists. According to Arsh Atharva Veda gives three therapies for evil dreams—the use of varan mani, anjan mani and jal chikitsa. In short the therapies suggested in Atharva veda for evil dreams are suggestion and auto suggestion, jal, amulet, medicines and the havana etc. religious therapies.

Shrap (श्राप) (A curse, or compulsive evil suggestion for bringing calamities and misfortunes on a person.)

AV II/7/1-4, VI/37/1-3 and VII/59, 61, 65 and 67 deal with *shrap*. The views expressed in these mantras are given by different commentators. Shende—'In Atharvanic ideology the curse plays an important part. It implies the disastrous effect of spoken words addressed to someone with a view to injuring or killing. These curses effect the person's life, progeny and wealth when the curses are uttered, their effect is gradually seen on the person, on whom they are inflicted."

Satavalekar— 'It is the pronouncing of evil words for somebody's destruction and calamity, charged with the energy of anger and ill-will."

Shrap is a suggestion to create evil effects, it is opposite of ashirvad, which is meant as good wishes or blessings. In *shrap* an evil psychic energy is emitted from the mind of the originator and hits or badly affects the mind of the receiver. The energy of anger, ill-will or atma bal of a rishi or man of prestige is behind it.

AV II/7/1 considers it like a sin and abnormality of the mind. Whitney considers it a sort of disease which has to be healed by expiatory rites. This ill-willed compulsive suggestion creates abnormality in the behaviour and life of the person on whom it is thrown. It is purely psychogenic and it is caused by tamas vritti.

Like *shrap*, evil eye (नजर) also produces bad effects. AV XIX/35/3 refers to the effects of evil eye.

Atharva Veda suggests several ways to ward off the evil effects of *shrap*. These are—

(1) Sending it back to the originator.
(2) To remove it by different forms of suggestion therapy, sankalpa.
(3) Wearing amulets of palasha and ingida trees, yava (जौ) and apamarg tree.

(4) Performing rituals by an Atharvanic priest.

(5) By transference.

Since *shrap*—both giving and receiving it are mental phenomena, they come under the scope of this book.

Personality Improvement, Integration and Health

These are the positive devices for the well being of people, and are mental health and hygiene programmes meant to prevent the occurance of mental diseases and disorder. Shaffer and Lazarus: "Actually the objective of psychotherapy is always the same, namely, to secure the soundest degree of mental or psychological health that is possible." Atharva Veda gives some ways to secure mental health and make improvements in personality.

Medha Vardhan (Improving Memory and Learning)

AV I/1/1-4, VI/108/1-3, VII/61 and VII/67 deal with *medhavardhans*. Whitney, Satavalekar, Shende and R. Sharma have commented on this. Medha is interpreted as intelligence by Satavalekar. The word meaning of medha is 'retentive capacity'. Out of the four factors of memory, given by modern psychology, learning, retention, recall and recognition, the first three have been emphasized. Atharva veda also deals with amnesia—a complete loss of memory, and suggests ways and means to improve memory. According to commentators AV VI/108/1-5, VII/61, 63/1-2, XIX/3/4 and XIX/4/12 deal with learning, AV I/1/1-4 deal with retention, AV VII/66, 68/1 and VII/67, 69/1 deal with recall.

Atharva Veda prescribes three methods to improve memory—

(1) *Sankalp*—self-determination to acquire and retain knowledge.

(2) *Tapa*—mental exercise, repetition, hard penances.

(3) *Havan, and prayer*—which act as suggestions.

Out of these, mental determination or readiness and exercise have been suggested by modern psychology also.

Paushtikarni— Making robust and strong. Here it means gaining strength of the ego or atma-bal.

Our sages, thousands of years ago, emphasized the need of strength in personality, both physical and mental strength. A strong energetic ego-atma—is necessary for mental health. Atharva Veda gives various procedures for strengthening the body as well as atma. But here we are concerned only with psychic energy, i.e., atma-bal.

Atharva Veda gives various ways and measures to increase atma-bal. These are given in AV II/12/1-8, II/17/1-7, V/10/1, V/9/1-7, VI/38/1-4, VI/41/1-3 and XI/8/4. The measures given in these mantras in summary are—

(1) To increases knowledge about ourselves and the world. (2) Sacrifice, (3) Self-control, (4) Sweet speech (*ce=og JeeCeer*), (5) Prayer to different cosmic powers devas, to increase different sorts of psychic powers in one self creates a sense of power and confidence in oneself. It works as auto-suggestion. (6) Sankalpa is determination within oneself to gain atmic-bal.

Samanasyani (Integration and Harmony with Others)

These special hymns are meant for social groups, not with individual personality.

Atharva Veda, in order to control and prevent incidence of mental illness due to social factors, propounded devices to check these social factors such as disintegration. They come under the mental health programme of fighting psychic disorders. The devices to create social harmony are given in three broad categories— (1) the family, (2) the friends and small group and (3) the whole nation or the country.

According to different Vedic scholars like Whitney, Bloomfield, Satavalekar and R. C. Sharma—the Atharvanic mantras are as given—

AV II/30/1-5, III/30/1-7, VII/38/1-5 deal with integration in family. AV VI/42/1-3, VI/64/1-3, VI/73/1-3, VI/94/1-3, VI/102/1-3, VII/52/1-2 deal with integration and harmony among friends and other small groups, AV I/15/1-4 and III/8/1-6 deal with integration in nation and country. All the above mantras mention 'manas' or 'mana', again and again, because social integration depends on the minds of individuals.

The measures suggested for samanjasya-harmony-are— (1) suggestions of different types, (2) performing rituals like havan, (3) prayer to different gods, (4) use of herbs have been suggested to avert disharmony and disintegration and to create harmony.

Modern psychopathology also emphasizes the importance of social factors in mental life. Social disintegration, wars, riots, social aggression, broken homes give rise to .behaviour abnormalities. Page (James D.) has discussed such causes of abnormality under environmental and cultural factors.

Maslow and Mittlemann also discuss cultural factors in etiology. They concludes that there is a definite relationship between psychopathology and social disintegration.

So measures to create social harmony must have been most welcome to Atharvans. They also realized that social harmony can be attained by individual minds that is why मानस. Manas is repeated time and again.

Five

Psychotherapy in Atharva Veda

It is clear by now that the general objective of Atharva veda is the welfare of all human beings. It wishes people "to live a long and healthy life for more than a hundred years and then attain Brahma i.e., merge in the cosmic energy". It is to fulfill this aim that Atharva veda seeks to remove all the barriers to a good healthy life to attain perfect robust health and to prevent and cure diseases of both body and mind. So in the field of psychotherapy too its object is to achieve sound mental health and for this objective, the measures it applies are mainly psychological. AV XIV/67.

Shende has rightly said, "The Atharvanic ideology aims at securing full enjoyment of life, for a period of hundred years and becoming free from all diseases, distress, sin and hostile witch-craft, which shorten the life of a person."

Psychotherapy— Weigel says— "Two interpretations of the word psychotherapy are possible—(1) the psychotherapy that uses exclusively the psychic means of personal contact, we can call identical psychotherapy, (2) the psychotherapy that uses every method in order to cure the psychic cause of a disturbance, we can call non identical psychotherapy."

—Weigel, J.A. 1958

Richards— "In its broadest sense this term psychotherapy is sometimes used to cover all the procedures that are used in handling maladjusted individuals."

—Richards, T.W. 1946

So, the term psychotherapy may mean—

(1) A therapy using mainly psychological methods,
(2) Which is concerned with functional mental disorders,
(3) Which is based on a theory that mental disorders are psychogenic,

(4) Which may include measures which are not strictly psychological.

Thus, psychotherapy has a broad meaning as well as a special meaning.

Atharva Veda tries to solve the problem of mental disorders. According to Karambelkar, Atharva Veda has made two kinds of therapeutic approaches —

Atharvanik— a psychological system. **Kaushik**— a physical system.

Atharva Veda is mainly psychological in nature, and applies the psychological or manas approach to all the problems of man. This manas approach is a unique feature of Atharvanik system. They claim to control, not only the psychic but also the physical world by means of manas or psyche. So, the basic Atharvanik approach to the treatment of mental disorders is mental, but at places it falls back on the kaushik or the physical system also. Here we are concerned with Atharva vedic manas chikitsa or psychotherapy mainly.

Classification of the Atharvedic Psychotherapies

Firstly, one observes that there is no hard and fast division or classification of therapies in Atharva Veda. There are several kinds of therapies for one disorder and one type of therapy for many kinds of disorders. The therapies are not mutually exclusive. Their features very often overlap such as havan-prayer etc. All the therapies in Atharva Veda include suggestion and re-education.

Shaffer and *Lazarus* say the same thing for western therapies— "While each method possesses certain unique and distinctive characteristics, they are not mutually exclusive. Within the framework of each distinctive therapy, certain features of other methods are utilized."

—*Shaffer and Lazaras, 1952*

In **AV** XI/4/16 a broad classification of therapeutic methods for mental diseases is given. It is as follows:—

Atharvani (अथर्वाणी) — psychological or manas chikitsa.
Angirasi (आंगिरसी) — endocrine (with body's own fluids or rasa).
Daiviya (दैवीय) — divine nature-therapy.
Manushyaja (मनुष्यज) — medicines prepared by human beings.

We may further classify these in Weigel's system.

I. Atharvanic Manas Chikitsa (Psychogenic or Identical)

1. Mantra-vidya—
   - (a) Sankalpa (self-determination or auto suggestion)
   - (b) Sadesh (suggestion)
   - (c) Samvashikaran (hypnosis)
   - (d) Rituals, drama
   - (e) Brahma kavach (psychological defensive belief)
2. Utarna—transference.
3. Ashwasana and upchar (assurance, desensitization, re-education).
4. Daiviya havan chikitsa—spiritual prayer with havan and rituals.
5. Prayashchitani— Sweekarokti (confession)
tapa (penance)
Balidan (sacrifice)

II. Kaushik or Bhautik Chikitsa (Somatogenic or non Identical)

1. **Angirasi**— endocrine or of juices of the body
2. **Daivya prakrat**— (divine and natural)
   - (a) Jal chikitsa—hydro-therapy
   - (b) Vayu chikitsa—air-therapy
   - (c) Agni chikitsa—heat-therapy
   - (d) Sour chikitsa—sun-therapy
3. Manushyaja or medicines prepared by human beings.

Here the basic interest is in the first category, that is identical therapies or Atharvanic manas chikitsa. Which will be discussed in detail. The equivalent or similar type of Western psychotherapies will be given side by side wherever possible, to present a comparison between the Eastern and Western systems of psychotherapy.

Atharvanic or Psychogenic Therapies

Whenever the therapy is based mainly on psychological factors it is called manas chikitsa. The Atharvanic therapy is mainly based on atma so it is psychogenic or manas chikitsa, i.e., the therapy comes from within oneself not from outside factors.

Main Features of Atharvanic Manas Chikitsa

The Approach— The approach of Atharva Veda is always psychological or psychosomatic, never purely somatic. Atharva veda is directly concerned with mana, manas, atma, buddhi and chitta. Satavalekar quotes Gopatha Brahman 3/2 and Aitreyi Brahman 5/33 which say that "vani and manas are the two sides of a man. The knowledge of the three vedas, Rig, Yajur and Sam, purifies and energizes vani, while the Atharva veda purifies and energizes the manas".

AV XI, according to Satavalekar, says that manas chikitsa is Atharvanic chikitsa in which mainly mantras and power of psyche (आत्म बल) are used to cure diseases. **AV** XI/4/16 clearly asserts that without the energy of psyche or manas, no other therapy such as medicines, prepared either by gods or by man, or angirasi (endocrine therapy) or any other therapy can work.

In Atharvanic therapy psychic energy is basically required in both the healer and the patient. The Atharvedic priest or healer is a true Brahma-vetta or one who has knowledge of Brahma, who has practical knowledge of Atharva Veda and who has attained oneness with the cosmic energy, i.e., Brahma. He possesses enormous mental energy of Brahma the creator, in himself, and uses this in his treatment along with his practical knowledge of Atharva veda. As Shende says, "Thus even in his scientific treatment of the diseases, he administers his medicine to the patient only in association with his spells."

—Shende, N.S., 1952

The message of Atharva veda is that all diseases whether somatogenic or psycho-genic should be cured by manas chikitsa or psychic method.

Karambelkar says, "The Atharva veda is a record of psychosomatic technique of healing by a combined procedure of charms, prayers, incantations, amulets and drugs." It can be said that the Atharvanic healer uses all the methods available to him (at his time) but his sole basis is psychic or manas chikitsa.

Atharva veda propounds that the psyche-mana has the capacity to cure and correct the psyche whether one's own or that of others. The logic behind this is that "when and if matter—medicines or drugs—can affect and cure matter, i.e., the body or its diseases, why can psyche not affect and cure psyche or conscious matter."

Satavalekar says that, "The vedas have given the greatest emphasis on manas chikitsa, than other therapies, and it is the best because it provides greatest freedom to the therapist."

The other therapies depend on outside help, the medicines, the availability of the drugs and other material things. Such therapies are bound by space time and the elements. But in *manas-chikitsa*, no such material help is required. The only thing required is psychic energy which lies within the therapist and is not bound by space time and elements.

Nagar says, "Pran or manasik chikitsa is scientific and best to attain mental health and cure of nervous diseases." It cures through psychic energy-manobal.

—*Nagar, S.D., Pran Chikitsa*

Methods or Branches of Atharvanic Manas Chikitsa

Mantra Vidya— Mantra is the main technique of manas chikitsa.

What is Mantra?— There are various meanings attached to the word 'mantra'. Let us examine some of them—

Mantra— is secret talk. According to Nirukt 7/12 mantra is silent talk.

Satpath Brahman 6/4/1/7 mantra is loud talk including sound.

Kapali Shastri— "Mantra, as is well known, is not a mere letter or a collection of letters with some meaning. It is the sound body of a power-charged with the intense vibrations of the spiritual personality of the creator or the seer of the mantra. The mantra is an ever living embodiment of the truth and power which have found expression in it through the medium of the rishi or yogin who has given it that body. The mantra may be in the form of coherent words or single letters arranged in a certain order."

—*T.V. Kapali Shastri, 1951*

"Mantras", according to Hans Jacobs, "or sounds pregnant with meaning, play a central role in the religious practices of the Hindus......A mantra is a combination of letters, sometimes it is monosyllabic, in which case it belongs to no particular language, sometimes it consists of one or several words, in which case the language used is always Sanskrit. A mantra, if it really lives, is always a powerful instrument."

—Hans Jacobs, 1961

Sri Yogendra says, "Mantra, therefore, is not only a conjoined word but a particular sound body of consciousness."

—Sri Yogendra, 1933

In summary, we can say that a mantra is—

- A silent or loud pronounciation of certain order of words.
- It may be in poetry prose or just syllables.
- It has definite meaning and connotation.
- It is infused with mental energy of the seer or rishi.
- Mantra is related to manas.

Kinds of Mantras

There are two kinds of mantras—

- Vedic mantra—found in the Vedas.
- Tantrik mantra—for special rituals of tantra.

The basic differences between the two are—

- Vedic mantras are as old as the Vedas, i.e., four to five thousand years old. Tantra vidya and its related mantras are of a much later origin. There are some scholars like Kapali Shastri, who believe that tantras originated in Atharva veda, most other scholars do not seem to agree to this.
- Vedic mantras are meant for recital, these are in verse form and have a specific language structure (छंद chhanda). These verses are quite long. The tantrik mantras on the other hand, may be monosyllabic or composed of just a few words.
- Vedic mantras were sung and learnt by heart to be passed on to the generations of disciples. The tantrik mantra are meant for—(i) Japa-inner recitation or (2) Keeping with oneself or tying around arms as Yantra-graphs etc.
- Vedic mantras are in Sanskrit verse and their meanings and sounds are very important to them. The tantrik mantras are very short and sketchy, may be of one syllable only, which is the centre and is known as "bijakshara"

(*yeerpee#ej*). These do not have meanings which are apparent these are the symbols of certain things. These may be found in the form of graphs called Yantra.

- Language meaning and thought have no importance in the Tantrik mantras. These are mechanically used and are supposed to be related to the psychophysical processes. They are more physical mechanical in nature.
- The Vedic mantras are related to Brahma the psychic power.
- Kapali Shastri says, "The vedic hymns are of a different order. They are all mantras where the meaning is as important as the text, and are generally meant for recitals, though a short verse may be selected for japa and meditation."

—*Kapali Shastri, 1951*

Value of Mantras

The Atharvedic mantras are based on psychic and sound phenomena.

Hans Jacobs says, ".....If a mantra is repeated either loud or at more advanced stages of the practice, silently, certain vibrations are produced within the organism, which depend in kind and in degree, on the particular letters used and on their connections. That is, some sort of ultra-sonic waves are produced in the organism by the japa of mantra. These waves have therapeutic value as has been discovered by modern science."

Karambelkar says, "Curative effect of charms is through their sound vibrations which are recognized to be effective by modern science also. So we can assert with some confidence that the charms were not simply witchcraft and deception but had scientific basis."

—*Karambelkar, 1961*

Karambelkar further says, "the charm was the best of all the hundreds and thousands of medical herbs."

Hans Jacobs says, "If well selected, the mantra is of such nature that by the vibrations it produces, it counteracts psychological drawbacks of the sadhaka, providing those elements which in his subtle body are lacking, countering those which are in excess. The atom bomb is as nothing compared with it."

—*Hans Jacobs, 1961*

Dr. B.L. Atreya says, "The effect of mantra is due to psychic feeling." (1963)

The Use of Mantras for Psycho-therapy

Mantras can be and have been used in various ways. Here we will discuss their use in psychotherapy. Some points have to be noted before we proceed further. The first is that there is no rigidity about the use of the mantras. They serve different purposes in different ways. The same mantra can be used for different occasions and in different ways. Secondly, in Atharva Veda the description of the diseases and their therapies are not given in detail and at one place. They are scattered all over and are sometimes very brief hints only. These have to be decoded, which means explained, and for such explanation, one has to seek the help of the commentators.

There are mantras connected with specific therapies. Five types of therapies will be taken up here:—

(i) Sankalp (संकल्प)
(ii) Sadesh (सादेश)
(iii) Samvashikaran (संवशीकरण)
(iv) Ritualistic Therapy (अपचार या अभिचार)
(v) Brahma Kavach (ब्रह्म कवच)

Sankalpa— Sankalpa is a sort of therapy by which the person tries to cure himself. In modern terms it can be called auto-suggestion. According to Satavalekar, "In AV II/9/5 it is expressed that the patient is himself the best physician, because he that caused the disease shall perform the cure." It is self-directive auto-therapy. It can be used as individual therapy as well as group therapy. In individual therapy the patient deals with his own psyche and gives suggestions to cure himself. In group situation, more than one person get together to sort out their problems, they deal with their own individual psyches, but at one place, in one group, it helps each individual of the group.

Sankalpa actually means atma-bal or will power. In terms of psychology it means strength of the ego. The Atharvans believed that the psyche or atma is the true therapist and manas is amrit which makes one immortal and healthy. It resides within and is directly connected with every part inside the body—so it can easily deal with every ailment of the personality. By the method of sankalpa, the ego can be made strong and energetic and able to deal with its problems. With a strong ego, there cannot be any disintegration in the psychic personality.

How Sankalpa Works— Sankalpa is a method which can work only in mild cases where the patient still has an active and conscious ego. Then ego makes suggestions and also accepts and acts on them. It means ego must branch out into two—one part acting as a therapist and the other acting as a patient. The therapist gives suggestions and other part follows its directions. At first there is this dual process, but after sometime when analysis is complete the duality also goes. Now only conscious strong ego remains and goes on acting on the suggestions given to it by itself.

The Stages in Sankalpa Method— This method has four stages—

- The ego comes in contact and converses with other parts, that is, the functions of mind such as learning, attention, memory intelligence or buddhi, dreams, sex etc. It tries to find problems and abormalities in their present and past roles. This way ego tries to bring any abnormalities of rajas and tamas within its control there is a sort of discussion and mutual agreement on their present and past roles.
- In the second stage the ego dominates, harmony in psychic life is established and differences are over (as a result of first stage). At this stage the suggestions are repeated again and again and intensify the hypnotic effect on itself. There are suggestions like "I am this, and not that" and "I should do this and not that" "that I am well without ailments."
- These suggestions are repeated, separately one after the other.
- The first stage is a negative one of breaking wrong type of old associations, second stage is of suggestions and the third stage is of unconscious faith created by suggestions, that I am without ailments, energetic and healthy.
- The fourth and last stage is a stage of determination and will, when future course of action is decided and adopted.

Here the ego is better adjusted, energetic and capable of dealing in a normal way with outside reality.

- Thus we see that sankalpa includes the processes of auto-analysis, auto-suggestion, auto-hypnosis and adjustment. It leads to ego-strength and better adjustment to life problems.

How Sankalpa is Applied— In Atharva veda sankalpa is a technique which can be applied to both mental and physical ailments. The main mantras are as follows—

- AV/12/1/9—are both for sankalpa. Sankalpa is said to be the main feature of manas. XIX/52/1—Vani (vocal power) is asked to create sankalpa in mind.
- AV VI/15/1-3—concerned with auto-suggestion and says that auto-suggestion is the best.
- AV I/34/2-3—asking auto-suggestion to create sweetness in vani, manas and behaviour.
- AV II/15/1-6 — deals with bhaya (phobia) and auto-suggestion is given to manas not to get afraid, be fearless, many things in the world do not get fear.
- AV XIX/14 and XIX/15/5-6 are auto-suggestions for fearlessness.
- AV VI/46/1-3, VII/100, 105/1 and VII/101/106/1- give mantras for auto-suggestions to stop evil dreams. First the causes of evil dreams are given, then dissociating these dreams and then finally the evil dreams are eliminated.
- AV XI/6/1-23, VI/45/1 and XX/96/24 are for auditory hallucinations and guilt pap bhawna. First a negative relationship is established, like saying 'go away' and then they are replaced by normal positive behaviour.
- AV/V/9/4-7 AV XI/4/1-5—give auto-suggestions for self-defense and long life.
- AV XI/6/1-23 — deals with group auto-suggestion (*mebkeauhe*) to drive away pap bhawana.
- AV VI/108/1-5— gives (*mebkeauhe*) which are to be repeated thrice a day morning, noon and evening to increase intelligence.
- AV II/12/1-4 and VI/38/1-4—are mantras for acquiring

psychic energy. In all these mantras law of association is used. Manas or the individual mind is shown the similarity and then given sankalpa to acquire energy like them or from them. For example, Atharva veda III/22/1 gives an auto-suggestion to acquire physical strength like an elephant. Similarly gods, fire, air, lion and bull are used as examples.

The Atharvedic Method of Sankalpa and Modern (Western) Psychotherapy

There is no single perfect equivalent of sankalpa. It is a mixture of three modern techniques of psychotherapy viz., auto-analysis, auto-suggestion and auto-hypnosis. It also includes the will and the training of the will, which is an additional advantage.

The Nancy School of Psychotherapy founded by Bernheim believed in the effectivity of auto-suggestion on mental abnormalities. Atharva veda propounded auto-suggestion thousand of years back and in an elaborate fashion.

About the usefulness of auto-suggestion, J.D. Page writes in his book *Abnormal Psychology* (1947) : "Some years ago, auto-suggestion or self-suggestion was made popular by Cove who instructed his patients to repeat 20 times each morning and night the following magic formula, 'Day by day, in every way, I am getting better and better.' This repetition will act as encouragement to himself, the patient, even in the absence of a therapist. The Atharvedins long ago believed in the effectivity of repetition of auto-suggestions to make the will strong, and a vivid imagination of a state of health will exclude all pathological reactions in the patient. The repetition of suggestion also produces a hypnosis like state. Indians specially Atharvans had long succeeded in discovering the value of self-hyphosis.

Swami Akhilananda, the outstanding exponent of Indian psychology in America writes, "the various methods prescribed by the Western schools of thought lack considerably in the technique of developing dynamic functioning of the will, in spite of their ameliorating effect. Psychoanalysis, self analysis of various types, autognosis, and insight, no doubt help in the understanding of the causes of mental problems, and may often help in removing a certain amount of tension. Yet they do not seem to unify the will."

—*Swami Akhilanand, Mental Health and Hindu Psychology, (1952)*

So it can be safely concluded that the Atharvanic method of therapy—Sankalpa—is scientific and in line with modern methods. It is far better because it includes positive ways of 'will training', which the modern psychotherapy seems to lack.

SADESH (Adesh or Suggestion)— In Sankalpa—there was no therapist. The patient gave suggestions or instructions to himself. But here the suggestion is given by an outside agent be it a guru or priest or therapist. The therapist plays a directive role in sadesh, the patient plays the passive role of a follower or a recepient.

P. Arsh has described Adesh as a form of Atharva vedic psycho-therapy. "Adehsis the name of energetic and successful assurances or effective suggestions which are used to cure different personality defects, including physical defects, but it is specially useful in mental disorders."

—*Arsh P., 1991*

The Theoretical Basis of Sadesh— According to P. Arsh it depends on two factors—

- The language—the sound plus the ideas produced by the therapist.
- The psychic energy of the therapist—his inner well wishing.

The practitioner of therapy or manas chikitsak is required to be a Brahma-gyani (ब्रह्म ज्ञानी) that is one who knows Brahma, and who works with the energy of Brahma. According to P. Arsh the Sadesh Chikitsak has to be serious, truth-speaking, self-controlled and of helping nature. Thus, by his own mental energy he exerts more effects on his patients.

In modern psycho-therapy, the influence of suggestion is the same, as Shaffer and Lazarus (1952) say : "The therapist, because of his prestige and authority as well as his helpfulness and protectiveness is in a position to exert unusual influence on the attitudes of the patient."

Thus, the views of modern psycho-therapy and Atharvedic conception of a Sadesh Chikitsak are nearly the same.

How Sadesh Chikitsa (therapy) Works

This is a directive therapy and the role of the therapist is more important. He is a guide, teacher, authoritative priest and the therapist all rolled into one. He had to learn the Atharvanic practices before becoming a therapist. To exert therapeutic effects on his patients, he must possess mental energy—Brahma gyan.

Sadesh (suggestion) therapy proceeds in stages, like follows—

- The First Stage—The therapist says 'he would do this and that and the disease will go away.' (in future tense)
- Second Stage — "That he is doing this........and the disease is going away." (present tense)
- Third Stage—The therapist talks about the problems and ailments with the patient.
- Therapist analyses patient's problems (not in the modern sense-discuss) then re-educates, i.e., corrects thinking, feeling and willing processes of the patient. It is done in confidential manner.
- The Last Stage — "That he (the therapist) has done this and that, the disease has gone."

The mantras may differ but the sequence of Sadesh Chikitsa remains the same. All the mantras are repeated daily in the same sequence. The cure is complete after some days. In giving Sadesh, the Atharvedin uses the mechanisms of symbolism, identification, personification and the laws of similarity and contrast.

In Atharva veda the Sadesh therapy stages are not given in detail. It is very flexible, sometimes stages overlap, sometimes one stage is missing. Actually the choice of stages, the time of their use depend on the severity of the disease, nature of the patient and the skill of the therapist. It seems the training of the therapists was more verbal and practical—all Vedic learning was verbal, so, may be, the written records did not have many details.

Applications of Sadesh to Mental Diseases— Sadesh as a therapy requires the patient to be able to understand the ideas being given. Sadesh can be used as a main therapy or as an aid to other therapies.

As a main therapy for mental diseases it can be used in Grahi, phobia, apasmar, pap bhawana, krodh, irsha, moh, shrap, samansayani and paushtikarni.

Examples from Atharva Veda on Application of Sadesh

AV VIII/1/	—	Sadesh for curing convulsion and grah
AV II/10/6, 8	—	„ „ „ grahi
AV veda VI 42, 43	—	„ „ „ for krodh rage
AV/VI/18/1-3	—	„ „ „ jealousy
AV/III25/1-6	—	„ „ arousing kama-sex urge-in women
AV/VI/101	—	„ „ to increase energy in the weak paushtikarni.
AV/V/34/4	—	„ „ „ bravery in a warrior or a ting.

Comparison and Contrast with Suggestion in Western Psychotherapy

Similarities in Sadesh and suggestion—

- It is directive therapy in both,
- The role of the therapist is active and directive, and
- The role of the patient is passive and of a follower,
- It is energetic and successful assurance to cure personality defects.

Points of Contrast

- Atharva veda believes that there is psychic energy in the therapist which works.
- That this psychic energy is transferred through Sadesh to the patient.
- Sadesh is more than suggestion, it includes analysis and synthesis also.
- Sadesh can be used negatively to eliminate grab, phobia etc. and positively to increase understanding saman sayani and energy पौष्टिकानी.

Thus, Atharvedic sadesh therapy is scientific and based upon the language sound+ideas, plus the psychic energy of the therapist. It seems to be in a better position than the suggestion therapy of modern psychotherapy, because it makes use of analysis, synthesis and psychic energy.

Samvashikaran-hypnosis

It is a special type of suggestion. Some definitions—

P. Arsh— "When suggestion is very effective it becomes SAMVASHIKARAN."

Dawson— Hypnosis is a method of applying suggestion.

Drake— Hypnosis is a condition of heightened suggestibility and the use of verbal suggestions is the technique to induce it.

Samvashi-Karan is the advanced effective stage of suggestibility in which the therapist's personality and psychic power are the main forces. Modern psychotherapy believes that suggestion is the basis of hypnosis. It does not believe in psychic power.

How Samvashi-Karan Works— It is a process of intense suggestions. The therapist gives suggestions to the patient as this— "Relax, let yourself go, listen only to my voice, relax and go to sleep. Your eyes are heavy and sleepy, close your eyes. Now you are asleep." etc. After this the therapist may give other suggestions.

Actually in Samvashi-Karan the therapist dominates and leads the mind of the patient like a charioteer. There are various techniques of Samvashi-Karan but Atharva veda uses mainly heightened verbal suggestions. Atharva veda does not give details, they become clear only after interpretation and explanation of the mantras.

In the initial stages the therapist passes his hands over the body of the patient. Then the patient is asked to check his own mental activities and follow the directives (आदेश) of the hypnotizer. Ultimately the patient surrenders his own ego to the will of the hypnotizer. The process has to be repeated until a state of mental submission is induced. During therapy there is a very close and intimate relationship or rapport between the therapist and the patient.

Uses of Samvashi-Karan— In Atharva Veda Samvashi-Karan is used for achieving minor aims. In Sanskrit mantras the words 'mohy', 'mohiyat' or sammohan are used as equivalent of hypnosis.

AV IV/13/6-7—These clearly show the procedure of Samvashi-Karan. VII/13/6 and III/8/6—which is like this establish rapport, give passes by hands to the patient, give suggestions until he is hypnotized. AV III/1, 2—is for hypnotizing the enemy to win him over. These mantras are to fill the warriors with bravery.

Comparison of Samvashi-Karan with Hypnosis in Modern Psychotherapy

Similarities

- Both use heighted suggestibility.
- Atharva Veda uses the word 'mohiyan' for hyphosis which means that hypnosis as a therapy was used at that time.
- Modern psychotherapy uses hypnotism for major mental diseases like hysteria, but Atharva Veda seems to use it for minor aims.
- In Atharva Veda it has been used as post-hypnotic suggestion to warriors, in modern times it has been used on players of competitive sports as well as on soldiers.
- The similarities in procedure of hypnotizing are also found.

These similarities are striking between a therapy which is thousands of years old and one which is quite modern.

Disimilarities

- Atharva veda uses Samvashi-Karan as a method of improvement for acquiring bravery, release from passion, and for promoting integration of personality. Modern psycho-therapy uses it as a major technique in diseases like hysteria.
- According to Atharva Veda some sort of psychic energy is transferred from the therapist to the patient. Modern psychotherapy does not believe in the phenomena of psychic energy.

Ritualistic Therapy—Drama and Demonstration

Drama and demonstration in the form of rituals form a definite and purposive technique, which can be used as a supplementary or as an independent method. It is meant to be used with illiterate, the insane and the children, who cannot grasp and understand their own mental processes properly. Mostly it is used as a supplementary technique of Sadesh. As in educating of a child a teacher has to dramatize and demonstrate, so is the case with rituals.

Atharva Veda is very rich in rituals. Kaushik sutra which is a part of Shaunakiya shakha, is the source of all Atharvanic rituals.

Here mantras are classified according to their purpose into ganas (groups). Then for certain purpose or work the mantras are chosen to be recited along with relevant ritualistic performances. Some writers had named these as "homopathic magic". But scholars like Sayanacharya, Satavalekar, Arsh, R.G. Shastri, R.C. Sharma and Jai Deo Vidyalankar have totally rejected any conception of magic in Atharvedic rituals. These ritualistic performances serve definite purpose. The rituals are always accompanied by the mantras. In Sadesh and mantras, the psychic energy produces effects. In drama somatic phenomena are also added and it becomes psycho-physical or psychosomatic process. Then some material things are also used in rituals which produce physical effects on the body of the patient. The ideas are symbolically demonstrated by the therapist to produce additional effect.

The Procedure— It is mostly enacted as a drama, of which the main participants are:—

1. The therapist
2. The patient
3. Other relations involved such as parents or spouse
4. Or a group as in Samansayani.

The role of the therapist—an Atharvan—is multi-faceted one. He is a director, actor, priest, physician, teacher at different times. Max Muller says, "Brahman (the therapist) is as it were the stage manager in the sacradotal drama". According to Shende— "The power of the priest depends on the knowledge of the practices, spells and on his penance (tapas) and the practice of the Brahman (ब्रह्मचर्य)."

Karambelkar says, "He is a physician, magician, priest, advisor, protector, philosopher and friend—all in one. Without him nothing can be done. He is equally helpful to man, woman, young and old in private and in public. Thus the whole field of the Atharvan practices is the stage for the activities of the Atharvan priest." The therapist or practitioner plays different roles, uses different materials, uses different places—room jungle, road crossing, river bank, any time—early morning, noon, evening, night or mid-night. The whole process is kept private and confidential.

Psychological Bases of the Rituals

The basis of drama and demonstration is symbolism. Karambelkar writes, "Symbolism is the soul of Atharvan practices"......"Thus throughout, the rites prescribed by the Kaushik Sutra are based upon transparent or obscure symbolism. The ceremonies are of greater interest on this account."

—*Karambelkar, 1959*

Some Examples of these Ritualistic Practices

- Max Muller on the authority of Sayan explains the procedure of AV VI/11/ which is for insanity and expiation of Grahs and demons—"Pulverised fragrant substances, mixed with Ghee are sacrificed and the patient is anointed with what remains. The patient is next placed upon a cross road (*chauraha*) wicker work of Darbha grass containing a coal pan upon his head, and upon the coal the previously mentioned fragrant substances are again offered. The patient, going into a river against the current, throws the same substance into a sieve, while another person from behind washes him off. Pouring more of the fragrant substances into an unburned vessel, moistening the substances with ghee, placing the vessel into a three footed wicker basket made of munja, he ties it to a tree in which there are bird's nest. The complicated ceremony is largely symbolic, it aims to purify and indicate the passing out of the unhealthy conditions."

—*Max Muller, 1964*

Effects of this Ritual— both on mind and body—

- The fragrant substances used in havan and for anointing the patient produce cooling and soothing effect on mind and body of the patient.
- He is put on cross-roads, so that the cermony may become public that people may consider him now as cured of the disease.
- A vessel with khas grass burning is put on his head—the head is made hot—and to contrast he reaches the cool river, and is washed in the water from behind.
- Throwing the hot pan from the head and getting washed

with cold water symbolizes the throwing away of mental disease and that the mind has become clean, calm and cool now.

- The substances are put in a wicker basket and tied to a tree full of bird's nests. This symbolizes that the disease is given to the birds to fly away with, and birds are offered eatables as a reward for that.
- All this drama is performed along with chanting of mantras. It produces a positive effect on patient, and he starts feeling cured.

Max Muller gives a second example— **AV** III/30 Samansayani—It is for establishing integration and harmony in a group. It is like this, "A jar full of water, anointed with the dregs of ghee is carried about the (quarelling) throng and poured out in their midst. The same proceedings are undertaken with a jar full of brandy (sura). They (who desire peace) are given to eat the pickled meat. Food, brandy and water from the public drinking place are anointed with the dregs of ghee and are consumed." This process goes along with mantras.

Its significance is as follows—

Water and ghee which are cool and greasy are poured in the midst of the fighting people.

Wine is also poured which symbolizes friendship.

Feasting on delicious food create erotic feelings.

Taking drinking water from a public place is meant to show publicly that the quarelling persons have established peace. Peace is public, so they will hesitate in fighting again.

Thus a broken fighting social group can be re-united by the rituals and mantras.

AV VI/112 is for removing pap bhawana. The priest sprinkles water on the person and the dwelling, while reciting mantras.

The examples given here are very simple ones, actually there may be more elaborate procedures, but havana is always performed. The Atharvan knows the proceeding by an intense practical training from his guru.

Conclusion— "The drama like music has been associated with mental healing since ancient times. In most instances, however, the drama has been considered as a therapeutic aid rather than as a special therapy in its own right."

—*Shaffer and Lazarus, 1952*

Drake, R.M. calls ritualistic method under the heading 'Miracles'. Drake says, "The belief in the miraculous power of a shrine, a certain person, or a certain ritual may be sufficient to affect a better psycho-biological integration, where the disorder is mainly functional."

—*Drake, R.M. 1959*

Moreno 1947 developed a technique called psychodrama which is used for certain problems of mental and social nature. The approach of modern psychotherapy is direct catharsis and a little redirection. The aim of Atharva veda is indirect, cathartic and more of demonstrative suggestion. The demonstration creates faith, corrects wrongly developed beliefs and makes ego unburdened or returned to normal. In Atharva veda the cure or removal of symptoms is through faith (demonstration) and suggestion (rituals).

BRAHMA KAVACHA— (Defensive Belief)—

The therapies discussed uptil now have some sort of equivant in Atharva veda and modern psycho therapies. But Brahma Karach is unique to Atharva veda.

BRAHMA KAVACH is a defensive measure. In English it can be called armour or protective device. It is sort of psychological defence against some danger real or anticipated.

There are two kinds of Kavachs in Atharva Veda—

(1) *Bhautik Khavach*— a garment worn over the dress, armour. It is physical it can be touched and seen.

(2) *Brahma Kavach*— psychological, which is belief in one self and support for self-confidence.

These are both subjective and environmental. It creates self-confidence within the person, a belief in perfect defence within oneself. According to Atharva veda Brahma kavach spreads some psychic invisible force in the environment, which acts as a resistance to the destructive forces which may be there.

In fact Brahma Kavach is not a therapy in the strict sense of the term. It is a device to defend and to improve the behaviour of the individual. Brahma Kavach can be for self or for others. It works through two things—suggestion and atma-bal. It is spread for one's own and other's protection.

Uses or Applications of Brahma Kavach

R.G. Shastri and Satavalekar call it, "a psychological defence from danger."

- It is used to bring energy and improvement in behaviour.
- It is most successfully applied whenever there is fear and danger in the environment.
- Satavalekar, explaining AV V/10/1-8 thinks it to be used against shrap and for self-defence against every possible danger.
- AV VII/2 is for creating Brahma Kavach for a weak client and for the defence against enemy, diseases and death. It makes a person feel fearless and energetic within and also protected from outside.

Conclusion— Importance of Brahma Kavach— There is no equivalent for Brahma Kavach in Western psychotherapy. Atharva Veda says a psychic energy is spread in the atmosphere for protection, modern psycho therapy does not believe in this type of derices.

Brahma Kavach is unique to Atharva Veda for personality improvement.

UTARNA— Transference— Utarna literally means shedding off. It is a process of sending the symptoms of disease or the diseases themselves, away. It is an Atharvedic method but its traces are found in practioners (ojhas) even today. Arsh has described this practice. He has proved it to be based on psychosomatic approach, and not mere magic or witchcraft.

Kinds of Utarna— In Atharva veda this technique has been used in two ways—

- Transfering the physical symptoms of disease to plants and animals.
- Transferring the psychological symptoms to all living beings—man, animal and plants.

Physical Symptoms— P. Arsh has dealt with physical aspect of utarna. He says it is on the basis of homogeniety of substances and elements involved in them. It has been proved scientifically and biologically that certain substances which are waste products of human body or injurious to it, may be useful to certain plants or animals, such as the air we exale with our breath contains carbon dioxide which is absorbed by the plants and is useful to them, and oxygen which is a waste product of plants and trees is useful for human beings. Atharva Veda emphasizes this type of give and take relationship of man and nature. Another example is germs of TB, dangerous for man, are very useful for cheer (चीढ़) tree, goat and monkey. Jaundice a disease for humans becomes useful for haldi tree (yellow pigment) and the parrot.

Atharva Veda gives this give and take in AV I/12/ and 1/22/4 that is physical symptoms of diseases are sent elsewhere.

Mental Symptoms— Atharva Veda uses the same technique of transference for the removal of mental symptoms and ailments. They are sent to both animate and inanimate objects. The basis of transfere being similarity or mere suggestion. According to Atharva Veda, the therapist can, by his command, transfer the psychic symptoms to other persons or objects through his own psychic power and suggestion. Whether the symptoms are actually transferred or the patient feels relieved of his symptoms—cannot be established as yet. It may be just the effect of strong suggestion. But transference is a therapeutic technique in Atharva Veda to relieve the patient of his ailments. The approach here is psycho somatic.

The Procedure— The procedure of transference is very simple—

First the objects or persons similar in nature to the symptoms of the patient are brought near either physically or mentally.

Then a ritual is performed with mantras etc. and a suggestion is given for going (उतरना) of symptoms to the brought up person (or his image) or an object. After this the patient feels that the symptom and disease have really gone.

Uses and Applications of Transference

Transference is not used in Atharva veda as independent or self-sufficient therapy. It is always used as a supplementary or supportive therapy. It is usually accompanied by suggestion, drama, demonstration and medicines.

AV prescribes transference for a variety of purposes such as—

AV II/7/5, V/14/IX/2/X/1— different shraps, calamities and mental abnormalities are returned to their originators or enemies.

AV VI/26, 45—sinful ideas are banished (transferred) to the forests.

AV VI/130, 131—the erotic strivings are sent to the object of love.

AV IX/2 and VI/46—evil dreams are transferred to enemies.

AV VI/112— according Max Muller, "sin, pap or guilt feeling is transferred from person to person in a long chain."

AV II/29—disease is transferred to some friend or menial.

Comparison with Transference in Western Psychotherapy

In Atharva veda the technique of transfer is totally different from the 'transference' of psycho-analysis. In modern psycho therapy transference has two meanings as James Drever in his "Dictionary of Psychology" states, "It is— (1) A term employed by psycho-analysis of the development of an emotional attitude, positive or negative, love or hate, towards the analysts, on the part of the patients or subjects. (2) Also used generally for the passing of an affective attitude or colouring from one object or person to another object or person connected by association in the experience of an individual person or animal."

The second meaning is a bit nearer to Atharva Veda, in that, the transfer is not to the therapist but from one person to another person or object. The second difference is that the therapist himself is not a part of the process, he makes arrangements and practices but he is not a party to the process but in psycho analytic transfer, he is a part.

In Atharvedic transference, whether the symptoms are actually transferred or is it the effect of psychological suggestion that the patient feels relieved—is a matter of further experimental study.

ASHVASAN AND UPCHAR (Persuation and Desensitization)

In Atharva Veda ashvasan and upchar are used as essential preliminary practices, and as supplement to the coming therapies, for mental problems.

P. Arsh has described ashvasan and upchar in detail as Atharvedic therapeutic devices. According to Arsh ashvasan is assurance, hope, confidence, satisfaction, upchar is to re-direct and re-educate the behaviour of the patient. These are both essential conditions or preliminaries for any sort of therapy. If these preliminaries are not there and the patient is not assured, hopeful, confident and satisfied then the therapy can never be successful. It creates a will in the patient to be cured. Ashvasan removes his false belief of hopelessness and nervousness and makes ego stronger. Upchar consists on the one hand in controlling or improving the environment in which the patient lives. On the other hand, it is to re-educate his daily habits, daily living. Thus ashvasan and upchar strengthen the will and the ego as well as reform the behaviour of the patient.

How It Works

Ashvasan and upchar is a directive technique in Atharva Veda, where the therapist plays an active and dominating role and the patient just follows him passively. This therapy starts as soon as the patient goes to see the therapist. The therapist by his words, his behaviour his total personality creates an atmosphere of hope and assurance. Then there are a few mantras in Atharva veda for this purpose. The meanings of these mantras are important. They give four points:—

- Only the relations and well-wishers remain with the patient to create confidence and sense of assurance in him.
- All that the patient eats his food and his medicines, should be prepared by his most near and dear ones spouse, father, mother, brother, sister etc.
- The medicines are to be regarded as amrit, life giving necter, however bad they may taste, and should be taken in a pleasant mood, with a faith that they will cure.
- Desensitization is that the patient must not think of his past and dead relatives—he must feel happy and be happy with his present people and present home life.

These are to create a congenial environment for the patient and changes his mental trend to a positive one with a will to live.

Applications and Uses

- As said earlier, it is a preliminary and supplementary technique to all other therapies. It can be used to—
- To educate and re-educate the patient.
- To create and increase a will to live.
- To strengethen the ego of the patient.
- It is most successful in ailments where ego becomes weak.
- It can be applied to all functional mental diseases.

Comparison with Modern Psychotherapy

Ashvasan and upchar techniques are quite similar to the modern techniques of persuasion, desensitization and re-education shaffer and Lazarus, Dubois and Dejerine have discussed the role of persuasion in psychotherapy. Here also the patient is given assurance, that he will get well soon. Payot, Walsh, Vittoz and Barret have given therapies in which will direction and regulation play a prominent role.

Points of Similarity Between Atharvedic Ashvasan and Upchar and Western Techniques

- Both are directive therapies.
- In both the role of the therapist is dominating, of the patient passive.
- In both the therapist-patient relations are emotional.
- Both try to make patient's ego strong by encouragement, surity of cure and confidence.
- Both use desensitization and re-education technique (though Atharva Veda is not very specific about it.)

Dissimilarities— The role of psychic power of the therapist is emphasized in Atharva veda. Modern psychotherapy does not believe in such powers.

DAIVIYA AND HAVAN CHIKITSA

This is a method of cure of mental ailments in which the blessings of different gods and goddesses is invoked. This trend started from Rig veda and was furthered by Atharva Veda. Actually it is a matter of spiritual healing. Modern clinicians like Shaffer and Lazarus have also discussed spiritual healing as a technique of psychotherapy.

This is a religious therapy by a religious priest. The priest-known as Brahma conducts the puja and all the rituals. The rituals may or may not be accompanied by Havana.

In Havan offerings and prayers are made to gods specially Agni, ghee and fragrant herbs are poured in fire as offerings.

Satavalekar has discussed Atharvedic Havan Chikitsa in detail. He says, "in Havan, the therapist, who is usually a religious priest, acts as a Brahma, the chief managing priest in the sacradotal ceremony of curing mental abnormalities. Prayers are made by the priest and the patient, and sometimes relatives etc. also join in prayers. This religious therapy is mostly accompanied by Havan or is also sometimes without havan."

Havan as psychotherapy is the originality of Atharva Veda. AV III/11/1, XIX/38/1-3 and XX/9/6 are clear evidence of this. These mantras show that in Atharva Veda not only known but unknown diseases, and even Yakshma (TB) can be cured by havan.

The science of Havan as a religious and therapeutic procedure was quite advanced in Vedic times. It was performed as a daily religious practice to appease gods and to cure diseases. It was used for other purposes as well, such as bringing in rains, growing of special quality in grains of crop, for the birth of son, to gain success in life, to achieve victory in war, to proclaim and celebrate victory in war, etc.

HOW HAVAN CHIKITSA WORKS

P. Arsh has eleborated the Havan Chikitsa in Atharva Veda. The procedure, in outline is as follows—"In havan there is sacred fire agni or Jativeda. Various fragrant substances herbs etc. along with ghee, are offered in the fire with mantras or prayers to different deities. The gods for havan and the substances offered in agni, depend upon the specific purpose of the havan. The offerings may be of eatables and other things like clothes, cows, gold and silver which are distributed among Brahmans and the poor. A monetary offer known as Dakshina is always offered to the priest and sometimes to the others as well. These offerings and prayers may be sometimes without havan."

There is no set procedure for it. There may be prayer with or without havan, may be with rituals. It may be with offerings

(Daan). The procedure may be individual or in group. Deities chosen differ with time place and purpose of the havan. The therapist acts as a liaison ageut between the deity and the patient. Many material things are offered to the gods which ultimately go to the priest. In mantras, the deity is profusedly praised, his powers and deeds in curing this particular ailment are defined and praised, and then finally a request is made that he may bless and cure the present suffering of the patient. The mantras also seek pardon for past mistakes, and promises are made for future good behaviour along with the request to be cured in the present.

These are just the outlines of the whole process. The details are innumerable and differ vastly according to purpose.

The whole process of havan produces faith and healing effect on the patient. The havan and prayer produce a mixed effect which is psycho-somatic. The fragrant substances burnt in havan agni produce smoke which has somatic effect on the body of the patient and all others present there. The prayer has an element of suggestion and faith. Thus the basis of havan and prayer therapy in Atharva veda is both physiological and psychological.

Applications for Diseases in Atharva Veda

Mostly for functional type of abnormalities—

AV VI/3/47-48—prayer and offerings for defence.

AV III/40—for phobia.

AV VI/112, 115, 116, 118, 119, 121, AV VII/34, 35—for removal of pap bhavna and inferiority feelings.

AV VI/132—for Kama or erotic anomalies.

AV VI/89 and VII/52, 54—for integration.

AV VII 23, 24—for evil dreams.

AV VII 32-33, 53-55—for long life.

AV VI/113 — for compulsions or grahi.

Comparison with Modern Psychotherapy

There are very few applications of this technique in scientific psycho-therapy. Shaffer and Lazarus have called these practices as "Spiritual healing"—which mostly works on the power of suggestions to the patient.

In Atharva Veda this therapy has been used to cure functional diseases believing in the therapeutic power of spiritual energy.

PRAYASHCHITANI

Prayashchitani show the unique psychogenic approach of Atharva veda. Prayashchitani consist of some special hymns or mantras. These hymns or mantras are found in both Pipplad and Shaunak Shakhas of Atharva Veda. These are its old literature — "Atharva prayashchitani". Atharva veda has 72 parisisthas (परिशिष्ट). On XXXVII (37) it is discussed as "Samuccya prayashchitani" (सम्मुच्य प्रायश्चितानि) or the whole of the prayashchitas.

—*Bolling, G.M. and Negelain J.V., Leipzig, 1910*

The Meaning— There are several meanings of the word प्रायश्चित. Some of which are as follows—

- "Whatever sublimates or catherises pap (sin) is prayashchitta."
- "Doing tapa after voluntary decision is prayshchitta."

—*Both by Radha Kant Dev Behadure*

- V.S. Apte, "Tapa done after voluntary decision for purity and sublimation is prayshachitta."

Thus the following features of praychchitt become evident—That—

- It is a tapa or penance — self-denial-self mortification.
- It is always self-imposed taken after voluntary decision.
- The purpose is to purify self, to get rid or pap bhavana.
- The tapa done is both mental and physical or monetary.
- Pap bhavan comes from any wrong deeds done against society culture or religion.
- In Atharva veda pap constitutes a large range of abnormalities of behaviour.

Psychological Basis of Prayashchittani— Psychologically prayshchitta is a means of purifying the ego to increase its strength 'Atma-bal'. Whenever the ego follows the path of 'pap' — denying the authority of the super-ego, going against social norms etc. it becomes weak. Defying super-ego by the ego leads to pap bhavana or feelings of guilt, inferiority and a mental pressure. To remove these feelings and to energize the ego, some kind of voluntary act of self mortification is undertaken. It is to be undertaken by the self by its own decision and must not come from any outside source.

This can be viewed in the light of Freudian psychoanalysis

also. According to Freudian dynamics, there is always an on-going struggle between the forces of Id and forces of superego. The forces of Id are libidinal and aggressive and want their own fulfillment. The super-ego is the voice of society and cultural norms which put controls on the urges of the Id. Now, the ego (Purush) has to adjust to the forces of three sides, Id, super-ego and outside reality. It has to maintain a harmony between them but sometimes some forces dominate and disharmony results. Whenever ego follows the urges of Id, superego is hurt and angry. It punishes the ego with feelings of guilt and shame. To atone for this and to pacify the super-ego the ego has to undergo self mortification. In a normal person there is a harmony in Id, ego and super-ego. But when the balance is lost, there is disharmony and abnormality results.

According to the Indian theory, the three gunas or vrittis of a psychic personality are sattava, rajas and tamas which are always struggling to dominate purush (ego). If purush works under the pressure of tamas, then feelings of guilt build up whenever sattva again takes over, it is a penalty for purush for letting the Tamas prevail upon him. After doing penances or prayashchittani the balance and harmony is again restored.

Thus the theoretical basis of prayashitta is quite similar in Western and Indian systems of psychotherapy. Both agree that feelings of guilt and inferiority, pap bhavana, have to be removed so that ego may function normally again. But how ?

The Atharvedic answer to this question is prayashchittani (plural of prayashchitta).

The main characteristics of prayashchitt according to Atharva veda are—

- These are cathartic and energy charging.
- Can help in reducing pap bhavan. The sense of guilt and shame, because here the ego consciously accepts the guilt. In prayashchitta ego has to play three roles, viz., —
    - It must realize and accept the authority of the super-ego and also appease it.
    - Must itself become the judge to Penalize its own self.

- Must execute the penalty seriously in the outside world.

Thus prayashchitta is an inner drama—a dynamic interplay of forces within the personality. There are three forces or players in this drama—the ego, the super-ego and the Id. And there is a happy ending also, as all the players are satisfied—the authority of the super-ego is regained, the Id resumes its old place as it has already satisfied some of its urges, and the ego has cleared off its sense of guilt. Now the mental harmony is restored.

Forms or Kinds of Prayashchittani

In most of the cases, it is ego-atma which decides on the form of penalty to be under taken, after analysing all the factors. But in some cases the ego becomes too weak to take decisions. In such cases some outside agency—a guru or a priest or some other prestigious person, may take the decision about the form of prayashchitta to be undertaken.

Anything, any act, which sublimates or catherises pap is prayashchitta so it can take many forms. Atharva veda mentions many forms and methods of prayashchitta. All these ways and methods can be classified in three broad categories—

- Sweekarokti स्वीकारोक्ति or confession
- Tapa तप or penance
- Tyag त्याग or sacrifice

Sweakarokti— Means a statement accepting one's own wrongful or immoral acts. It can be done before—

— the deity if the action is against religion or god.

— the public if the action is against or harmful to society.

— the family if it has been against the family members.

— the person who has been harmed by the act.

The person (patient) himself discloses his wrongful deed, gives a promise not to repeat ever in future and also asks for pardon. In this way the suppressed act gets purged out and the ego is relieved of the burden. Outwardly it seems very humiliating for the person but it requires a lot of moral courage and self-confidence to make such public confession. But after this traumatic trial all the suppressed matter is flushed out and after the catharsis, the ego feels clean, unburdened and energetic again. Sweekarokti is done by the person himself but sometimes another person a guru or a priest may act as a guide in the process of confession.

Tapa— It is the penalty ego avows to take on itself. It may take either physical or mental form of penalty. The physical forms of tapa are fasting, standing on one foot, lying prostate or rolling down a certain distance, bearing the extremes of heat and cold or other ways of causing pain and discomfort to the body. The psychic tapa may take the form of strict self control and abstinence, controlling one's drives, motives, and emotions. It may also mean Japa or constant chanting of certain mantras.

Tapa has been variously emphasized in Atharva veda as energy producing device. The exercise and control involved in mental and physical tapa, suppress all types of wrong desires, unburden the ego and charge it with energy. The Hindu mythology abounds in the tales of Tapa bala or the energy gained by tapa. Tapa charges the energies of ego. Tapa can also be successfully used for removal of ailments and abnormalities and for gaining health, wealth and prosperity.

Tyag— While Sweekarokti was social-mental, tapa was physical-mental, tyag is more worldly or material possessions, arthic. It means giving up worldly possessions valuables, money etc. It is enonomic-mental. Here the victim or patient, as an atonement for his wrong deeds, vows to sacrifice some or all of his valuables, wealth or property, land, house, property, cattle (mainly cows) etc. In this sort of sacrifice or tyag the ego feels relieved of the guilt, unburdened and normal again. Tyag may be used positively to gain health, wealth and prosperity.

Prayashittani— as Therapeutic Technique

In Atharva veda prayashchitta is mentioned as a technique for relief in mental ailments and abnormalities. Karambelkar gives 40 mantras of Atharva veda which give the use of prayashchitta for 40 different purposes. Some of these are—

- **AV** VI/45—for expiation of mental delinquency.
- **AV** VI/26—for evil.
- **AV** VI/16—for sin
- **AV** 38/22—(Kaushik sutra) for evil eye effects.

- AV VI/140—for unlucky stars.
- AV VII/23/100-101, XVI/5, and XIV/56-57—for evil dreams.

Similarly Bolling and Negelain have given twenty sins for which prayashchitta has to done (Boiling, G.M. and Negelain, J.V., 1910).

Sweekarokti — or confession has been used for removal of schizoprenia, evil deeds and guilty feelings.

- AV 1/7/5—for expiation of evil deeds.
- AV 1/10/4—for public confession of pap for its removal.
- AV VI/45 — applied on schizophrenia paranoid type and the confession is made to 'agni' for past deeds.
- AV VI/115 and VI/120—are used to avert sin and sins are confessed to all gods and deity 'agni'.

Satavalekar has explained three Atharvedic mantras as a high type of mental prayashchitta, and also praised them as highly courageous.

Tapa— It is done both ways—negatively to get rid of past sins and positively to gain energy of the ego. Mentions in Atharva veda about tapa are as follows—

Max Muller has described tapa as creative fervour. According to him AV XI/5/1, 8, 10, 11, 17, 19, 26, XII/1/1, 39, XIII/1/10 and XIX/53/8 give the purposes and powers of tapa.

Whitney has also discussed the same hymns in the same manner. Both these scholars show that in Atharva veda tapa is depicted as useful for gaining wisdom and energy.

According to Satavalekar, AV I/13/2 tapa used to stop downfall, VII/61 to increase memory and learning, in AV XI/5/5 tapa mentioned as all powerful and wins calamities and death, and in AV XI/7/9, 17 to increase prosperity.

In Atharva veda thus, Tapa, is not used as a therapy for severe mental disorders, but for medha vardhan memory and learning, paushtikarni increasing atma-bal, ayushayani or promoting longer life, that is for personality improvement, integration and better health.

Tyag— Tyag is not used as a therapy for mental diseases, but for other purposes in Atharva veda. Shende has given a detailed version of Tyag. Max Muller gives as follows —

- AV VI/110—for child born under unlucky star.
- AV VI/14—for defects in ritualistic performance.
- AV XI/7—for attainment of power.

Whitney gives AV IV/14 for sacrifice of goat.

- AV V/26 and VI/14—for prosperity, AV VII/70, 73 for attainments.
- AV XIX/6/13, 14—describe the powers of sacrifice (tyag).

Evaluation of Prayashchittani in the Light of Modern Psychotherapy

Prayashchittani, specially Sweekarokti is a unique psychotherapeutic device of Atharva veda. In modern psychotherapy we find its equivalent in the cathartic therapy of Freud. In cathartic therapy of Freud, the discharge of emotions, under hypnosis was considered to be of great therapeutic value.

Another reference to confession technique is found in Shaffer and Lazarus, who say that the Catholic church recognised the value of catharsis in the technique of confession. The feelings of guilt and shame in the mental patients are greatly relieved if given an opportunity to discuss them openly.

For the Atharvans the value of prayashchittani is that they are cathartic and energy giving. Sweekarokti brings back the balance of the ego, while Tapa and Tyag basically aim at energising the weak ego.

Atharva Veda has given a unique and dynamic concept of prayashchittani whose equivalent is not found in modern psychotherapy, except passing references to the cathertic value of confession.

VEDIC TERMINOLOGY

Agantuj— Psychological, an exogenous cause of insanity.

Agnivesh— An Aryan rishi who wrote Agnivesha Tantra on Ayurveda text which was presented to Arya Vrata Ayurveda Congress in Himalayas in 7th century A.D.

Alzheimers Disease— A dreaded disease of the brain. Its cure has not yet been found.

Amrit Veda— Another name for Atharva Veda—because it is supposed to contain nectar of life.

Angiras— The name of a rishi who was born from the bodily secrations of Brahma, while he was doing severe tapa. Hence the name Ang+rasa=Angirasa.

Apasmar— Epilepsy or mirgi which is characterized by convulsive fits and locking of jaws of the patient.

Aptantrak— A severe disease characterised by convulsions somatogenic.

Arjuna— Name of a tree. Also the name of a famous warrior of Mahabharata whom the famous Geeta was preached by Lord Krishna, who volunteered as a charioteer of Arjuna.

Asatma Indriyarth Sanyoga— A contact of senses with sense objects which is not true or real cognitive defect.

Ashtanga Hirdaya Ashtanga Sangraha— Both treatises on Ayurveda written by Vagabhatta, at the time of Gupta empire in 6th century A.D. Ashtang Hridaya is the abridged edition of Ashtanga Sangraha.

Ashwini Twins— Characters in Indian mythology to whom Ayurveda was taught by Daksha Prajapati.

Ashvasan and Santwana— Assurance, persuasion and desensitization. A form of Atharvanic therapy.

Atatvabhinivesh— Paranoia. One of severe mental abnormalities.

Atharva— The name of rishi Bhrigu who was born out of the tapa of Brahma, and who later become the main exponent of Atharva veda, literal meaning is uncunning and non-violent. The auspicious aspect of Atharva Veda.

Atharva Angirasa— The original name of Atharva Veda. For meanings see Atharva and Angirasa.

Atharva Vigyan— The science of Atharva—Mana or psyche.

Atharva Veda— The fourth and last veda. It is said to combine the knowledge of Brahma, of other world, as well as that of this world.

Atma— Soul also used for self or ego.

Atreya— One of the original disciples of rishi Bhardwaj, who took Ayurvedic learning from Indra. Vagabhatta gave credit for his thoughts to Atreya.

Ayurveda— A science of life Ayu+veda. Considered to be a branch or upveda of Atharva Veda. It is being practised even today by the Vaidyas.

Batcheet and Vishleshan— Talking out and analysing—a method of psycho-therapy mentioned in Charak Samhita.

Bhagat— Literally devotee. A line of practitioners of Indian psychotherapy.

Bhagwat Geeta— Literally the song of the lord. It is part of the Mahabharata epic. It was preached by Shri Krishna to Arjuna during Mahabharata. Teaches Karma Yoga.

Bhaya— Phobia.

Bhaya Chikitsa— Fear shock therapy in which artificial emotional shock is given to the patient.

Bheshaj Veda— Another name for Atharva Veda, as it contains the bheshajya or the knowledge of medicines.

Bhishag— A practitioner of medicines—a physician.

Bheshajayani— A particular section of Atharva Veda which contains knowledge about medicines.

Bhoot— Past, to become, born, gone, true, real fact.

Bhoot Dhara— Retaining in the mind or remembering the past.

Bhoot Vidya— Indian psychopathology or psychotherapy. One of the eight branches of Ayurveda, based in Atharva veda. That branch of therapeutic knowledge, which is psychogenic in approach, and which deals with morbid psychic functions and disorders.

Bhoot Grah— These are the names of abnormal psychic symptoms or syndromes, personified and given symbolic names.

Brahma— The Hindu god of creation. One of the trinity of highest duties. Also the universal psychye. The Highest office in vedic religious and sacrificial ceremonies.

Brahma Gyani— One who has knowledge of Brahma. The priest, the therapist or vaid who knows Brahma.

Brahma Veda— Another name for Atharva veda, because it was revealed to Brahma and it deals with the knowledge of Brahma and Atma.

Brahma Vigyan— Knowledge or science of Brahma.

Brahman Granthas— Are many and serve as supplement and commentaries of the main vedas.

Brihad Trayi— The Big three main samhitas of Ayurveda—Charak, Sushrut and Vagabhatt.

Buddhibhransh— Deranged intelligence or destruction of intellect understanding and cognitive processes.

Chakra— In modern terms the plexuses, are referred to in Yogic exercises.

Charak— One of the main propounders of Ayurveda.

Charak Samhita— The main treatise of Ayurveda, given in the form of questions by the disciple Agnivesh and the answers by the teacher Atreya. Discusses mental and physical ailments and their therapies.

Charan Vaidya— One of the nine schools or Shakhes of Atharva veda.

Chinta— Anxiety functional mental ailment.

Chitta Prasanna— Recreation therapy.

Chittavritti— Mind stuff, mental trends. Five chittavrittis are given.

Chittavritti Nirodh— Control of mental trends by Yogic exercises or Yogic way of dealing with mental complexes.

Condensation— A mental mechanism, given in psychoanalysis where the actual content is made very short and dense.

Daivya— Godly or religious therapy, such as hawan, prarthna pooja uphar etc.

Daivyavipasrya— Divine therapy with psychogenic approach— having recourse to psyche or atma for therapy.

Dev Devta— Psychic energy personalised and given names.

Dhanvantari— One of the earliest proponents of Ayurveda. Took the learning from Indra and gave it to a group of disciples one of whom was the famous Sushrut

Dhratbhramsh— Derangement of the will, lack of will power, motivation and effectivity of ego. A loss of sankalpa shakti (will power).

Devansat— Sin against gods—one of the causes of unmad (insanity).

Durmana— New asthenia. A kind of severe mental abnormality.

Dushswapna— Evil dreams. One of the mild ailments discussed in Atharva Veda.

Ego— The self the socio-cultural aspect of personality.

Etiology— The science of searching for causes.

Gaman— Environmental change, literally 'going'.

Gayan, Nritya— Music and dance therapy.

Ghrena— Hate. One of the vices or ailments of mind.

Gopath Brahman— The Brahmana or supplement and commentary of Atharva veda.

Grah— Compulsive neurosis. A kind of disorders.

Grahi— Hysteria or seizure.

Id— The inner most unconscious part of personality. First Sigmund Freud discovered the unconscious and the significance of Id. Id the reservoir of primitive instincts and desires.

Ida— One of the two 'nadi-s' in left nostril.

Irsha— Jealousy a mild disorder of behaviour.

Ishwar— Parmatma. The Supreme energy.

Jajal, Jalad— Both are Shakhas or schools of Atharva Veda.

Japa— Inner recitation of some mantras.

Jambh— Lock-jaw personified as demon Jambh.

Jatukaran— The name of a rishi whom Atreya taught Ayurveda.

Kama— Erotic instinct personified as a deity Kama (cupid).

Kapha Phlegm— One of three basic elements which constitute the body.

Kaya-Chikitsa— Somatogenic therapy and medicine.

Krodh— Rage, a mild behavioural disorder.

Kumbhak— The middle stage in pranayam in which the breath is retained. There are eight kinds of Kumbhak.

Kundalini— The coiled up serpant or vital energy of the nervous system is aroused by Yogic exercises.

Lobh— Greed—one of the milder behavioural disorders.

Mada— Mania—a behavioural disorder mentioned in Atharva Veda.

Madatya— Alcoholism.

Manas— Mana, psyche.

Manas Chikitsa— Psychogenic therapy.

Manas-pap— Schizophrenia.

Manibandhan— A type of therapy in which a precious or semi-precious stone is tied on the arm of patient.

Mantra— A verbal lyrical form of divine instructions, emerging from the deep process of meditation.

—Also a medium to worship divine or light element, mantras are also known as Richas.

Richa— A prayer, with which you worship gods.

Mantra Vidya— Mantra is silent talk it may include sound.

A sound body of power, charged with intense vibrations of the spiritual personality of the creator or the seer of the mantra.

An embodiment of truth and power.
Mantra may be in the form of coherent words or single letters arranged in a certain order.
Mantras are sounds, pregnant with meanings.
A combination of letters in a certain definite order.
The sounds produce vibration which affect body and mind, and also produce a psychic energy.
A sort of therapy which produces psychic effect or Atmic Shakti-psychic energy.

Medha Vardhan— Improvement of learning and memory.

Moh— Erotic tendency or attachment.

Murcha— Fits, losing consciousness for sometime.

Nagarjuna— Redactor of Sushrut Samhita.

Naturo Therapy— One of the four therapies described in Atharva Veda.

Nosology— Naming or listing.

Ojha— Practitioner of Indian psychotherapy even today.

Organotherapy— One of the four therapies described in Atharva Veda.

Palipplad— Name of a rishi. A shakha of Atharva Veda.

Panini Mahabhashya— A treatise by the sage Panini, which has reference to Atharva Veda.

Pap Bhavana— Sense of guilt and inferiority.

Parirameshti— The effect of past actions. A cause of abnormalities.

Paushtikarni— Some ways suggested for energising the ego in Atharva Veda.

Personality Types— Sattvik, Rajasik and Tamasik in Atharva Veda.

Pingla— One of the nadis in right nostril.

Pitta— Bile, one of the three basic gunas or elements in body.

Pragyapradh— Volitional transgression, doing wrong willingly.

Prakriti— nature or natural tendency. Rajas and tamas gunas are in Prakriti.

Purush— The Atman or pure self.

Note— Human personality according to Yoga is composed of Purush and Prakriti. Prakriti has three gunas— Sattva, rajas and tamas. Purush has sattva guna, it is pure.

Prakshepan and Shodhan— Projection and Sublimation therapy. The ritualistic therapy in Atharva Veda is meant as projection and sublimation.

Prayashchitta— Suggested as a therapy in Atharva Veda to remove pap bhavana—to sublimate and catherise pap or guilt. Prayashchitta may take three forms—Sweekarokti (confession), Tapa and vrata (penances) balidan and dan (sacrifice and charity).

Psychic Energy— Atma-bal or ego-strength.

Psychogenic— Which is born out of the mind or psyche.

Poorak— The first step in pranayam drawing in of breath.

Puranas— The epics. Two main Hindu epics are Ramayana and Mahabharata.

Punarshikshan and Vicharna— Re-education and insight therapy.

Parivarik Upchar— Family treatment.

Rajas— One of three gunas— Love of sensual things of life.

Rakshaspari— Caused or influenced by demons.

Rechak— The last step of Pranayama—the expelling or exhaling of the breath.

Rig Veda— One of the four vedas.

Rishi— The sage a term denoting special abilities of some one who can see the hidden truth of this world मन्त्र दृष्टा.

Samansayani— Ways and means suggested for social integration.

Samoohik— Group therapy.

Samvashikaran— Hypnosis.

Sam Veda— One of the four vedas.

Sanskaras— The mental complexes (arising from cultural factors).

Satpath Brahmana— One of the interpretations or commentaries on vedas. Known as Brahmanas.

Sattva— One of the three gunas—the pure uncorruptible one.

Sattva Vajaya— Mental control and exercise—A therapy.

Sayana— A sage, a commentator of Atharva Veda.

Shantipath and Kanna— Recitation to propitiate—a therapy in Atharva Veda.

Shaunak— A Shakha or school of Atharva veda named after sage Shaunak.

Shok— Distress or depression, one of the minor disorders.

Shrap— Compulsive evil suggestion.

Sushumna— Spinal cord.

Siddhi— Super natural achievements obtained by Tapa.

Siddh-sadhit— A therapist or practitioner who has attained siddhi in mantras.

Smritibhransh— Derangement of memory-amnesia.

Suktas— The whole saying of a rishi is known as a Sukta. Suktas vary according to their subject matter, meter suchas Rishi-Sukta, arth Sukta, Chand-Sukta etc.

Tamas— Literal darkness. One of the tree gunas — the dark evil one.

Tantrik Mantras— Some rituals to attain some aims.

Tantrik Therapy— Cure of mental ailment by tantra or the aparajita vidya.

Totka— An evil deed to cause harm to others.

Unmad— Insanity.

Upanishad— Treatises giving philosophic analysis of veda mantras parts of vedas.

Utarna— Transference therapy.

Vata— Wind one of the three gunas.

Veda— The sources of all knowledge for Indians see note.

Vedant— The end of vedas—a particular branch of Indian philosophy.

Virodhi Bhawana— Opposite passion therapy.

Vritti— Tendency (of the mind).

Yajur Veda— One of the four vedas.

Yoga— A particular philosophy—a therapy, a life style.

Yogic therapeutic exercises called Asanas.

Yuktivipashrya— Organic therapy.

A Note on Vedas

According to Hindu belief the Vedas came from the mouth of the creator—Brahma—himself. They are believed to be not of human origin. Then they were handed down from one generation of rishis to another, in a verbal form. These were chanted and are mostly in lyrical form.

Vedas are four—

Rig Veda— Considered to be the oldest. It contains prayers to the gods and praises of gods Indra, Agni, Sun (Savita).

Yajur Veda— It is mostly in prose form. It deals with methods and the correct procedure to perform 'Yagya'.

Sam Veda— Deals with ways to fight and ward off the forces that disturb 'yagya' and also ways to appease the vedic gods.

Atharva Veda— Contains more worldly knowledge like

living a long and healthy life, medicines, ways and means to eliminate the enemy, fight common and chronic diseases etc.

Rishi denotes a person with special abilities who can see the hidden truth of this world मन्त्र दृष्टा. Vedas are also known a 'Shruti' because all the knowledge of vedas was communicated by reciting and hearing. Vedic richas were heard and retained in mind as there was no writing material or printing technology 4-5 thousand years ago. The Atharvana prays for a long lasting and large memory to retain all the wisdom (Atharva veda I/1/2-3).

The Divisions of the Vedas

Dr. Vachaspati Gairola says, "The long heritage of Vedic knowledge which is available to us today is not the work of any one rishi, or one group, one ashram, one mind, one time. This is a long tradition of centuries, of many groups of rishis, many charanas or shakhas, many ashramas and many minds."

Each veda is divided into ten kandas or sections.

Every veda has 4 parts—Samhita, Brahman, Arnayaka and Upanishad.

Samhitas— Are collections of mantras, as divided into Shakhas or branches. Pt. Satyavrata Samshrami says, "It seems that in ancient Vedic charanas or schools, for sake of convenience of the study, the whole lot of mantras were divided into sections known as the Samhitas."

Brahmanas— Supplements or commentaries giving interpretations of the mantras. Every veda has one or more than one, brahmanas. Gopath Brahmana is the Brahmana of Atharva Veda.

Arnayakas— Give the rituals for those Aryans who have attained a mature age and have retired to forests.

Upanishads— Give philosophical analysis of ved mantras.

Mantras are poetic expressions of vedic wisdom in very concise form.

Sutras are also mantras but in very brief form. The mantra sutra technique become necessary because all the material was to be learnt by heart and retained.

Yajya or Yagya (Havan)— The worship of devas deities, to sacrifice, give alms, later on it came to mean the special offerings of fragrant herbs and ghee to the agni devta along with chanting of mantras.

Devta— Divine energy but personalised. The real God is only one known as Ishwar or Parmatma. He is one and unique. The other devtas represent the various aspects of his energy. These are the forces which make the world go or move. Vedic devtas are from the nature—the sun, moon, varun (water), agni (fire). There are some immaterial devtas also as Kala (time), Kama (eros). In Atharva Veda these devtas occur again and again. Those devtas are given more importance who can help in destroying the demons, eliminating the diseases and vanquishing the enemy.

Atharva Veda

The Atharvans or Atharvedic rishis, when they pondered on matters relating to spirituality, went into poetic form. But sometimes when they discussed the matters relating to this world, they used prose also, specially 15th and 16th kandas are mainly in prose.

Atharva Veda presents a beautiful harmony between this world and other world, reality and spirituality.

Samskaras— Atharva Veda in the Grahya sutras gives all the sixteen samskaras of Hindus which are prevalent even to day. These samskaras start from the early pregnancy known as Punsawan samskara, then coming of the body into the world and giving him a name of Kula (कुल) and identify of gotra (गोत्र). Anna prashan (feeding cereals), Vidyarambha (starting education), Yagyopveet (यज्ञोपवीत), vivaḥ (marriage) are some of the more important samskaras. They go upto after death rituals (shraddh).

Thus Atharva veda presents a full of life picture of the vedic Hindus. It is vast in its canvas and scope. It presents the early Aryas the people at that time as devotees worshippers, performing the holy yagya. But also their more natural and human aspect as greedy, as those who believe in demons, who are fearful, hateful and revengeful who can fall in the grip of sexual pleasures and do tricks to entice cold maidens. They can also perform Ghor (घोर) or ill harmful rites for their enemies. On the whole they are human and peace loving.

Psycho Therapy in Atharva Veda—A Summary

Atharvanic science of healing Chikitsa Vigyan has eight branches called Atharvediya Ashtanga. The main branches are

शरीर रचना (anatomy), क्रिया शरीर (physiology), भेषज (pharmacy), रोगोत्पत्ति (origin or sources of diseases), रोग-विनिश्चय (determining the diseases), निदान (diagnosis), उपचार खण्ड (treatment), भूत विद्या (psychiatry). Bhoot vidya forms the sixth khand or branch. It mentions unmad (insanity) khshipta rog (a kind of mental infliction) dhanurvat (form of convulsions) etc.

In the upchar khand (section on treatment of diseases) eight types of treatment or therapies are mentioned. These are:—

(1) Pani Sparsh पाणि-स्पर्श—Touching by hand. Somewhat like Reiki.

(2) Suryakiran सूर्य किरण—Solar therapy by rays of the sun as sun bathing.

(3) Pavanopchar पवनोपचार—Treatment by wind or air.

(4) Pavakopchar पावकोपचार—Treatment by fire.

(5) Jalopchar जलोपचार—Treatment by water—hydro therapy.

(6) Mantropchar मन्त्रोपचार—Treatment by mantras.

(7) Havanopchar हवनोपचार—Treatment by havana.

(8) Ashwasana आश्वासन—Assurance—a verbal method of treatment.

The second chapter of 6th khand gives manas rog chikitsa or the treatment of the disease of mind what is known a psycho therapy today. The origin of mental disorders is said to be Pragyapradh or the crimes of the conscience. Dushswanpna is mentioned as one of the many mental diseases. Other minor ailments mentioned are krodh, moh, shok (depression), irshya-dwesh.

Unmad is called a disturbed state of mind caused by pap (sin), jwara (fever), krimi (small insects). There is a prayer to Agni, "O jataveda please destroy these specific kriamis (which are causing me pain)." Bhoot and pishachas are also said to cause loss of a sense of balance and judgement (विवेक).

Treatment for unmad suggested is prayer to Agni devta. May the Agni devta give you peace.

Medicines suggested for unmad and other mental ailments are herbs (in different combinations and proportions for different ailments). The herbs suggested are—ajashrangi, guggul, pippli, jata mansi etc.

References

Apte, V.S., *Sanskrit English Dictionary*. Motilal Banarsi Das, Delhi, 1963.

Arsh, P., *Atharvediya Chikitsa Shastra*. Arya Sarvadeshik Sabha, Delhi.

Arsh, P., *Atharvediya Mantra Vidya*. Gurukul Kangri Press, Hardwar, Samvat 1999.

Bloomfield, M., *The Atharva Veda*, Gurundriss.

Boiling G.M. and Negelain J.V., *Parishishthas of Atharva Veda*. Leipzig. 1910.

Brown, J.F., Psycho-dynamics of Abnormal Behaviour. McGrow Hill Co. Inc., London, 1940.

Dawson, W.S., *Aids to Psychiatry*, Bailliere, Tindall and Cox., London, 1944.

Drake, R.M., Abnormal Psychology. Little Field Adams & Co., Paterson, New Jersey, 1959.

Drever, J., *A Dictionary of Psychology*, Penguin Books Ltd., 1952.

Freud, S., *New Introductory Lectures on Psychoanalysis*. Hogarth Press Ltd., London, 1949.

Griffith, *the Hymns of Atharva Veda*, Vol. 1.

Hans Jacobs, *Western Psycho therapy and Hindu Sadhna*. George Alien and Unwin Ltd., London, 1961.

Henery Lefever, *The Vedic Idea of sin*.

Karambelkar, V.W., *The Atharvedic Civilization*. Nagpur University Press, 1959.

Karambelkar, V.W., *The Atharva Veda and the Ayurveda*. Usha Karambelkar, Nagpur, 1961.

Lindermann, Erich, *The Encyclopaedia of Mental Health*, New York.

Max Muller, *The vedas*. Sushil Gupta, Calcutta, 1956.

Max Muller, *Sacred Books of the East* Vol. XI Hymns of Atharva veda. Motilal Banarsi Das, Delhi, 1964.

Maslow and Mittlemann, *Principles of Abnormal Psychology*. Harper and Row Pub., New York, 1951.

Nagar, D.S., *Pran Chikitsa*.

Page, James D., *Abnormal Psychology*, McGrow Hill, London, 1947.

Priya Vrat, *Veda ka Prshtriya Geet*. Gurukul Kangri Press, Hardwar, Samvat 2012.

Radha Kant Dev Bahadure, *Shabd Kalpadrum* (शब्द कल्पद्रुम) Hindi dictionary. Baptist Mission Press, Calcutta, 1886.

Richards, T.W., *Modern Clinical Psychology*. McGrow Hill, London, 1946.

Satavalekar, S.D., *Vedic Chikitsa Shastra*. Saudhyaya Mandal Satara, 1927.

Satavalekar, S.D., *Atharva veda ka Subodh Bhasya* Part I, Saudhyaya Mandal, Pardi, Surat, 1958.

Sharma, R.C., *Atharva veda Samhita*, Sayan Bhashya, Mathura.

Shastri, R.G., *Vedon me Ayurveda*, Ayurvedic Anusandhan Trust, Delhi, 1956.

Shaffer and Lazarus, *Fundamental Concepts in Clinical Psychology*, McGrow Hill Pub., Kogakusha, Tokyo, 1952.

Shende, N.J., *The Religion and Philosophy of Atharva veda*. Oriental Research Institute Pune, 1952.

Singh, H.G., *Psychotherapy in India*. National Psychological Corporation, Agra, 1977.

Swami Akhilananda, *Mental Health and Hindu Psychology*, George Alien and Unwin Ltd., London, 1952.

Vedalankar, B.D., *Vedic Swapn Vigyan*. Gurukul Kangri Press, Hardwar.

Weigel, J.A., *Psychiatry in General Practice*. Elseview Pub. Co., London, 1958.

Whitney, W.D., *Atharva veda Samhita*. Motilal Banarsi Das, Delhi, 1962.

Winternitz, *A History of Indian Literature*.

Swami Ajaya, *Psychotherapy East and West*. The Himalayan International Institute of Yoga Sciences and Philosophy. Honesdale Pennsylvania, U.S.A.

अथर्व चिकित्सा-विज्ञान—ले॰ डॉ॰ हीरालाल विश्वकर्मा व डॉ॰ उपेन्द्र नाथ द्विवेदी, कृष्णदास अकाडेमी, वाराणसी (221001) 1984.

मानस रोग विज्ञान—ले॰ आचार्य डॉ॰ बालकृष्ण अमर जी पाठक, प्रकाशक श्री वैद्यनाथ आयुर्वेद भवन, झाँसी, चतुर्थ सं॰, 1983.

Six

Ayurveda

"Ayurveda is a rich heritage" says Pt. Shiv Sharma, Ayurvedacharya. It is a vast scientific system. But this very vastness makes it rather difficult and unweildy. Secondly the language in which it is treasured—Sanskrit helps make it a sealed book, not only to the foreigner but even to the educated intelligensia of modern India. People do not want to grapple with the complexities of Sanskrit and there is hardly any authoritative book in English which actually describes the system of Ayurveda in a comprehensive and simple way.

These days the interest in Ayurveda is growing. It is a part of Indian renaissance as also a sign of increasing disillusionment with Western systems of medicine. The world has to know the real worth of this system and how it can contribute to the health and well-being of mankind.

This book will describe psychotherapy or the Manasrog-vigyan part of Ayurveda.

The Origin

Ayurveda is the indigenous system of medicine. Its origin dates back to the Vedic times. Even the recorded history of Ayurveda goes back to eight hundred years before Christ. It was called Ayurveda or the knowledge of life. (Ayu = life) like all other vedas, it also had the tradition of being passed over from one generation of gurus to their shishyas, then to another, orally. Thus, in the whole Ayurvedic literature, in fact in whole vedic literature, we find not a single author who claims "I say this......." There is always a chain of guru-shishyas before, and the 'sayer' seems to express the views of not one, but a long unbroken sequence of his predecessors.

Then about 700-600 BC Ayurveda starts taking a definite shape and form. It was held in such a high esteem by the intelligensia of that time, the rishis that they called it an 'upveda' or the junior form of the Holy Vedas, and some even called it the fifth veda.

A Brief History of Ayurveda

Actually there is no agreed history. The scholars differ in their views. Here we can safely take the path taken by Charak.

Like all other vedas Ayurveda is said to have come out from the mouth of Brahma the creator. Then Brahma taught it to Daksha Prajapati, who imparted it to the Ashwini twins. From them it was learnt by Indra. Then Atreya and Dhanvantri took the training from 'Indra'. Now from here the branching out begins—one set of scholars led by Sushrut believe that Dhanvantri began this learning, while the other group claims that Bhardwaj approached Indra and requested for the learning of Ayurveda from him. Actually Bhardwaj was the first mortal to learn Ayurveda. Bhardwaj in turn imparted this knowledge to some of his disciples. Among them Atreya Punarvasu was one. Now according to Charak, Atrey Punarvasu taught it to six of his prominent disciples—Agnivesha was one of them. Actually Charak Samhita is in the form of a dialogue between the Guru Atreya and the shishya Agnivesha, with Agnivesha asking the various questions and Atreya, the Guru replying.

At about 7th century AD the thoughts crystillized into Samhitas. It was the need of the hour. In the 7th century an all Arya Vrata Ayurveda Congress was held in Himalayas. It decided about compiling and writing the teachings of Atreya. Several texts were presented to the august assembly of rishis. Here the text prepared by Agnivesha was adjudged as the best. Thus Agnivesha's text became the standard text for Ayurveda, and afterwards many commentaries of this text were written, including one by Charak and Drudbal. Atri Deva Vidyalankar, P. Roy and H.N. Gupta, support the fact that Charak samhita is the redaction of Agnivesha Tantra. Three samhitas of Ayurveda were written each in a special field of its own— Charak in therapeutics, Sushrut on surgery and Vagabhatta on general principles of medicine. Together these three samhitas are known as the 'Brahadatrayi' 'the Big three' of Ayurveda. Even today they form the basic texts for Ayurveda students every where.

The time of Charak samhita is put in pre-Buddhist era, i.e., before 600 BC.

About the authorship of Charak Samhita, as said earlier, there is a line of rishis not only Charak. At the beginning and at the end of every chapter of C.B. is given—"...as explained by Atreya, compiled by Agnivesha and redacted by Charak and Dradbal, the matter is given here." So the original author is not Charak, but a long chain of rishis before him. Charak is just one of the interpreters of the learning known as Ayurveda, which originated in Atharva Veda—Gulab Kunverba Society of Gujrat has remarked—"Thus we see that Atreya Samhita was the seed which was watered by Agnivesha and nurtured by Charak."

The first text of Ayurveda available at present is "redaction by Drudbal in the 9th century A.D. Sushrut Samhita comes a bit later although most scholars think that Sushruta was a contemporary of Charak. Vagabhatta's Ashtang Sangraha is the last of the three treatises. It's time is placed as the time of Gupta empire i.e., 5th century A.D."

All the three samhitas are very exhaustive. But here only those portions will be taken up which deal with psychotherapy. Before taking up the samhitas one by one, it will be better if some salient points of Ayurveda are discussed.

Salient Points of Ayurveda

It is to be noted at the very outset that Ayurveda developed side by side with Indian philosophy. It had a close affinity with the developing or developed Indian systems of thought of that time like Sankhya, Yoga, Nyaya, Mimansa etc. Not only that, Ayurveda had a healthy give- and-take relationship with the new streams of thought current at that time, such as materialism (पदार्थवाद), evolutionism (सृष्टियुत्तपत्तिवाद).

Secondly the propiciators of Ayurvedic Samhitas were deeply concerned with the basic issues facing the thinkers of that time such as sources of knowledge, aspects of truth. It regards both direct experience and inference as Pramanas, as also aptopdesh

(आप्तोपदेश) and Yukti (युक्ति). Yukti has been given extra emphasis, because Ayurveda is concerned with the person being treated, who has both body and mind.

Then there are basic differences in Indian systems and Western systems. Indian systems tend to be tilted towards spiritualism, while Western system is based on positivism and materialism.

A basic tenet of Ayurveda is the emphasis it gives to the relationship of all mental and physical phenomena and tridoshas. Tridoshas are the malfunctions of the three basic elements in body वात, पित्त, कफ (wind, bile and phlegm). This point is unique to Ayurveda and is to be understood and explained fully.

(1) Ayurveda is the Science of Life—It deals with life in all its forms and aspects. It takes both the positive and the negative view, in that it positively suggests a life style in which the diseases do not emerge and then shows the ways and means to the treatment of diseases once they attack a body. This positive aspect, adopting a healthy life style, by paying attention to diet etc. is a unique contribution of Indian systems of medicine.

(2) The approach of Ayurveda is patient-oriented. It is not disease oriented like the Western medicine nor is it based on diagnosis of symptoms like homeopathy. It caters to the individual, his nature, his vrittis and then suggests therapy according to the patient's needs. Thus it is a wholly patient-oriented system.

(3) The approach of Ayurveda is also holistic. It treats body, mind and soul as one whole system. As Charak says—

सत्त्वमात्मा शरीरं च त्रयमेतत्त्रिदण्डवत्।
लोकस्तिष्ठति संयोगात्तत्र सर्वं प्रतिष्ठितम्।।

चरक सूत्र अ. 7/46

"The mind the soul and body form the three pillars on which not only a human being's existence rests, but also that of the world." The Western science is coming to this holistic approach now.

(4) Ayurveda believes in harmony and equilibrium. As Sushruta says—

समदोषः समाग्निश्च समधातुमलक्रियः
प्रसन्नात्मेन्द्रियमनः स्वस्थ इत्यभिधीयते।।

सुश्रुत सूत्र अ. 75/41

"Balanced doshas (humours), healthy agni, a good state of tissues and their metabolic end products lead to a balanced state of senses, mind and spirit, all of which lead to health."

To be healthy every aspect of the total organism, that is the doshas, tissues, sense, mind and spirit have to be in a state of equilibrium—even the disposal of waste products should be balanced.

(5) Ayurveda gives importance to mind also. It emphasizes the need to keep a healthy mind, free of worries and tensions to keep fit.

(6) Ayurveda is also environment-friendly. It .lays stress on the need to live in harmony with nature. There is a constant give and take between man and nature in various ways—for example, in Utarna (transfer) the things which are harmful to man are given to plants and birds to whom they can be beneficial. In joundice man gives the yellow colouring which is harmful to him, to turmeric plant which can get a richer colour, to a parrot etc. It is never with an intention to harm any one but an exchange mutually benefitting both.

(7) Ayurveda lays great stress on the role of the mind in causing both physical and mental disorders. It is called प्रज्ञापराध which literally means 'crimes of intelligence' but can also be interpreted as going astray of the mind or some guilty feeling lying deep in the mind. So the causes of all types of disorders lie in the mind.

Similarly in treatment of diseases stress is laid on mental factors such as conquering of sense pleasures and the control of mind.

The Basic Tenets of Ayurveda

One basic tenet is giving importance to body, mind and soul in the science of healing. Health can result only when the three are in harmony with each other.

Ayurveda emphasizes the need to keep a healthy mind to keep fit.

Ayurveda emphasizes the relationship of all mental phenomena and tridoshes (the malfunctions of the three basic elements in body— वात पित्त कफ).

Role of mind in causing both mental and physical ailments is stressed.

Includes both positive and negative aspects of therapy. In positive aspect a healthy life style, diet, exercise are given importance while on the negative side, treatment is suggested when diseases do arise. So it includes both prevention and cure of diseases.

Attention is paid to the individual patient, his needs, his vrittis and then to arouse in him a will to live.

It advises man to live in tune with nature in harmony with nature, not to harm any living thing.

Ayurvedic therapy includes herbs, Yoga and Panch Karma.

Proper natural diet and good digestion are the pivots on which Ayurveda is based.

Basic components of a human body are—

(1) Panch mahabhoot	पंचमहाभूत	the five elements.
(2) Doshas	दोष	the controlling forces
(3) Dhatus	धातु	the tissues
(4) Mala	मल	the metabolic waste products
(5) Agni	अग्नि	the fire within (which digests food)—the metabolic process

All the Ayurvedic philosophy is contained in these 5 concepts. These are illustrated below—

Each individual has a specific प्रकृति constitution. Any one can know his or her own Prakriti and act accordingly.

Ritucharya ऋतुचर्या means adopting one's behaviour patterns according to the seasons.

Dincharya दिनचर्या is the best way of adopting a daily routine of life—eating, sleeping etc.

Branches of Ayurveda (as given in Charak Samhita)

There are eight branches known as Ashtang of Ayurveda.

Kaya Chikitsa— somatology internal medicine.

Kumarbhrtya— pediatrics or bala roga chikitsa for young and very young.

Salakya— or science of special diseases of eye, ear, nose, throat etc.

Salya pahartaka— surgery or shalya chikitsa.

Agodatantra— visagra vairodhika prasamana-toxicology.

Bhoot vidya— psychiatry or psycho pathology. Manas rog Chikitsa.

Rasayana chikitsa—rejuvination. Gerontology.

Vaji karana chikitsa — study of sexual function and reproduction.

In all these emphasis is on prevention, but side by side methods to diagnose and cure the diseases are also given. First of all it continued in guru-shishya parampara, but later on crystallized into Samhitas. The well known basic texts are *Charak Samhita, Sushrut Samhita, Vagabhatta's Ashtanga Sangraha* and *Sharangdhara Samhita.*

Why Ayurveda did not Grow?

Somewhere in the fourteenth century, for different socio-political reasons Ayurveda as a system stopped growing and fossilized. Successive Muslim and British occupation of the country for six centuries, did every thing to undermine its growth. If it is living on even today, it is because it has become a part of every man's life. His very way of life is guided and governed by these rules.

Another major drawback has been the language in which Ayurvedic texts are written in Sanskrit. It has become a non-used language and is far away from the understanding of the common man. So the real wisdom was hidden in the texts of Sanskrit, while quakes with half-truths ruled the roost.

One more difficulty is the form in which it is written. This is small Sanskrit stanzas axioms or sutras. Due to the nature of the language these sutras are open to various and often conflicting interpretations. Take for example the word 'rasa' is Sanskrit. It can have thirteen different meanings depending on the context in which it is used such as 'sap', 'juice', 'body fluid', 'primordial tissue', 'emotional tone' etc.

Also the small axiomatic sutras become a problem. These are always packed with enormous information. Some one has compared the Samhitas to a 'zipped' computer file. If properly and systematically interpreted and translated, it could be 'unzipped'. It would then be enormous information occupying phenomenal memory and space.

Ayurvedic method of preparing the medicines is very slow and cumbersome such as Kadhas (concoctions) or asavas (fermentations). They seem entirely out of place in today's ready to take capsules and pills.

Only now Ayurveda has started attracting attention.

— due to side effects of most of the allopathic drugs.

— its easy methods for reducing tension, deep-breathing, Sunbath.

— because it gives a formula for healthy living.

In India the Ayurvedic literature is still in its original form of Sutras in Sanskrit. The material is all scattered and mixed up. One has tow ade through the whole lot of them to find the real descriptions and prescriptions of mental diseases. These are in Sanskrit language and thus, far removed from general reading public. That is why many quacks exploit simple uneducated people in the name of medicines or 'utarna' or 'Jhad-phoonk'.

Now the three Ayurvedic Samhitas will be taken up one by one. This is to be remembered that the basic tenets are coming down from Atharva veda and so remain the same. Only the special features will be discussed and only psycho-therapy will be dealt with.

Seven

Samhitas

Charak Samhita forms one of the three pillars of Ayurveda. As stated earlier, Charak Samhita is the redaction of the original Agnivesha Tantra and rendered by Charak and Drudbal. It is written in the form of question and answers, questions being put by the Shishya Agnivesha and answers given by Guru Atreya. Although there is no consensus on the time of Charak, most of the scholars think Charak's time to be before 600 BC. The text available at present is a redaction by Drudbal in the 9th century AD.

Scope and Contents

As in all ancient Sanskrit literature, Charak Samhita also covers a large number of subjects besides main Ayurveda. The main topics on which views are given are metaphysics, cosmology, ethics, philosophy, physio-chemistry etc. Among the medical subjects it gives detailed discussions of all sorts of physical and mental diseases—their etiology diagnosis, prognosis, treatment etc. In treatment also it gives medicines as well as psychotherapy. Charak Samhita has touched topics like embryology, anatomy, mental and physical hygiene, training and duties of the physicians, theoretical and practical aspects of medicine etc.

Branches— Charak in sutra/30/-8 describes eight branches of Ayurveda (as given in last chapter) viz. Kaya chikitsa (medicine), Salakya (ENT diseases), Salyapahartaka, visagravairodhika prasomana (taxicology), Kumarabhrtya (pediatrics), rasayan or the science of rejuvenation, vajikarana (sexual diseases) and bhoot vidya or psychiatry, science of mental diseases.

Scope— Charak Samhita is sut/30/32 gives 10 topics as the scope of Ayurveda which has been further classified into 8 sections. The ten topics are—

(i) Sharir	शरीर	anatomy
(ii) Vritti	वृत्ति	physiological and psychological make-up.
(iii) Hetu	हेतु	etiology
(iv) Vyadhi	व्याधि	pathology—both physical and mental.
(v) Karma	कर्म	therapy both somatic and psychic
(vi) Karya	कार्य	objective
(vii) Kala	काल	climatology
(viii) Kratr	कृत्	the physician (or Karta)
(ix) Karna	कारण	pharmacology
(x) Vidhiviniseya	विधिविनिशेय	the procedures

The eight sections as given in Charak Samhita are as follows—

(1) Sutrasthan	सूत्रस्थान	general principles and philosophy
(2) Nidansthan	निदानस्थान	etiology of various physical and mental diseases.
(3) Vimanasthan	विमानस्थान	general pathology
(4) Sharirasthan	शरीरस्थान	anatomy—both physical and psychic
(5) Indriyasthan	इन्द्रियस्थान	diagnosis and prognosis
(6) Chikitsasthan	चिकित्सास्थान	therapeutics
(7) Kalpasthan	कल्पस्थान	pharmaceutics
(8) Siddhisthan	सिद्धिस्थान	chances of success in treatment

Main Features of Charak Samhita— As seen above, the scope of Charak Samhita is very vast. In fact it is the first scientific documentation of all the medicinal knowledge available at that time—600 BC.

The basic approach in Charak Samhita is psychosomatic unlike Atharva Veda where it is mainly psychic.

- Although psychosomatic in approach, it gives proper place to psychic approach also, in following Atharva Veda.
- Thinks physicians must have compulsory knowledge of Atharvedic therapeutic practices—Sut/30/21.

- Considers the main cause of even bodily diseases to be mental—sut/25/11. Gives due importance to mental factors.
- Sut 11/46-47— clearly shows that bhoot vidya or psychiatry was a separate and specialized branch of medicine at that time and was practised by specialists in those days.
- One very important feature of Charak Samhita is the scientific and correct classification of the subject matter. All the medical (as also other) information available at that time has been systematically classified by Charak. An example is the description of mental personality types he gives in Sha/4/36. His originality for such classifications is to be praised.

Another very special feature of Charak Samhita is its very detailed and exhaustive descriptions of the diseases, and all things related to them, such as symptoms, medicines, preparing medicines etc. Charak always goes to the depth of the matter and discusses his subject from all possible angles and all points of view.

Charak must also be praised for presenting an unbiased view of things. His opinions are not biased against others, nor are they tilted in his own favour. He gives due importance and praise to his opponents as also points out the shortcomings of his own views.

Charak is a very respected name among medicine men not only in India but other lands also. Charak Samhita has been translated into many foreign languages including German.

Psychic Disorders in Charak Samhita— As already mentioned the scope of Charak Samhita is very vast. For the purpose of this book we have to confine ourselves only to the section on psychic disorders. Mental and psychic disorders are known as Bhoot Vidya in Atharva veda as also in Charak Samhita.

Bhoot Vidya in Atharva veda as well as in Charak Samhita is that branch of medical knowledge which deals with abnormal psychic functions and mental diseases. It forms one of the eight branches of Ayurveda as given in Sut/30/28. But as in Atharva veda, so in all the Samhitas of Ayurveda this branch or any other branch is not given separately. The whole matter is scattered and it is very difficult to go through the whole Samhitas to find the relevant material.

Another point to be mention here is that the approach of Charak is basically Kaya-pradhan or somatogenic. Bhoot vidya is basically psychogenic so it does not find much space and attention paid to it as such. Bhoot vidya does find place in Ayurvedic Samhitas, but not in details. The descriptions are short and confined to the symptoms of mentally ill persons called "grahas" or 'bhoot grahas'.

Bhoot vidya as originally conceived in Atharva veda and developed in Ayurveda and as present in the public eye today are not only very different but poles apart from each other. Bhoot vidya has been a victim of many misconceptions which led to 'jhad-phook' and 'tona totkas' practised by the semi-literate quakes and ojhas. The misconceptions regarding bhoot vidya are—

- grahas are some evil spirits which cause mental problems and disorders.
- that grahas or bhoot grahs enter the human body and cause this body to act in abnormal ways.

But Charak in Nidanasthan says that mental disease is caused by agantuj or exogenous factors. Insanity or unmad is mentioned as mental disease, its causes being agantuj—Nid./7/19-22

So bhoots here are not evil spirits.

What are Bhoot-grahas?— The word 'bhoot' actually means past or gone. It also means retaining in the mind or remembering the past. So it might have meant 'past deeds of the individual'. These bhoot grahas may be symptoms caused by past acts. The grahas do not actually enter the body of the patient from outside. These are not pathological germs either. Charak has mentioned twenty (20) types of germs or parasites which enter the human body, but they do not cause insanity or unmad.

So bhoot-grahas are neither evil inhuman spirits, nor are they pathogenic germs. These are the names of the syndromes of abnormal mental personality types—which are caused by the disharmony of different mental vrittis—sattva, rajas and tamas. These syndromes are symbolically personified and given names. Their names also are given on the basis of mental personality types. Actually this is a continuation of the personificatory tendency of Atharva veda where gandharvas and apsaras represented these bhoot grahas.

In Chik./9/20/1-8 Charak has described eight types of unmad. We find a perfect similarity between these types and symptoms and the characteristics of different gods and devils after whom these are named.

Bhoot Vidya— Bhoot vidya originated in Atharva veda. It is that branch of medicine, in Indian systems, which deals with mental illnesses and abnormalities. Its English equivalent is 'psychiatry'. There are two main causes for misconceptions related to basic bhoot-vidya. Firstly, bhoot-vidya originated in Atharva veda, and there was a vast gap of several centuries before Ayurvedic samhitas arrived. This vast gap of time might have led to the confusions and misconceptions about bhoot vidya. Secondly, the Ayurveda is mainly kaya-pradhan, i.e., somatogenic. So Ayurvedic samhitas failed to give proper space and importance to bhoot vidya which is psychogenic in approach.

Bhoot grahas are the names of abnormal psychic symptoms or syndromes, personified. This is a process of psychic symptom formation. Grahas as in Atharva veda so in Ayurveda mean the psychic compulsions which compel a person for a certain type of behaviour. Grahas resemble in modern terms, the complexes, which come under neuroses or cause neuroses.

Concept of Normality and Abnormality— Ayurveda conceives of personality as a functional whole, which has two aspects—soma (body), psyche (mind), diseases may attack any one aspect, but the other side gets affected as well. "Here the vital relationship subsisting between psychic and somatic life is emphasized. Thus a somatic transgression has psychic repercussions and likewise psychic transgressions lead to somatic disturbances. Therefore volitional transgression of either kind leads to disorders affecting the entire psycho-somatic unit."

Charak adopts the Atharvedic concept of the three gunas vata, pitta and kapha as the constituents of the body and three vrittis as constituents of the mind—sattva, rajas and tamas.

Mental personality is composed of these three gunas or vrittis. Sattva is pure, the rajas is passionate erotic and the tamas is ignorant and destructive. In a normal personality there is an equilibrium among these three. Whenever this equilibrium is disturbed mental abnormality is the result.

According to Charak the aim of Ayurvedic science is to maintain and restore this equilibrium of the personality. Charak lays down a practical code of behaviour called Sadvrat or Swasthya-vrata. It is a constant vigilance and a regular daily and seasonal routine (दिन चर्या, ऋतुचर्या) of prophylectic hygienic measures given in Sut/5-8 chapters.

The mental functions like greed, anger, fear, vanity, hatred, harsh speech all exist in a small degree in normal persons. But when they increase they injure the body as well as the mind. In human personality also sattva, rajas and tamas are present. Sattva is true and never gets corrupted but when rajas and tamas get out of proportion, abnormality occurs. Thus mental normality and abnormality is a matter of degree of the same elements or vrittis. This concept of Ayurveda exists in Atharva veda and agrees with the modern psychological concept of abnormality.

Concept of Personality in Charak— According to Charak (lnd./1/5) personality is the sum total of these hereditary, family, climatic seasonal periodic and ideosyncratic tendencies which make the individual variation among persons. Due to lifferent degrees of interactions in different persons there arise differences in personality make up. Charak has described normal personality types on the basis of the three basic gunas as sattvik, rajasik and tamasik. These three have further varities so there are 16 (sixteen) personality types. This is shown in the table below 7.1.

Table 7.1
Personality Types as Given in Charak Samhita

Satvik	*Rajasik*	*Tamasik*
(1) Brahma	(1) Asura	(1) Pashav
(2) Rishi	(2) Rakshas	(2) Matsya
(3) Indra	(3) Pishach	(3) Vanaspatya
(4) Yama	(4) Sarp	
(5) Varuna	(5) Pret	
(6) Kuber	(6) Shakun	
(7) Gandharv		

Similarly in Vim. 6/3 and Sut. 19, 20 Charak has given classifications of diseases on various bases such as their effect, their intensity, the seat of affection, etiology etc. All of these classifications do not come within the scope of this book. Here only two or three basic classifications will be taken up.

In Sut. 11/45, Sut 7/51-54 and Vim. 6/1-22 diseases are classified according to their etiology—as—

Nij— endogeneous—arising out of imbalance of body humours

Agantuj— exogeneous — arising from outside sources.

Manas— psychic—arising due to imbalance of rajas and tamas.

Sut./7/51-52 says that the endogenous are mainly somatic while the exogenous and manas are both primarily psychogenic. We are concerned with the latter or the exogenous category. In Sut./20 severe diseases are classified Vim/6/5 (2), Sut./7/51-54 give mild diseases. The table below 7.2 gives the classification of psychic diseases on the basis of Sut./20/3 (2).

Table 7.2
Classification of Mental Abnormalities in Charak Samhita

Severe Abnormalities	*Mild Abnormalities*	
(1) Unmad—Nij— (somatogenic)	(1) Agantuj (exogenous and psychic)	
(i) Vatonmad	Anxiety	चिन्ता
(ii) Pittonmad	Fear	भय
(iii) Kaphonmad	Jealousy	ईर्ष्या
(iv) Tridashajonmad	Hate	घृणा
Agantuj— (psychic)	Eros	*Keaece*
Bhootonmad	Anger	*>eaesOe*
8 varieties	Greed	लोभ
Anubandhonmad (feigned or	Manic	मोह
para insanity)	Depressive	विषाद
(2) Apasmar (epilepsy)		
Nij—somatogenic		
(i) Vataj		
(ii) Pittaj		
(iii) Kaphaj		
(iv) Tridoshaj		
Agantuj—(endogenous psychic)		
(3) Atatvabhinivesh (paranoia)		
Agantuj—exogenous and psychic		
(4) Durmana (neuresthenia)		
(1) Nij		
(2) Agantuj		
(5) Murchcha— fainting fits		
(6) Aptantrak— Convulsions		
(7) Madtya— alchoholism (somatogenic)		

General Etiology of Psychic Disorders

Three general causes of mental disorders are given—

Nij— endogenous somatogenic—doshas (discordance) of bodily humours—vata, pitta, kapha

Agantuj— exogenous psychogenic—such as trauma.

Manas— psychic—discordance of sattva, rajas and tamas.

Sha./4/34 says that the same disease unmad may be caused by somatic factors or outside factors or psychic factors. In Sut./19/7 Charak says that, "exogenous disorders may be consequent upon endogenous disorders and similarly increased endogenous morbidity may combine with exogenous effects." So the physician has to carefully find out 'the primary cause' and secondary complications before beginning actual treatment.

In Sut./20/7 (1) Charak gives the recognition points of primarily exogenous and endogenous diseases as—"the exogenous one begins with anxiety and leads to disharmony of vata, pitta, kapha in endogenous ones the order is reversed."

According to Charak, apart from the three immediate causes, there are some remote or pre-disposing causes. These pre-disposing causes are described in Sut./20/5 as—

Asatmaindriyath— sanyog—unwholesome interaction between the object and the sense organs.

Pragyapradh— volitional transgession.

Parirameshti— the effect of one's past actions.

Charak in Sh./1/116-117 explains that past actions and behaviour affect the personality, but the ultimate cause even of bodily disorders is mind. In Sut./25/11 he says that the real cause of the origin of body and its diseases is the Mana (mind) known as Purush enveloped by Rajas and Tamas. So the ultimate cause of all diseases of body and mind are the rajas and tamas types of behaviour. In modern psycho-pathology also over throwing of the super-ego authority and giving free rein to Id urges leads to mental abnormality.

Now we can summarize Charak's views —

Three kinds of mental diseases Ref. Sut./11/45—

(i) Nij
(ii) Agantuj
(iii) Manas

Three kinds of remote or predisposing causes Ref. Sut./20/5, Vim./6/6, Sha./1/987—

(i) Asatamyaindriyarth samyoga—a cognitive defect
(ii) Pragyapradh—volitional transgression
(iii) Parirameshti—effect of past deads

Three kinds of immediate causes (Ref. Sut./19/4, Sut./11/45, Vim./6/5)—

(i) Sharirdosha—vatta, pitta and kaph—morbidity of three humours.
(ii) Shrap-Graha—complexes and compulsions.
(iii) Manas desh—rajas and tamas, labh and alabh.

Three kinds of causes of pragyapradha (Ref. Sha./1/102, Sha./1/98, Sha./1/99-108)—

(i) Buddhi bhransh—derangement of intelligence
(ii) Smriti bhransh—derangement of memory
(iii) Dhrat bhransh—derangement of will.

Three kinds of therapies (Ref. Sut./11/54)—

(i) Yuktivipasrya— scientific organic medicine
(ii) Daivyavipasrya— divine therapy
(iii) Sattva vajaya—mental control and exercise.

Three means of diagnosis of psychic disorders (Ref. Vim./4-7, Vim./4/3-5)—

(i) Aptopdesh—theoretical knowledge of all possible causes
(ii) Pratyaksh—observation and examination of symptoms
(iii) Anuman—inference based on previous experience.

Symptoms of Psychic Disorders

I Severe Abnormalities

Unmad— insanity—psychosis.

Unmad is dealt with in Charak Samhita as—pathology in Nid./7, Symptoms in Ind./5/18-21 and therapy in Ch./9.

Etiology of Unmad

(1) Endogenous— 4 sub. types—produced by somatic morbidity of (i) vata, (ii) pitta, (iii) kapha, (iv) all three combined.

(2) Exogenous— 8 sub-types produced by grahas or the compulsions and by psychic morbidity of rajas and tamas.

Nid./8/11— causes of insanity given as fear, anxiety and grief.

Upadhimanbandhan is a type of feigned insanity. It has been discussed by B.A. Pathak and Chakrapani both. Charak in Vim./5 calls it false, para or pretended type. It is mentioned to make the therapist aware of such possibility.

Nid./7/11 gives symptoms of premonitory stage of unmad.

Nid./7/5, 12, 13 gives acute state and Ind./5/18-21 gives symptoms of the fatal state.

In Chik./9/21 Charak gives the description of grahs of many types. Of these the 8 more common grahs—or symptoms are—

(1) Devonmad, (2) guruonmad, (3) pitronmad, (4) gandharvonmad, (5) yakshonmad, (6) rakshasonmad, (7) brahmrakshasonmad and (8) pichachonmad. These are the symbolic names of the symptoms found in the disordered personality. Nid./7/19-22.

The detailed descriptions of the symptoms of these 8 kinds of grahas are given in Chik/9/20 (1), 20. These symptoms match the names of grahs for example the devonmad symptoms are like gods gentle, pure clean. Pitronmad is using harsh language, angry. Gandharvonmad shows erotic symptoms while all the rakshas types are aggressive destructive and mean.

Apasmar— (epilepsy)— It is translated as epilepsy, but the symptoms of apasmar as given in Charak Samhita include other types of fits also such as hysteric fits.

Apasmar is discussed in detail in Charak Samhita—pathology in Nid./8, its fatal symptoms in Ind./5/22-23 and therapy in Chik./10.

Etiology of Apasmar is (1) endogenous mostly caused by the disturbance of body humours—it has 4 sub-types—vata, pitta, kapha and combined, (2) Exogenous or psychogenic causes—rajas and tamas.

Nid./8/4 refers the causes as both combined, that is, the remote cause is somatogenic and immediate is psychogenic. "When the humours, lying dormant are aroused by a sudden outburst of काम, क्रोध, लोभ, भय, मोह infatuation, manic excitement, Meeskea depression or anxiety, they restrict the channels of the heart and internal organs and the patient has a fit." According to

Chik./10/4, 5 sattva guna gets abscured by rajas and tamas and mind is oppressed with worry then apasmar results. Charak has not mentioned anywhere Pragyapradh as one of the causing factors. So it is not a functional disorder of behaviour but the pathogenic disorder of the organism. As in Charak in modern psycho-pathology it is mainly somatogenic.

Mahagad— Atatvabhinivesh—paranoia. The word meaning of ATATVABHINIVESH is 'the faith in what is false, wrong or untrue'. Delusions and perversions are the two special features of it. Chik./10/57-60 gives its cause as psychogenic the excessive increment of rajas and tamas gunas—unnatural and immoral behaviour or suppression of urges, anxiety etc. The somatogenic causes are impure diet which vitiates body function.

The main symptoms of this disease are feeble mindedness, wrongful or clouded understanding, increase in aggressive tendencies passions, frequent delusions, wrong judgement of true and false etc. The tendencies are perverse. This is mainly a psychogenic disease. Its therapy is both psychogenic and somatogenic.

Ref.— Mansik Rog Aur Chikitsa in Sachitra Ayurveda, Jan. 1965, article by Som Deva Sharma Sarsvat.

Durmana— neuresthenia. The other name for this disease is Anjakshaya. It is discussed very briefly in head-diseases in Sut./17/73-77. The symptoms given are depression, anxiety, timidity, nervousness, discomfort nervous exhaustion, dryness emacipated look etc. The causes are mental strain, over-exhaustion, anxiety, no meals or scanty meals, fear, grief, sexual excesses and effect of grahas. The therapy given is psychosomatic.

Murchha-sanyas— Syncope— It is a short fainting fit. It has been very summarily discussed by Charak in Sut./19/4 (5) and Sut./24/25-60. This disease is called psychosomatic like apasmar. The somatic cause is the discordance of vata, pitta and kapha while the psychic causes are morbidity of rajas and tamas. Its main symptoms are fainting, hallucination paralysing the functions of speech body and mind, unconsciousness. Therapies prescribed by Charak are psychosomatic.

Aptantrak— Convulsions—Given in Sut./9/11-24. The causes are both psychic and somatic. Somatic causes are the three gunas humours and psychic causes are the vrittis, rajas and tamas—their morbidity clouds mental functions and brings about convulsions. The symptoms are—bending of body like a bow, convulsions of limbs, fixed and wide eyes, difficult breathing, makes some voices (coos) and becomes unconscious. For the convulsive stage medicines are applied and after that psychic therapy is given for improvement in daily behaviour.

Madatya— alcoholism. In Charak Samhita madatya is discussed in a full chapter with all details— Chik./24. According to Charak wine in mild doses is like Amrit—promoting long life and happiness. But its use in excess causes physical and mental disorders. In Chik./24/53-56 Charak says that excessive wine agitates the mind like a storm shaking trees and then it causes morbidity of rajas and tamas. The man who is enslaved by wine is deprived of all sattvik qualities and of wisdom. Two types of therapies are suggested of all sattvik qualities and of wisdom. Two types of therapies are suggested in Chik./24/191-193, behavioural and psychological.

Mild Abnormalities

These have not been discussed separately but mentioned in Vim./6/5 (2) as diseases caused by morbidity of rajas and tamas. These are treated as symptoms of mental disorders and not as diseases.

These are functional abnormalities and to check them—there should be no volitional transgression or pragyapradh, also sadvrata—proper code of behaviour must be adopted.

Psycho-therapies in Charak Samhita

Charak explains in Chik./1/14 that therapy means any such measures as can be applied against diseases. Therapy is called treatment, disease remover, medicine, prayashchit of any sedative, restorative agent, in short any measure to restore health is therapy.

Main Features of Psychotherapy in Charak Samhita

- It may be psychogenic or somatogenic herbal etc.
- It is a continuation or rather extention of Atharvedic therapies. Atharva veda is the source of all therapies for Charak.

- It is rather mixed up with religious practices such as havan, fast, prayashchit, mantra etc.
- That by Charak's time psychotherapy was so advanced that it was practised by separate specialists and mental patients were asked to go to these specialists.

Aims and Objects of Therapy According to Charak

- Sut./1/53—the maintenance of equilibrium in the elements of body and personality, i.e., gunas.
- Sut./30/26—maintaining health in healthy and removal of disorders in the ailing.
- Chik./1/4—therapy can be of two kinds—one for promoting health and vigour in the healthy-preservative, two, for removing or destroying diseases in the ailing-curative.
- Charak presents a dynamic view of the health condition. Health is not static, it is dynamic and creative. It must grow like life.

Classification of Psychotherapies in Charak Samhita

In Sut./1/54 (1) — 54 three classes of psychotherapies with their sub-classes are given in Table 7.3.

Here we will be concerned with the first, that is, the psychogenic therapies of mental disorders. These are two. Some points are to be remembered here—

- That there are a number of such therapies which are given at different places in Charak Samhita.
- That the names of therapies and diseases on which these are applicable are given but the details of the procedure have been left out, that is because the people in India generally know them such as pooja and havan, only some specialisation is required, and secondly because Charak is mainly kayapradhan (somatic therapist) so only a mention of psychogenic medicines is found.
- That these therapies directly relate to manas chikitsa of Atharva Veda.
- That the specialists of psychogenic therapies were expected to have sound theoretical knowledge of Atharva Veda and acquire the practical knowledge by experience and practice.

TABLE 7.3
THERAPIES IN CHARAK SAMHITA

Psychogenic	*Somatogenic*
Divyavipasrya Sattva vajaya Chikitsa	***Yuktivipasarya Chikitsa***
(1) **Mantra-vidya** (a) Sankalp—vow (b) Japa—repetition of mantra (c) Mangal-karma—auspicious rites (d) Shanti karma—propitiatory rites	(1) **Shalya (surgery)** (a) Aghat-shock— mental or physical (b) Shiravedh (venesection) (2) **Aushadhi (medicines)** (a) Manibandhan— amulets massage external appliances for eye, ear etc.
(2) Religious practices (1) Pooja (worship) (2) Uphar (offering) (3) Prarthana (prayer) (4) Havan (3) Punarshikshan—re-education (4) Gaman—going away or a change in environment (5) Virodhi bhawana—opposite sentiments (6) Prayashchita—Bali and dan, tapa and vrat.	(b) Herbs and their concoctions (c) Drugs or chemicals—for oral consumption

The Two Main Psychotherapies

Mentioned in Charak Samhita in Sut./11/46, 47 and Sut./30/21 are—

Daivya Vipasrye— The word meaning is Daivya-divine or atmic. Vipasrya=have recourse to, refuge or shelter. (as given by V.S. Apte) So the meaning of the term is that the person or patient has to seek the refuge of the divine or Atma or psyche for therapy. It is found in modern psychotherapy. Drake says, "The belief in the miraculous power of a shrine, of a certain person, or a certain ritual may be sufficient to effect a better psychological integration, where the disorder is mainly functional."

—*Drake, R.M. Abnormal Psychology, 1959*

Sattvavajaya— Sattva = the Sattva guna, Vajaya = the victory

It is clear that mental diseases arise when rajas and tamas gunas get out of control. So here the effort is to harmonize rajas and tamas in personality and to make Sattva guna superior to them. By so doing the mental balance is restored and the disorder is eliminated. It is to control the mind and save it from unwholesome deeds. It is a psychogenic therapy working from within the mind. It is like psyche treating the psyche itself.

The sub-therapies or techniques within these two are—

Mantra-vidya— Mantra vidya has been discussed in detail in Atharva veda. In Charak Samhita also one full chapter No. XIV is for mantras. It emphasizes "the curative effects of specially arranged hymns and incantations called Mantras."

In mantra vidya the mantra or a group of words are first made siddha that is, made sacrosanct by some sacred person, who then uses them for therapy. Such mantras form part of psychic therapy. These mantras can be used or uttered only by those persons who possess siddhi or higher psychic qualities in them thus strictly preserving the sanctity of the mantras. In Charak Samhita there is a special name given to the therapists, who achieves mantra siddhi and who practice mantra therapy. They are known as siddh-sadhit (those who have attained siddhi) Sut./11/50. But Charak gives very few mantras unlike Atharva Veda, which is full of mantras. The treatment of mantra vidya in Charak Samhita is very scanty and mostly mention is made not giving the full procedure.

Mantra vidya has been called effective for unmad, apasmar and atatvabhinivesh. Modern psycho therapy does not have any equivalent of mantra vidya. Under mantra vidya come—

- Sankalpa—self determination taking, a vow for something.
- Japa—repetition of some hymns, words, mantras.
- Mangal Karma—auspicious religious rites.
- Shanti Karma—propitiatory rites for atonement.

Sankalpa— It is taken fully from Atharva veda and nothing new has been added by Charak. It is non-directive therapy said to be useful in unmad and apasmar.

Japa— It is a new practice and is not mentioned in Atharva veda. In this some mantras words or syllables are repeated a given number of times say sava lakh (or one lakh twenty five thousand times) by the patient.

This type of repetition for a large number of times is said to create psychic effects on the mental make up of the patient, who is made to repeat them. It combines auto-suggestion and faith, the sounds also produce the desired effect. Since Japa is not found in Atharva veda, it seems to be a tantrik influence. Japa is said to be the Tapa of vani (speech). It is also non-directive therapy and its equivalent is not found in modern psychotherapy. Charak recommends Japa in milder forms of unmad and other mental diseases.

Mangal Karma Shanti Karma— These are performed by the patient but mostly presided over by the priest or purohit. They may be done publicly in large groups, small family groups or the patient alone. These are supposed to bring 'mangal' welfare and happiness and shanti karma is done to pacify gods and goddesses or grahas so that they may relieve the patient of his symptoms.

Atharva veda gives these practices under different names, together with mantras and rituals. It is a sort of directive therapy. Charak recommends it for milder mental disorders.

Religious Practices— Apart from the above, other religious rites are also recommended for mental disorders. These are—

(1) Puja—worship
(2) Uphar—offerings
(3) Prarthana—prayer
(4) Havan—

These are also found in Atharva veda. They are based on faith and are called "faith healing or spiritual healing" by Shaffer and Lazarus.

Pooja is done to please gods and goddesses, one or more than one, then offerings are made of some material things like food items, which are then given to the priest or poor. Prarthna or prayer may be offered with these rites and alone also. These three are done together in most of the cases. The suggestions and faith act as curative agents. It is directive therapy, and can be effective in unmad, apasmar and atatvabhinivesh.

Havan— This practice originated in Vedas. In havan several herbs, mostly fragrant, are poured into the secred fire along with ghee and recitation of mantras. The priest performs it and the patient makes the offerings. It is fire worship but the smoke from the burning herbs and ghee also produce effects in all those who inhale it. Thus it is a mixture of faith and medicinal healing, psycho-somatic effect. It is useful in disorders of psychogenic origin.

Punarshikshan and Vicharna— Charak in Sut./11/46 (1) 47 has discussed punarshikshan or re-education. He has emphasized the need for re-educating mental patients to correct their values and conceptions. The cause of abnormalities lies in corrupt knowledge and understanding and vitiated memory. So the understanding and knowledge of the patient must be corrected and he should be re-educated. These things are mentioned in the following—

Sut./11/46-47— Charak says that the man afflicted with mental disorders must get the association and help of the experts of psychic disorders to get the knowledge of his own personality, and knowledge of good and evil from philosophers.

Sut./11/46 (1)— Charak says that the patient must think intelligently on the problem, get proper guidance and must get an insight into his conditions, environment and ailment. He must reform his habits and actions through insight (vicharna).

Chik./9/85— Charak says that any one who has lost his mind due to the loss of some dearly loved object or person must be consoled by words of sympathy and comfort.

As explained by **Charak**, re-education must include analysis, advice teaching and practical training of the patient.

Re-education— punarshikshan is a directive therapy—its scope starts from heredity upto the present factors — environment, physical and mental study of values, religion, pleasures and also areas of conflict within.

In modern psychotherapy Shaffers and Lazarus have discussed re-education which is equivalent to punarshikshan and insight which is equivalent to vicharna.

"Re-education may be broadly viewed as the re-training of the individual in his habits of response to both situations, ideas, etc. And that Franz (1923) Lashley (1929) and others have supplied information regarding such processes of re-education."

—*Shaffer, G.W. and Lazarus, R.S.*

They have also explained insight therapy. Wolpe's behaviour therapy also comes very near to these.

It is generally applicable to all psychic disorders, but Charak lays stress on the ability of the patient to make association with the therapist. He must not be totally insane. Charak specially recommends it for atatvabhinivesh (paranoia) and Durmana (neuresthenia).

Gaman— It means 'going' but actually stands for environmental change. Charak has mentioned it many times as a method of treatment for mental disorders. Gaman may mean going away from the present environment (and its problems) may be on pilgrimage, to some relations, to holiday resorts etc. It is meant to get the patient away from his present environment.

Comparison with Modern Psychotherapy— It means environmental change and is given importance as such by Shaffer and Lazarus—They quote Austin Riggs.......'therapy was directed to the psychoneurotic, for whom he advised temporary environmental change. He believed that the patient should be removed from his vocational, social and home environments, since it was in these environments that the stress developed.' Charak has recommended environmental change for unmad, apasmar, durmana, atatvabhinivesh specially and for all other psychic disorders generally.

Virodhi Bhawna (Opposite Emotions)— This is Charak's unique contribution to psychic disorders. In Chik./9/86 he suggests that when psychic disorders result from excess of emotions like eros, grief, fear, rage, envy and greed—they can be cured by bringing in its opposite emotion (virodhi bhavana) to influence it, so that it can be neutralized. In this way the effect of the causing emotion will be neutralized. It may be called a balance or neutralizing therapy or an indirect repression therapy. On surface it seems a symptomatic cure, it tries to change the feelings directly but in the long run the autonomic nervous system and thus the whole body is affected, and the cure is of mind and body both.

There is no equivalent of this in modern psychotherapy. But Wolpe (1966) has mentioned, "reciprocal inhibition"—which is not the same—the approach is quite different from Charak in Wolpe.

Patanjali in his yoga sutra 33, 34 section II has given a method, "pratipaksha bhawna", which may have been adopted by Charak later.

Prayashchit— These are the same as given in Atharva Veda. Sweekarokti, tapa and tyag. All the three are found in Charak Samhita. Charak also mentions bali (sacrifice) dan (giving alms) and tapa and vrata (fasting) under penances. We have discussed all these in detail in the section on prayashchitani in Atharva Veda. It is a unique Indian approach to mental disorders and there is no equivalent of this in modern psychotherapy. Charak recommends prayashchit for all mental disorders but specially unmad (mild neurosis) atatvabhinivesh (paranoia) durmana (neuresthenia) and excessive emotions kama, krodh, moh, bhaya, irshya, ghrina etc.

Sushruta Samhita

As stated earlier, Sushruta Samhita is one of 'the big three' of Ayurveda. Its specialisation is in surgery as Charak is in medicine. To some the Gulab Kunverba Society of Gujrat—Sushrut was a contemporary of Charak, but according to A.D. Shastri, Sushrut was the son of Vishwamitra and his time is 2000 BC.

The historical basis of Sushrut is the same as Charak, both owe their origin to Atharva Veda. It is said that Ayurveda came from the mouth of Brahma himself—who taught it to Daksha Prajapati—who gave it to Ashwini twins. From them it was learnt by Bharadwaj. Bhardwaj imparted it to some of his disciples like Atreya Purnarvasu and Dhanvantri. It is claimed that Dhanvantri took Ayurvedic training from Indra directly. Dhanvantri had a group of disciples and Sushruta was the leader of this group. They took Ayurvedic training with special reference to surgery.

The learning thus received was compiled in the form of Sushruta Samhita—Sut./1/18, 28. Like all other Vedic and Ayurvedic treatises Sushruta Samhita is also in the form of questions and answers, the questions being put by the shishya Sushruta and the answers given by the guru Dhanvantari.

The Sushruta Samhita available now is a redaction of the original redacted by Nagarjuna much later. It is very similar in approach and content to Charak Samhita, except in the surgery section, in which it specialises. Sushruta Samhita is divided into two parts, which cover all the eight branches of Ayurveda. In Chapter Sut./3 the summary of all the contents is given. The first part has 120 chapters divided into 5 groups, viz., Sutra, Nidan, Sharir, Chikitsa and Kalpasthan. The second part of Sushruta Samhita is known as UTTAR TANTRA and has 66 chapters divided in 5 groups, viz. Shalakya, Komarya, Kaya-chikitsa, Bhishan and Bhoot-vidya. This bhoot-vidya is equivalent to modern day psychiatry and psychotherapy. We have already discussed bhoot-vidya with reference to Atharva Veda and Charak Samhita. Here we have to concentrate on bhoot vidya. It is worth noting here that in Surgery Sushruta is superb. He has given detailed descriptions of Yantras or instruments of operation, the ways of doing operation, places of surgery and the healing medicines etc.

According to Sut./3/43-45 Sushruta Samhita deals with Shalakya-tantra, i.e., the diseases of eye, ear, nose, throat and mouth, Komar tantra diseases of the young or pediatrics, Kaya-chikitsa somatic medicine, and Bhoot-vidya psychiatry or psychotherapy.

Sushruta seems to be more influenced by Atharva Veda. He shows the same tendency of symbolising and personifying and naming according to similarities. Sushruta has named diseases, human personality types and even surgical instruments on the basis of their similarity with gods, demons, animals or birds.

Although Surgery is the speciality of Sushruta, he has given ample attention to unmad and grah diseases. Sushruta has given mental grah diseases of children separately. In the field of therapy also Sushruta is directly influenced by Atharva Veda. He has given ritualistic therapy with mantras etc. in detail.

Sushrut's surgical methods are being used in the Ayurvedic hospitals even today. Sushruta Samhita has been translated into many foreign languages also.

Psychic Disorders in Sushruta Samhita— Psychic disorders are given in Bhoot-vidya Sut./1/6, 7. Sut./3/41 defines it as that branch of therapeutics which deals with abnormal or grah diseases like apasmar (epilepsy) and unmad (insanity).

Sut./1/12 is more relevant here. He defines Bhoot-vidya with reference to therapy, as "that branch of the Ayurveda which makes psychological approach of sacrifice, hawan, mantra etc. for the treatment of grah and other psychological diseases. So, in all three chapters of uttar tantra have been devoted to the therapy of grah diseases, epilepsy and insanity (Utt./60-62). This portion of Sushruta Samhita is known as Bhoot-vidya. What is known as modern psychiatry or psychotherapy is Bhoot-vidya of Ayurveda".

Points of Dissimilarity between Sushruta and Charak with Reference to Bhoot-vidya

- Sushruta clearly defines bhoot vidya and therapy related to it.
- Sushruta distinguishes between grah diseases (neuroses) and unmad (psychoses) which Charak had mixed up.
- Sushruta has described eight grahas—which are not found in insanity types.

Similarities in Sushruta and Charak— With reference to bhoot-vidya—

- Both believe that grahas never enter the human body.
- Mental personality types described by both are the same (Sha./4)/

Sattvik	*Rajasik*	*Tamasik*	
Brahma, Mahendra, Varun, Kuber, Gand-harva, Yama and Rishi	Asur, Sarp, Shakun Rakshas, Pishach and Pret.	Pashu, matsya Vanaspati	
= 7	= 6	= 3	Total = 16

- Both believe in the Ayurvedic tenet—the three humous of the body—vata-pitta-kapha. Three gunas of the mind, sattva, rajas, tamas.
- Normality in the physical personality is the equilibrium of vata, pitta and kapha (Sut./16/48) and abnormality is their discordance (Sut./25/9).
- In mental personality, normality means the equilibrium of sattva, rajas and tamas, and abnormality is increase or decrease in the degrees of rajas and tamas (Sut./24).
- Both prescribe swasthya-vrat (Utt./64) for a long healthy life.

Classification of Diseases in Sushruta Sahmita— The psychic diseases are dealt in Utt./46, 47, 60-62.

- According to Sut./1/32-33 the psychic diseases are of 4 kinds—

- Agantuj — due to outside causes, exogenous.
- Sharirik—due to discordance of vata, pitta, kapha—physical.
- Manasik—due to excess of rage, sorrow, fear, sex, grah etc.
- Svabhavik— natural due to suppression of natural bodily needs.

—Sut./1/45-46 says exogenous diseases may arise in body or mind.

- Sut./24/3—he gives two types of diseases on the basis of cure—those curable by surgery or curable by other means.
- Sut./24/4—describes diseases of three types on the basis of etiology—
  1. Adhyatmic—caused by heredity, mother's abnormality or dosha's etc.
  2. Adhibhautic—caused by outside factors.
  3. Adhidaivic— caused by grahas—cured by mantras.

Mental disorders have been classified by Sushrut as—

— Nij—somatogenic—discordance of bodily humours.
— Agantuj—exogenous—grahas complexes or compulsions.
— Manas—psychogenic—discordance of rajas and tamas.

This etiology is dealt with more exhaustively and clearly in Charak.

Sushrut does not give diagnosis of psychic disorders separately, these are found mixed up. In general the somatogenic and psychogenic disorders are diagnosed on the basis of imbalance of body humours or rajas and tamas gunas. Agantuj are diagnosed on the basis of symptoms similar to the grahas.

Symptoms of Psychic Disorders According to Sushrut Samhita

Severe abnormalities—
Grah—8 types
Apasmar — epilepsy— nij — agantuj
Unmad — nij — agantuj
Others — Murchha — fainting
Sanyas—coma
Panatyay — alcoholism

Grah Diseases— neuroses and compulsions.

In Sushrut Samhita Utt./60 is wholly devotes to grah diseases. Sushrut has clearly distinguished between grah diseases (neuroses) and unmad (psychoses) which Charak had mixed up. Utt./60/6, 7 gives the names of eight grahas as the most important ones. These are simply the names given to the group of symptoms of the diseases. In Utt./60/22 he emphatically says that the disorders are caused by the immoral, irreligious and unnatural behaviour of the patient and causes symptom formation Utt./60/1, 27. This naming and personifying tendency of Atharva veda and Charak has been followed by Sushrut in naming the grahas. These are just the diseased personality types.

One point noteworthy in Sushrut is that he has discussed the mental disorders of children separately. These are also named as grahas on the basis of their symptoms. The inability of the children to tell as also of adult abnormals, makes it necessary that ailments are described on the basis of their symptoms. Sushrut in Utt./60/8-15 gives detailed descriptions of these grah diseases. Here some examples are being given of 8 grahas.

- Dev graha—clean, gentle, pure, pleasant, truthful, benevolent.
- Daitya—sweating, criticizing elders and gods, mean, evil.
- Gandharva graha—erotic, music and fragrance loving, dancing etc.
- Yaksha graha—red eyes, speaks less, tolerant.
- Pitra graha—silent, talks like dead forefathers.
- Sarp graha—characteristics like snake, licks by tongue, like milk and milk products.
- Rakshas graha—like meat, wine, blood, is shameless and obstructive.
- Pishach graha—thin, with strong body odours, dirty, crying and wandering.

Different therapies are suggested for graha diseases.

Apasmar— Epilepsy—Sushrut gives one whole chapter Utt./61 for apasmar. It has been defined as Ap—without or loss of, smar—memory,—hence apasmar is loss of memory or past associations. The causing factors are given in Utt./61/4, 6 as—

(a) a hypo, hyper or para functions of sense organs, speech etc.

(b) living a dirty evil and mean life.
(c) discordance of vata, pitta, kapha on one hand, rajas and tamas on the other.
(d) having sexual intercourse with menstrual woman.
(e) corruptions of mind due to emotions of fear, anger, sex, sadness etc.

According to Charak apasmar is more somatogenic. Sushrut considers it both somatogenic and psychogenic. Utt./61/7 gives the symptoms of early stages as trembling of heart, sweating, blankness, loss of consciousness and fit or coma. Utt./61/8-10 gives the symptoms of the acute stage as—the three gunas vitiate the nervous system, rajas and tamas cloud the consciousness, the patient throws hands and feet, eyes are twisted, grinds teeth, foam forms around mouth and falls unconscious on the ground. He regains consciousness after some time. Therapies are suggested according to the causative factors. These are shocks, venesection, mantra, prayashchit and ritualistic therapies.

Unmad— (psychoses—insanity)—The importance of this mental disorder is evident by the fact that Sushrut Samhita devotes one full chapter to unmad—Utt./62. This chapter gives in detail all the causative factors as well as the therapies.

Unmad is a functional disorder of long duration in which the mental functions are deranged. The main predisposing cause is wrong past behaviour of the person himself—living a life of evil, immoral irreligious nature, Utt./62/3. It means giving a free rein to Id tendencies, and going against the superego. Some marked symptoms are found in the patient before the actual onset of the disease. These symptoms are excess of eroticism emotionality, auditory hallucinations, manic behaviour, debility, insomnia, bad dreams, aversion to food, giddiness, anxiety etc. These symptoms are mentioned in Utt./62/6, 7. In the acute stage all these symptoms are increased, patient talks irrderautly releventently and incoherently, his memory, associations and intelligence are lost. He may be singing or weeping and laughing, his consciousness is fully lost. Utt./62/13.

According to Sushrut there are two main causes of the disease— (1) somatogenic and toxic, (2) Agantuj or psychogenic that is due to the discordance of rajas and tamas, some mental trauma, sex frustration, anxiety and fear. Then the different types of psychogenic anxiety are given Utt./62/12-38. The main types are—

Aghatonmad or traumatic—due to some trauma—loss of money or dear ones, business, prestige.

Kamonmad— caused by sex frustration.

Shokajonmad— anxiety neurosis caused by worry due to losses.

Bhayonmad— caused by feeling of fear from enemies etc.

Vishonmad— caused by toxic elements—poisons go to brain.

The main therapies suggested are—medicines, shocks, venesection, mantras, prayashchit, religious rites, recreation and re-education.

Murchha— fainting fit—Sushruta gives one full chapter to this disease also Utt./46. In this diseases there are fits of fainting for short duration. It is psychosomatic and resembles apasmar—with one difference that here the locking of the jaw and foaming at mouth are not found. The main causative factors are—the discord of three gunas decrement of Sattva and increment of rajas or tamas, toxins and alcohol. The main symptoms of this disease are clouding of the consciousness, a temporary paralysis of all bodily, and mental functions, falling fainted for a short time. After this fit the patient regains consciousness.

Several medicines to cool and sooth the patient are prescribed, but no psychotherapy is given.

Sanyas— coma—Sushrut has dealt separately with Murchha and Sanyas—Charak had combined the two. This disease is given in Utt./46/21-26. It is the last and acutest stage of murchha and is very dangerous—because if immediate medical aid is not given the patient may never regain consciousness and dies in the coma. For this medicinal aids are prescribed, no psychotherapy is given.

Panatayaya— alcoholism—One full chapter is devoted to panatayaya in Sushruta Samhita—Utt./47. The description is the same as in Charak. Here the approach to the disease is purely somatic. Psycho-therapy is not prescribed by Sushrut.

Psycho-therapy in Sushruta Samhita

In Sushruta Samhita 'manas chikitsa' means psychotherapy or the treatment of mental disorders through psychogenic methods like mantra, havan, prayashchit etc.

In this Sushrut is nearer to Atharva Veda than Charak. Sushrut has used Prayashchit and mantra etc. for somatic diseases like fever as also for pediatrics and surgical cases along with surgery— Utt./39/265-267 and Sut./5/19-35 and Utt./27-37.

Sut./1/11 Sushrut defines bhoot-vidya, "as diagnosing mental diseases and treating them through psychogenic practices of propitiatory rites, havan mantra etc. Again in Sut./l/46 he says that mental, exogenous and psychic disorders must be treated by speech, talks or words group of practices." It means non-medicinal therapies of psychogenic nature, in which speech talks and, words are used such as mantra, japa, re-education suggestion persuasion and analysis are found in bhoot-vidya. Thus it is very near to modern psycho-analysis.

In Sut./1/22 Sushrut has expressed the aim of Ayurveda as—(1) the cure of diseases in diseased and (2) the maintenance of health in the healthy. On this basis the given therapies are also of two kinds— (1) curative, (2) preventive. The aim of Sushruta Samhita psycho-therapy is also two-fold, namely, the cure of mental diseases in diseased and the preservation of health in the healthy. Utt./64 is chiefly for the health and hygiene and the other whole of Sushruta Samhita is for the cure of psychic as well as the somatic diseases.

Classification of Therapies for Psychic Disorders

These therapies 'are scattered in Sushruta Samhita mainly in Sut./1/12, 46; Sut./3/18-26; Sut./5/19-36; Sut./6/22; Sut./19/27; Sut./29/74 and Utt./27-37, 60-62'. These scattered therapies are being classified in Table 7.4.

As one can see, there is much similarity in the psycho therapies prescribed by Charak (Table 7.3) and Sushrut, so we will not go into the details of these, except where there is something new in Sushrut Samhita.

Psychogenic Therapies— These are the therapies in which psyche itself treats psyche and medicinal approach is avoided. This originated with Atharva Veda and came to Charak and Sushruta. Some of these are more elaborate in Sushrut than in Charak and for some, name of therapy and name of the ailment in which they can be used are given—say pooja or japa. It may be for two reasons, one, because these practices were so well-known to people that it was needless to elaborate them, second, the main interest of Sushruta was surgery, so psychogenic therapies did not come under his field. That is why they are only briefly given in Sushruta Samhita.

TABLE 7.4
CLASSIFICATION OF PSYCHO-THERAPIES IN SUSHRUTA SAMHITA

I Psychogenic therapies—

(1) Mantra Vidya—
- (l) Shabd or vani—suggestion
- (2) Shanti-path— auspicious readings
- (3) Shanti-karma—propitiatory rites
- (4) japa—repetition.

(2) Religious practices—
- (1) Pooja—worship
- (2) Upahar—offering
- (3) Prarthana—prayer
- (4) Havan—

(3) Updesh and Santwana—re-education and assurance

(4) Chittaprasadan—recreation

(5) Gaman—environmental change

(6) Prayashchit—Bali and dan—sacrifice
Tapa—penance

II Somatogenic therapies—

(1) Shalya—surgery—
- (1) Aghat—shocks—mental and physical
- (2) Shiravedh—venesection

(2) Aushadhi—medicines
- (1) Manibandhan—amulets and other applying medicines
- (2) Herbs and drugs—for external and oral use.

Mantra Vidya— This has already been dealt with in Atharva veda and Charak Samhita. Sushruta has included some new practices and prescribed siddha mantras even for the somatogenic diseases like fever, for child diseases for healing wounds and for use along with surgery. Sut./5/19-35, Utt./39/265-267 and Utt./ 27-37. One speciality of Sushruta is an elaborate use of mantra therapy for children's diseases. Utt./27-37 gives the use of mantras for child therapy. Detailed procedures are given separately for separate diseases. Charak has not dealt with psychic diseases of children.

As far as mantra vidya is concerned Sushruta is nearer to Atharva veda practices than Charak. Sushruta prescribes elaborate mantra therapy for unmad, graha diseases, apasmar, child diseases, certain types of fevers and wounds.

Sabd or Vani— suggestion.

Sut./1/46 lays down that mental diseases must be cured by sabd group of therapies. Here sabd means those therapies in which speech or language is used for curing purposes. Thus it includes suggestions, mantra japa, talking, analysis etc. This is a psychogenic approach taken from Atharva Veda—Sushruta has not added to it anything new.

Shanti-path— pacifying. This is for pacifying, soothing, quietening and consoling the patients. It is used on patients who are excited, uneasy and full of anxiety. In this some mantras or some passages from religious books are recited or read out. The patient may do the reciting himself or listen to recitings by the priest. Thus it can be antotherapy. It has no equivalent in modern psychotherapy although it is really useful in some cases like Durmana.

Shanti-karma— propitiatory rites—This is not new but its use is wider in Sushruta. In Sut./3/26 he uses Shanti-karma as synonym for therapy. It is given a definite therapeutic status. In shanti-karma some religious rites along with mantras are performed. There is a long progression of rituals—in which cooling and soothing things like khus baths, sherbats are used. Then prayers are recited. This is a mixture of mantra, shanti-path and rituals. Sushruta has dealt with these in detail-stating why when and how these are to be used. These rituals are more useful in graha diseases and so the procedures are given in details for separate grahas. The effect produced on the patient is a joint one of faith-healing, dramatization, recitation and herbal effects.

Japa— recitation—Japa may be done by the person himself or by some others reciting while he is listening—but sounds must reach the patient. Some mantras or only syllables are to be repeated for a large number of times. It is the same in Charak and Sushruta.

Religious practices—These includes pooja, uphar, prarthana and havan. These are the same in Charak and Sushruta. Sushrut has prescribed one or many religious practices for all the mental diseases.

Updesh and Santvana— Sushrut has dealt with these in Utt./62/37. Here 'updesh' means giving good teachings and suggestions, and 'santvana' means consoling or assuring. It is a sort of directive therapy in which the thought processes concepts and values of the patients are corrected. The equivalents of updesh and santvana in modern psycho-therapy are re-education and desensitization. It is meant to re-orient the patient towards life.

Chittaprasadan— recreation—Sushruta has used this as a therapy and discussed in Utt./62/38. It has been prescribed for all sorts of unmad or insanity. This is not found in Atharva Veda and Charak Samhita. This is new in Sushruta. The meaning of the word 'Chittprasadan' is 'making mind happy'—it may mean some recreation or entertainment in any form. It is meant to divert the attention of the patient from his present problems, to reduce his anxiety and sufferings. In some sort of recreation or entertainment he forgets his own problems, temporarily and finds some freedom for himself in this way conditioning is broken and he can proceed towards normalcy.

The equivalent of chittaprasadan in modern psychotherapy is recreation therapy. R.M. Drake and J.F. Brown, both have discussed the role of recreation and entertainment therapy. "Quite frequently individuals who have isolated or peculiar personalities, have not learnt how to get along in social affairs........it is possible to do a great deal with what has been called a recreational and entertainment therapy."

—Brown, J.F. Psychodynamics of Abnormal Behaviour, 1940

Gaman— environmental change—The mention of this is the same in Charak and Sushruta.

Prayashchita— repentence—In Sut./3/26 Sushruta calls prayashita a method of therapy. It is a definite therapeutic method in Atharvaveda and Charak also. Although Sushrut has not given its varieties but he has discussed bali and dan (sacrifice) and tapa (penance) and prescribes these for all sorts of psychic disorders. Sweekarokti or confession has not been mentioned in Sushruta.

Ashtauga Sangraha

Out of 'the big three' or Brihadtrayi of Ayurveda, the last to appear was Ashtaga Sangraha of Vagabhatt. While specialisation of Charak is in medicine, of Sushruta in surgery, so the special field of Vagabhatt is general principles of medicine. It was composed during the time of Gupta empire. Vagabhatt was the son of Singh Gupta and was born in Sindhu Pradesh. His time is given as 6th century AD and by Atri Dev Guptà as 5th century A.D. Vagabhatt had written two books *Ashtanga Hridaya* and *Ashtanga Samhita*. Both are available Ashtanga Hridaya is just the abridged form of Ashtanga Sangraha. For our purpose Ashtauga Sangraha is followed here.

Vagabhatta was devoted to Ayurveda and read a lot about it. He believed Ayurveda to be an upveda of Atharva Veda. He compiled the teachings of Atharva Veda, Charak and Sushruta and all other material about Ayurveda available at that time. In Sut./1/15-20, 22 Vagabhatt describes the purpose of writing the Ashtanga Sangraha—in short as—(1) Combining the important learning of all different specialized writers, because reading them separately takes up a very long time. (2) The basic books are difficult to understand—so to make them easy. (3) Make one volume of all learning at one place. (4) No unnecessary repetitions—concise and clear matter. Vagabhatt has given few original thoughts. His job had been to select and rewrite the matter in easy and meaningful words. Thus it is a sort of summary of all the writers on Ayurveda uptill that time. Vagabhatt was a Buddhist, so some of the vidyas of Buddhists have entered his treatise. His being Buddhist also explains the fact that he was not very popular in North India—where Brahmanism prevailed and Charak-Sushrut duo reigned supreme. He became popular in South India.

Ashtanga Sangraha—as is evident by its name—contains all the eight angs or branches of Ayurveda, although some names are changed. These eight branches are—(1) kaya chikitsa (medicine), (2) bal-chikitsa (pediatrics), (3) graha chikitsa (psychiatry), (4) urdang chikitsa (therapy of the upper part of body), (5) shalya chikitsa (surgery), (6) danshtra chikitsa (toxicology), (7) jara chikitsa (therapy of early decay), (8) Vrash chikitsa (rasayan).

Special Points in Vagabhatt

- — Names of some anga-s have been changed such as Danshtra and Jara.
- — Some branches are not mentioned such as eye, ear, nose, throat.
- — In graha diseases he has increased the number of grahas from 8 to 18.
- — All mental diseases like unmad and apasmar have been taken under the name 'graha' diseases.
- — New therapies have been added—
- — Vagabhatt being a Buddhist has added Aprajita vidya.
- — Added Tantrik mantras for therapy which is not found in Atharva Veda, Charak or Sushruta.
- — Samadhi for the first time added as a therapeutic technique.

The most important feature is the inclusion of procedures in all details for example how, when and why to use the different mantras and rituals.

Ashtanga Sangraha thus combines the prevailing two trends of that time viz., Brahminic trend of Atharva Veda and Buddhist trends, as also all the trends of Ayurveda prevalent at that time, i.e., Gupta period.

Approach of Vagabhatt to Psychic Disorders

It should be made clear at the outset that Vagabhatt has followed traditional path of Ayurveda—that is Atharva Veda, Charak and Sushruta. Hence there are many similarities in Vagabhatt with these traditional treatises of Ayurveda.

Similarities

- Bhoot-vidya is mentioned as one of the eight branches or anga-s of Ayurveda Sut./6/42-44 and Utt./7.
- Bhoot-vidya is said to be related to grah diseases.
- All agree that the grah diseases are the names of different syndromes of psychic diseases or symptom formations.
- Agrees that the super beings never enter the human body and the syndromes have been named after them because of the similarity of behaviour.

- In line with Atharva Veda, Charak Sushruta, to Vagabhatt also 'bhoot-vidya' is the science of psychic diseases and their cure.
- Agrees on the basic principle of Tridosha—tridiscordance—on both physical and psychic levels.
- Agrees that disease may begin in soma or psyche—but later on it affects the other side also and the whole organism will get disordered.
- Gives swasthya vrat, i.e., the daily routine for a healthy life in Sut./4.

Dissimilarities

- Has given psychogenic diseases of children and called them 'graha'.
- These diseases are called 'bhoot-graha' among the adults.
- Unmad and apasmar have been discussed as separate psychogenic diseases—Charak had mixed up the two and called them 'grahonmad'. Vagabhatt follows Sushruta in this matter only he adds bhoot-grah to diseases of adults.
- Vagabhatt describes 18 bhoot grahs, and for children 12 grahas in Utt./3/7.
- Vagabhatt has not mentioned personality types, whereas all others have given these types.

Classification of Diseases— In Ashanga Sangraha, the diseases are broadly classified into Somatic and psychic—Sut./1/44—as curable and incurable—Sut./2/26, as hij—(endogenous) and agautuj exogenous—Sut./1/43. One chapter Sut./22 is devoted to this type of classification. Here he states that diseases are of 7 kinds according to their causes such as heredity, pregnancy, defects, physical shock, weather, divine curse and natural urges etc.

Vagabhatt has included all mental disorders into Agautuj—Sut./6/41. These are the same as given in Charak and Sushruta. All mental diseases are put in two kinds—severe and mild ailments.

Etiology

— has been taken from Charak and does not go beyond him.

— the cause for all psychic disease is increase or decrease in rajas and tamas Sut./1/43, 44.

— the cause of all somatic diseases is discordance of the three humours Utt./9/2.
— Sut./6/41 describes the causes as nij, agantuj and psychic.
— Sut./22/24 describes the causes as nij, agautuj and psychic.
— Utt./8/32 gives Shrap—curse which may cause psychic disorders.
— Utt./9/12 sex and anxiety are also given as psychic causes.

These are the immediate causes.

TABLE 7.5
CLASSIFICATION OF MENTAL ABNORMALITIES IN VAGBHATT

Severe Abnormalities	*Mild Abnormalities*
(1) Bhoot-grahas— neuroses and compulsions 14—named	(1) Srap— compulsive evil and bad curse 4 grahas— rishi grah guru grah vriddh grah siddha grah
(2) Unmad— psychoses-insanity (i) Nij— vatay pittaj kaphaj and tridoshaj (ii) Agantuj— psychic due to rajas and tamas (iii) Vishjanya—toxic	
(3) Apasmar— epilepsy (i) Nij—vataj, pittaj, kaphaj, tridoshaj (ii) Agantuj—psychic	
(4) Murchha— fainting fits	
(5) Sanyas—coma	
(6) Madatyaya— alcoholism	

The general and basic causes are given in Sut./22/11-13. Same as in Charak and Sushruta—as three—

(1) Asatamindriyarthsanyog—wrong sort of contact of senses with their objects.
(2) Pragyapradh—volitional transgression or sins of intelligence.
(3) Pariram—effects of past deeds.

As far as diagnosis is concerned Vagabhatt does not come at per with Charak. Diagnosis and symptoms are discussed. By Vagabhatt—here only additions are given.

Bhoot-grahas— neuroses and compulsions—Neuroses or Bhoot grahas are taken up separately by Vagabhatt like Sushruta. Ch. Utt./7, 8 deal with bhoot-grahas—but while Charak and Sushruta give only eight grahas Vagabhatt has given six more in severe category and four in mild category thus making eighteen bhoot-grahas in all. He also emphasises that grahas are not actual beings—but the names of symptoms after whom the behaviour is named Utt./7/4. And in Utt./7/6 Vagabhatt says that pragyapradh or wrong behaviour give rise to abnormality, by spoiling the equilibrium of rajas and tamas. Symptoms and diagnosis of each graha are given. Vagabhatt prescribes japa, tapa, bali, dan, havan, mantra and prayashchit along with medicines for these diseases.

Unmad— insanity or psychoses—Utt./9 in Ashtang Sangraha gives description and therapy of unmad—It is similar to Sushruta. The causes given are—(1) discordance of three body humours, (2) Abnormality of rajas and tamas, (3) toxins. The psychogenic kinds of unmad are the same as given in Sushrut.

(1) Aghatonmad—born out of some trauma.
(2) Shokajonmad—from anxiety and depression.
(3) Kamonmad—from frustration of sex urges.

Vagabhatt has not given bhayonmad. He prescribes medicines, shocks, re-education, mantra, japa, tapa and prayaschita. For these—

Apasmar— is dealt in Utt./10. It is exactly the same as in Sushruta.

Murchha— found in Nid./6/32-38 and Utt./9/58-60. There is nothing more than Charak and Sushrut here.

Sanyas— coma—is given in Nid./6/39-41 and Utt./9/62-63. Here also nothing new is suggested only one thing recreational therapy to the patient after the fainting fit is over.

Madatyaya— given in Nid./6/1-31 nothing new is added dealt with somatogenically like Charak and Sushruta.

Mild Abnormalities

Shrap— is given with bhoot-grahas in Utt./8/32. It is a curse, not a disease. Neither Charak nor Sushruta have mentioned it—but Atharva veda has given it. Vagabhatt prescribes psychotherapies for shrap.

Psychotherapy in Ashtaug Sangraha— Here we will try to take up only Vagabhatt's contribution to psychotherapy, and will try not to repeat what has already been given earlier in Charak and Sushruta.

Meaning of Psychotherapy

Prayashitta is included in therapies. Vagabhatta gives 2 kinds of therapies—

(1) Dravya—materials—medicines.
(2) Adravya—non-material—like *upvas*, japa, mantra, prayashchitta etc.

Sut./12/5 describes 3 kinds of therapies like Charak—

- Daivyavipasrya— divine
- Yukti vipasrya— medicinal
- Sattva vajeya—mental control—dominance of sattva guna.

To Vagabhatta— Sut./1/49— the best therapies to cure mental disorders are—correction of intellect, patience and knowledge of one's own self.

In Sut./6/42-44—sloping immoral behaviour, quietening of sense organs, correct knowledge of time, place, memory, one's own self and Atharvedic practices of worshipping gods are prescribed.

In Vagabhatt mantra—vidya is given more importance Charak and Sushruta take it from Atharva veda and do not go any further. But Vagabhatta, being a Buddhist, adds the use of Aparajita vidya of Buddhists and prescribes it both for psychic and somatic disorders. Use of any non-materials or psychogenic method is psycho-therapy for Vagabhatt.

Object of psycho therapy is given in Chik./24/39 as lessening any sort of pain or suffering physical or mental. Charak and Sushrut have described it in a better way.

Classification of Psycho-therapeutic Practices— There are several practices and many ways of classifying them. Some of these are—

Dravya— material and adravya—non-material.

Daivyavpasarya Yukti Vipasarya and Sattvavajaya. Of these adravya, daivya ivpasary and sattvavajaya are psychotherapies and they will be discussed here along with their sub-classes.

Classification of Therapies

Somatogenic

1. Shalya-surgery
   - (i) Aghat—mental and physical shock
   - (ii) Shiravedh-venesection.
2. Aushadhi-medicine
   - (i) Manibandhan—amulete etc. for external use
   - (ii) Herbs drugs for oral use

Psycho-genic— Daivya vipasary and Sattvavajaya.

1. Mantra-vidya
   - (i) Tantrik mantras—Aparajita vidya
   - (ii) Japa—recitation repeatedly.
   - (iii) Mangal-karm auspicious rites.
   - (iv) Rituals—bath, drama and demonstration.
2. Religious rites—Pooja, uphar (offering) havan.
3. Santvana—ashwasan and gyan—consoling reassuring persuading and insight.
4. Chittaprasadan—recreation.
5. Virodhi-bhavana— opposite tendencies.
6. Gaman— going away, environmental change.
7. Samadhi—concentration, meditation.
8. Prayashchitta
   - (i) bali and dan—sacrifice.
   - (ii) Tapa and upvas—penance.

We will discuss only psychogenic therapies.

Mantra Vidya

In Vagabhatt mantra-vidya is taken from Atharva Veda and is the same as in Charak and Sushruta. But Vagabhatta combined the Atharvanic mantra vidya with Buddhist and other vidyas of that time and prescribed them as psycho-therapies. Second point to be noted in Vagabhatt is that, he gives in full details, all the procedures for use of mantras, as to when, where, how and which mantra is to be used for the purpose.

Tantrik Mantras

At the time of Vagabhatt two trends were prevalent—one Brahminic and the other non-Brahminic. The Brahminic trend was represented by Atharva veda, Charak and Sushruta. The Brahminic mantras were said to derive their energy from Brahma—God himself. The non-Brahmins did not believe in Brahma or Supreme god. The Buddhists and the Tantriks believed in cosmic psycho-physical energy. They were energy worshippers—Shakti-poojak and their mantras derived their energy from Cosmic psycho-physical elements.

We can compare tantrik mantras with other mantras here. The Tantrik mantra's are short and mechanical often composed of monosyllables or sounds. These are technical and very difficult to understand. These can be used only by those practitioners who have made them. Siddha by severe penances. The Brahmanic or Atharvanic mantras on the other hand, are often full Sanskrit stanzas or Sutras. These are lyrical and meaningful and can be easily understood by anyone who knows Sanskrit. Although they require being made Siddha—still they can be used by ordinary Brahman priests.

The Aparajita vidya of the Buddhists has Tantric mantras which are made siddha by given procedure and then used for purposes of therapy.

Modern psycho-therapy does not have any equivalent of Mantra vidya.

Japa— recitation and repetition.

Japa therapy is given in Utt./8/2 and Utt./1036. Like Charak, Vagabhatt also prescribes Japa therapy for grah diseases, epilepsy etc.

Mangal-karma— given in Sutt./12/5. Nothing new.

Rituals— bath, drama demonstration.

One full chapter Utt./5 is given to it. This has been taken by Vagabhatt straight from Atharva veda, as Charak and Sushrat do not mention this. Rituals are often accompanied by Mantras, sometimes medicines are also used as in bath water. In this way it is directive psycho-somatic therapy. The bath is accompanied with rituals drama etc. It is recommended for grah diseases of the children, because they are more sensitive and receptive to drama and demonstration. Vagabhatt has given full details of bath the herbs and oils used—the temprature of water, place and time of bath, duration etc. Some Ayurvedic clinics in South use these methods even today.

Religious Practices— Only two religious practices uphar and havan are given in Sut./12/6, Utt./10/36, Utt./8/2. There is nothing new here.

Santvana, Ashvasan, Gyan— Vagabhatt in Utt./9/35 and Utt/8/2 has prescribed consoling assuring and giving insight. These are to be used in cases of insanity—unmad—caused by anxiety—as loss of loved one or loss of material wealth etc. These are more directive therapies. These are here as given in Charak and Sushruta. The equivalent for these therapies can be found in modern psychotherapy in the techniques of re-direction and desensitization.

Chittaprasanna— recreation.

Vagabhatt prescribes these as subsidiary therapies to be used after fit in apasmar and sanyas Utt./10/40 and Chik./9/62. Sushrut used the word chittaprasadan. This is not found in Atharva veda or Charak. Sushrut and after him Vagabhatt has used it. It is recreation therapy in modern terms.

Gaman— going away—environmental change.

Vagabhatt gives it in Sut./15/5. This has been found in Charak and Sushruta and nothing new is added by Vagabhatt.

Virodhi Bhavna— opposite passion—In Ashtanga Sangraha Utt./9/36 it is prescribed for unmad caused by over-functioning of some passions such as kama (erotic) krodh (rage).

Charak first used virodhi bhavana as a therapeutic technique Vagabhatt took it up and made it more clear and specific. He clearly mentions the passions which are to be encouraged in place of the undesirable ones. The opposite passion acts as an antidote to eliminate or minimize the effects of passions like envy grief etc. The detail of this have already been given.

Samadhi— concentration, meditation—It is not found in Ayurvedic literature from Atharva veda to Charak and Sushruta. The original source of Samadhi is Yoga Sutra of Patanjali. In Ayurveda it is introduced by Vagabhatt in Utt./8/2. It has been prescribed for grah diseases.

Samadhi is a sort of mental exercise using meditation and concentration. It is non-directive auto-therapy that is, the patient uses it on himself—after some guidance of guru. It is meant for over-excitation, nervous tension anxiety and restlessness. After

Samadhi the patient feels relaxed fresh and energetic. But children and totally insane cannot take advantage of it.

It is a purely Indian contribution to the world of psychotherapy. It is cathartic hygienic, economic and of high scientific value. Vagabhatt has just mentioned it. In fact this is a technique of Yoga.

Prayashchitta— is given in Sut./12/5, Utt./8/2, Utt./10/36 and Utt./9/38. It is like Atharva Veda Charak and Sushruta. Only one difference is that Vagabhatt describes the procedures of the devices in full and rich details. He adds practical and procedural notes to all these devices of prayashchitta.

Eight

Yoga

Yoga! well the name rings a bell not only to Indian but foreign ears as well. The word 'Yoga' has become a household name irrespective of nation, caste and creed. It has found medical recognition also and is being practised as a reliable technique for relaxation.

Is Yoga just a technique then ?

No! It is a philosophy a metaphysics and a way of life too. But here we have to confine ourselves to Yoga and its therapeutic practices not going into the philosophical nuances of the term.

What is Yoga?

The dictionaries give more than 80 meanings of the word Yoga, some are general and some specific. The general meaning of Yoga comes from the Sanskrit root "Yuj", which means 'to join' or 'to yoke'. So Yoga is a means of joining one thing to another or yoking two things together.

Felix Guyot says, "The word Yoga means : Union. Its equivalent in English is the word 'Yoke', from the Latin 'Jugunu'".

—Felix Guyot, "Yoga : The Science of Health"

Swami Pavitranand says, "Yoga literally means 'connection' or 'union'. Technically the word Yoga has been used to refer to the system of philosophy propounded by the sage Patanjali."

—Pavitranand, "Common Sense about Yoga"

Shri Yogendra describes Yoga as—"that which makes it possible to achieve anything is Yoga."

Thus Yoga is "the science that teaches the method of achieving unity of the individual soul with the Supreme Soul." The traditional doctrine of Yoga has the object to unite. In this broad and general sense, it can take innumerable meanings.

In its second and more specific sense Yoga is a system of Indian philosophy as propounded in the Yoga Sutra of Maharishi Patanjali.

Yoga is a complete system of self-culture, realisation, conscious unfoldment of inner energies. It is equally applicable to people of all castes, creeds, nationalities, religions, sexes, ages and times. It is a technique for enlightening the mind and upliftment of total personality.

The Origin of Yoga

To most scholars, like Kapali Shastri "Yoga is as old as the Vedas." The Indian philosophy has been divided roughly into three periods—

(1) The Vedic Period—About 1500-600 BC which was the origin of the four vedas, Upanishads, as also of Yoga.
(2) The Epic period—about 600 BC to 200 AD
(3) The flourishing period—from 200 AD anwards.

The origin of Yoga can be traced to the first attempt of Aryans towards civilization. Some elementary yogic practices existed even in the times of Vedas. Then the yogic teachings were handed down, through thousands of years, by word of mouth, from rishi to his shishyas. The mention of Yoga is found in Upanishads also, such as Kath, Mandukya, Jaittriya upanishads. This Vedic and upanishadic form of Yoga is known as Puratan (or old) Yoga. It contains the essence of Yoga and is in the form of small sutras.

The formalised form of Yoga, as it is found today was propounded by Patanjali some three hundred years B.C. Patanjali, a great sage and called 'the father of Yoga', collected and compiled old writings and oral teachings into a treatise named 'Yoga Sutra'. It is known as 'sutra' because it consists of small axiomatic condensed statements, which give a written and co-ordinated account of the whole Yoga philosophy.

Patanjali presented Yoga as an independent school of metaphysics and a science of psychic development. Yoga as it is known and taught today is based on 'Yoga Sutra' of Patanjali. It is also a fact that the teachings have remained basically unchanged and as they were originally in Vedas and Upanishads, even though thousands of years have passed, many generations of thinkers and philosophers have come and gone, and man in general has developed considerably. Yoga remains the same. It goes to show that the teachings of Yoga are timeless and are as valuable and effective today as they were thousands of years ago. It shows a way to man to find true happiness and inner peace and joy which comes with true knowledge.

It is in the 20th century that the true worth of Yoga has been realised by Westerners also. Various Western writers and thinkers like Max Muller, Hans Jacobs, Behanan, Flagg, Moore, Havall, Geraldine Coster as also Indian scholars like Kapali Shastri, Swami Akhilanand, Shri Aurobindo, Swami Shivananda, Swami Ajaya have compared Yoga to Western systems of psychology and mental health. It is found that it far excelled in effectivity than other methods of modern psychotherapy. It has been accepted as a very useful technique for relaxation for modern maladies of hypertension and anxiety.

Let us clear some misconceptions about Yoga, first—

- Yoga is not other-worldliness. It is inwardness—in that it seeks to turn the search light of consciousness on one's own inner most self. It does not recommend going away.
- It is not running away from home—from duties, eschewing human relations. It is cultivation of all embracing love, living in world.
- Yoga is disciplined and ceaseless performance of one's duty. योगः कर्मसुकौशलम्
- Yoga is not a pessimistic approach to life. It is a most intense hopeful positive optimistic approach to life.
- Yoga is not a religion. It has basic human fundamental teachings and it welcomes people of all races, religions and creeds without any bias whatsoever. Theists, a-theists, agnostics can all use Yoga equally effectively, to find peace and joy.
- Yoga is not a cult of asceticism, of self-denial and negation, of self-mortification. It is a path full of life, full of joy. A true Yogi enjoys the fruits of earth and of spirit. We have examples of such Yogis in Shri Krishna and Rajarishi Janak.

What then, is Exact Nature of Yoga?

Yoga is a specific philosophy—one of the six basic Indian systems.

It is an endeavour to join individual soul to the Universal Soul or union of personal spirit to Supreme Being. Yoga teaches that such union can be achieved by rigorous training and observances. This union is possible while the spirit is still in the body or in this life itself.

Any person can achieve a state of spiritual advancement, if he leads the right kind of life and studies and practices assiduously the ways and means by which such spiritual advancement can be possible.

Ernest Wood, Professor of American Academy of Asian Studies, says, "Yoga is a system of spiritual and physical culture, practised from ancient times in India. Its exponents combine religion, philosophy psychology and physical culture into one complete science and art."

"Yoga has been applied not only to the central aim of attaining heightened consciousness, but also to the development of every human faculty—physical, emotional and ethical, which may conduce to that end."

"Yoga is a method by which to obtain control of one's latent powers. It offers the complete means to self-realization."

—Dennis Dunne, Principal, London School of Yoga

"Yoga is a way of life which can be practised by any human being regardless of age, sex, state of health, religion or nationality. It is based on general physical or spiritual laws which operate on all mankind alike."

—James McCartney

The ideal of Yoga can be summarised as, 'having a fit and healthy body, strong in all its parts, under the control of an informed and cultured mind and a masterful will, animated by the highest ideals.'

Yoga is the subject of such breadth and depth that it covers every possible phase of human existence. The fact that it has existed unchanged for thousands of years speaks clearly of its veracity and usefulness to mankind.

It must be emphasized that it is not sufficient merely to study Yoga—for this will be an intellectual pursuit only. This type of academic knowledge would not be of any practical benefit. One has to bring Yoga to life to really profit by it—it must be taken to heart in every sense of the word, and lived as an essential part of one's daily life.

The author of Yoga Sutra Patanjali has stated in clear terms that the main aim of this philosophy is "attainment of Moksha" as such, there is no place for emotions in it. Patanjali gave chittavrittis. Then he gave 9 vikshepas interceptors in samadhi, as 1. vyadhi (illness), 2. akarmanyta (or lethargy of the mind), 3. sanshay (doubt), 4. pramad (forgetfulness), 5. alasya (laziness), 6. avirrati (non attachment), 7. bhranti darshan (wrong perception), 8. not gaining ground for samadhi and 9. unsteadiness of mind. Patanjali called these nine vikshepas as chitt-mal or dirtiness or waste product of mind, because they are hinderances in the way of yoga. There are our chitta-kleshas-sorrows of the mind, avidya (ignorance), asmita (ego), rag (attachment), dwesh (jealousy) and aninivesh (non-approachable) they also create hinderances in Samadhi. According to Patanjali, "Mana or Chitta (psyche or mind) is a sort of battle field in which different forces try to exert their control over the functions of psyche. Yogi has to avoid these and go ahead. He has to give a proper direction to his psychic functions."

What Yoga can do for You?

- Encourage positive thinking and faith.
- Remove negative attitudes like avidya (ignorance) asmita (ego) raga-dwesh (attachment and jealousy).
- Effective assessment of inner consciousness—antahpragya—which is consciousness of the inner world.
- Proper channelisation of inherent energies.
- Relieving tensions and pressures of every day life.
- Physical and spiritual rejuvenation.
- Control over mind by choosing your response to environmental stimuls.
- Managing stress through a greater awareness of the self.

Schools or Branches of Yoga

Yoga is a way of attaining self realization. It is intended for every type of man, woman and child, ever likely to exist. And no two people in the world are alike in their physical and mental make up, so to cater to the huge variety of mankind several different schools of Yoga have developed. It is to be remembered that all these branches have a common aim which is self-realization.

TABLE 8.1
BRANCHES OF YOGAS

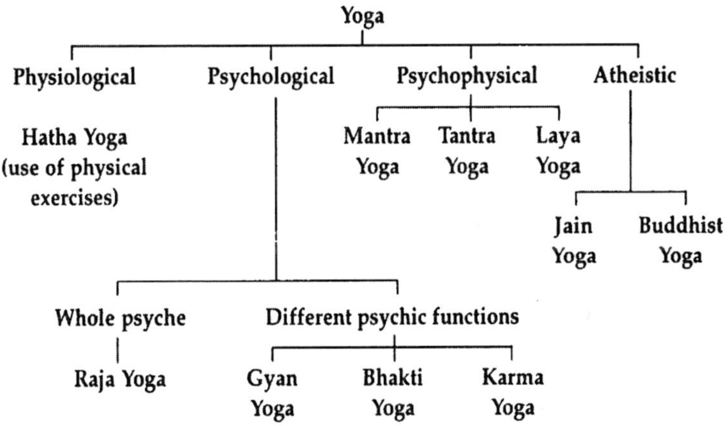

TABLE 8.2
BRANCHES OR SCHOOLS OF YOGA GIVEN BY EVANS WENTZ

School or Branch	*Gives Mastery Over*	*Leading to control of*
Hatha Yoga	Breath	Physical body and vitality
Dhyana Yoga	Thought	Power of thought process
Bhakti Yoga	Love	Power of devotion
Shakti Yoga	Energy	Power over energizing forces of nature
Laya Yoga	Will rhythm	Power of the mind
Mantra Yoga	Sound	Power of sound vibrations
Tantra Yoga	Form	Power of geometric form
Raja Yoga	Method	Power of discrimination-vivek
(i) Gyan Yoga	Knowledge	Power of intellect
(ii) Karma Yoga	Activity	Power of action
(iii) Kundalini Yoga	Kundalini	Power of Psychic and nerve force
(iv) Samadhi Yoga	Self	Power of ecstasy

Branches of Yoga

Hatha Yoga Physiological— It is said that originally Hatha Yoga with its techniques were taught by Lord Shiva to his consort Parvati. Later on Gorakshanath (popularly known as Gorakh) practised and perfected it. Its basic principles are contained in Gheranda Samhita. It is actually the outward form of Tantrik vidya, which became more popular in Buddhist period.

This is basically physiological approach the emphasis being on physical body—its purification and exercises. The word Hatha (ह+ठ) Ha—the sun principle, the pingla nadi—pran vayu of right nostril, tha—the moon principle—the ida nadi-pran vayu of left nostril.

"It recognises the concept of the wholeness of man and proposes to achieve psychosomatic sublimation through a system of physical culture which, inter alia includes physical education, hygiene, therapy and biogenic control of the autonomic nervous system, effecting the hygiene of the mind and moral behaviour."

— *Yogendra*

"Hatha Yoga selects the body and the vital functionings as its instruments of perfection and realisation; its concern is with the gross body."

—*Shri Aurobindo On Yoga*

There are seven stages of Hatha Yoga which include— (1) the purification of the body, then (2) asanas and (3) mudras, bodily posturers (4) pratyahar (5) pranayam (breathing exercises) (6) dhyan—concentration (7) samadhi. The Yogi tries to arouse Kundalini—the coiled serpent, the source of vital energy.

There are supposed to be 84 lakh asanas—out of which only 84 have been found and only about 25-30 are in practice.

Thus Hatha Yoga has a somatic approach and reaches to the autonomic nervous system.

Psychological Approach

Raja Yoga— This is the branch propounded by Patanjali in Yoga Sutra. Raja Yoga literally means "the royal path to Union (with God)."

This is the most scientific and practical of the other branches. It starts from the subconscious depths of mind and tries to reach its super conscious heights. It tries to reach the spirit. At the very outset Patanjali declares —

"Yogah chittavrittinirodh" that is Yoga is a means of controlling the conscious and unconscious psychic functions, to make Chitta-psyche free from bondage of its own vrittis. The five vrittis given are —

Pramana— perceptual stimulation, getting attached to perceptual experience.

Viparyaya— illusion, that is, getting false knowledge from the senses.

Vikalpa— effective imagination, getting attached to something which is not present there.

Nidra— sleep—which is tamas. Sleep and dreams stimulate chitta.

Smriti— memory—all memory traces of long past which may come to disturb Chitta.

The Ashtanga or Eight Limbs of Yoga

Actually these are the eight stages of Yoga practice. The students start from the first stage.

1. Yama—don'ts—negative ethical code of conduct or abstentions.
2. Niyama — do-s positive ethical code of conduct or observances.
3. Asanas—postures and exercises.
4. Pranayama—control of breathing by exercise.
5. Pratyahara—withdrawal of senses from their respective objects.
6. Dharana—concentration.
7. Dhyana—meditation and contemplation.
8. Samadhi—spiritual or higher stage of consciousness.

The five Yamas are—non-injury, truthfulness, non-covetousness, continence and non-receiving of gifts. The five niyamas are—cleanliness, contentment, austerity, study of scriptures and surrender of self to the god.

Patanjali's Yoga— Sutra is divided into four sections. The first section gives the meaning of Yoga and Samadhi. The second section, gives the positive and negative preliminary qualifications for a Shishya or a student of Yoga. The third section describes the stages and powers of samadhi, and the fourth section states the aim of all yogic philosophy which is Kaivalya.

Gyan Yoga— Yoga of intellect or cognitive functions.

Bhakti Yoga— Yoga of emotions of love and devotion affective.

Karma Yoga— Yoga of willing and doing conative motor functions.

These three are psychic approaches, but whereas Raja Yoga deals with whole psyche—these deal with different functions of the psyche. These are also suitable for three different types of personalities—intellectual, emotional and doer or volitional.

Gyan Yoga is the lofty types only intellectuals can follow this path. We have Vedanta Philosophy of Shankaracharya as an example of Gyan Yoga. This is a path of knowledge which leads to vivek and pragya. Union with god is attained by methods of intelligence.

Bhakti Yoga is based on emotions. In this intense love and devotion of god leads one to the attainment of union with God. Chaitanya Mahaprabhu and Meera Bai are examples of this Yoga.

Karma Yoga is the path of action and will, it means doing one's assigned duty in the world, without any egoistic aims. All work is dedicated to the Supreme being without any wish for a reward. This is what Lord Krishna advocates in Geeta.

All the three have the same purpose—Union with the Supreme being.

Mantra, Tantra and Laya Yoga

All the three represent the psychophysical approach. The machinary of the body is an reservoir of energy which is utilized in these three. Here the psychophysical approach is like that of Atharva veda.

Mantra vidya is repeating certain words or mantras—which combine sound vibrations and meanings.

Tantra Yoga is more mechanical and technical. It is related to cosmic energy. The individual energy seeks to be united with cosmic energy by using mantras also.

Laya Yoga is seeking Supreme union with the help of laya or rhythm. One can listen to one's own sound 'nada' and then the union with the ultimate can be attained.

"........Laya Yoga consists in fixing the attention on some interval object and becoming absorbed in it, to the extent of forgetting oneself completely. The best way to begin with is absoption in the sound (Nada) which is heard on closing the ears."

—*M.N. Dwived.*

The Atheist Approach

Yoga started traditionally in the Vedic-Brahminic culture but with time it became very popular and influenced the people outside the Brahminic fold. At that time about 300 BC two powerful trends were present in the society. They were Jainism and Buddhism. Buddhism and Yoga, in fact have a common origin and common aim. Buddhism adopted many teachings and techniques of Yoga. Even the objectives of both are the same. 'Nirvana' for Buddhists and 'Kaivalya' for Yoga. This particular branch of Yoga is known as Buddhist Yoga. It advocates self-control, meditation and samadhi to attain Nirvana. Buddhism does not believe in a god as such.

Another branch of Yoga is called Jain Yoga. It developed along with main Yoga and Buddhist Yoga. They also have Yoga practices, but in their own way. The stages in Jain Yoga are Gyan (knowledge), shraddha (faith), charitra (character) which all lead to the ultimate goal which is Moksha.

Of all these branches of Yoga, Raja Yoga became the most popular. It has been used variously not only to attain Moksha or Samadhi but for more worldly objectives, such as gaining health, hygiene, happiness etc. and for removal of ailments. The uses of Yoga for practical everyday life are innumerable. Even today Yoga is being used for relieving the tensions of modern day living.

Nine

Yoga and Psychotherapy

Yoga is the highest product of Indian Psychology. Its central theme is psyche (mana) and consciousness. It endevours to strengthen the psyche and to elevate consciousness to the uppermost levels. To normals it helps in leading a long happy and healthy life and to the abnormals, it offers relief from suffering and gives solace. In the field of psycho-therapy also it touches all sorts of behaviour from mild to very abnormal or psychotic behaviour. Raja Yoga of Maharishi Patanjali specially deals with mind and its functions.

The Concept of Normality and Abnormality in Yoga

The yogic concept of normality of persons is taken down straight from the Atharva veda, but it has been much modified and advanced.

According to Yoga human personality is composed of Purusha and Prakriti, roughly translated it means man and the nature. We will be coming to the finer nuances of the terms later. Purusha is pure, but may get corrupted. Prakriti has three gunas—sattva, rajas and tamas. Purusha becomes impure when it comes in contact with rajas and tamas. Abnormal behaviour starts when Purusha, the ego, comes in contact with rajas and tamas. Yoga thus takes a very wide view of abnormality. Abnormal behaviour starts from the birth, because as soon as the Purusha takes human form—becomes a body, it has to come in contact with rajas and tamas gunas.

Patanjali says all behaviour is abnormal when Purusha comes in contact with rajas and tamas.

Normal and abnormal is degrees of deviation of these gunas. Their disequilibrium gives rise to psychic disorders or abnormality.

Purusha = Ego in modern psychological terms.

Vritti = mental trends or channels of mental functions.

The gunas give rise to vritti-s which vitiate chitta (psyche). So in the very first sutra of Yoga Sutras, Patanjali says "Yogaschittavrittinirodhah". Yoga is control of these vrittis—because they lead the mind to abnormal channels.

Yoga does not offer any clear cut causation or classification of mental abnormality as Atharva veda and Ayurveda do.

The techniques offered by Yoga can be broadly classified into—

- Health and hygiene programme—both cure and prevention.
- Attainment of higher or supernatural powers of mind.
- Teaches Samadhi—the state of pure being or bliss.

In the first the approach is mainly somatic, but in the second it is psychological and third is spiritual. Thus, Yoga has a holistic approach encompassing body, mind and soul.

Causes of Abnormality— as said above—rajas and tamas gunas of Prakriti unite with Purusha—which cause the vrittis to arise and vrittis constitute abnormal behaviour. Sattva guna is pure and can never cause abnormality, rajas and tamas can and do.

Diagnosis of Mental Disorders— Yoga has developed very clear and scientific tests—like clinical tests for different mental disorders. Felix Guyot in *Yoga—The Science of Health*, gives a number of such diagnostic tests. The tests are for morbid fears, for nervous debility, for different complexes etc.

"Hatha Yoga psycho-analysis unearths these complexes by means of very simple and traditional methods, such as, short tales and stories of immemorial origin, that Indian doctors have handed down from generation to generation."

—*Felix Guyot*

These tests are technical and scientific.

Symptoms

Clear cut symptoms of diseases are not found in Yoga. In the name of symptoms vrittis are given, which are neither diseases nor symptoms, but the remote causes or promotors.

As said earlier Yoga treats a person as a human composite.

TABLE 9.1
THE HUMAN COMOOSIL

Atman	*Brahman*	*Purush*
Buddhi—intelligence Manas—mind Indriya—senses	Sharir	Prakriti

In this composite the Indriyas—senses are lowest on the ladder, then man goes upwards to manas and buddhi. All these three make up the Sharir (soma or body) while Atman is upper most, it is the spirit or the essence.

On the psychological level it is manas—buddhi which combine and control behaviour levels—it is the Atman or the soul—which directs the whole affair. Yoga begins by taming the Sharir with asanas and exercises, and then leads the mind towards an inner vision. A man can get the full radiance of Atman if he can manage to free himself from the bondage of desire or Sharir.

Yoga is cessation of all mental activity *UeesieMUeefoeoeje=efoe efvejesOe*. Once Sharir is tamed then all the controls move upwards until the ego gains strength to achieve higher aims.

Yogic Psychotherapy

All Yoga therapy is psychotherapy as its objective is "chittavrittinirodh". It seeks to cure the psyche by controlling its own vrittis, which may lead it astray—as said in Geeta *JeeUegvee&JeefceJeecceefme* (2/67). Vrittis take away the psyche like a strong wind takes a boat in water. This is a hinderance in the way to Samadhi. So, the different kinds or branches of Yoga differ in their objectives as also in the means adopted to achieve these objectives. Individuals may take up the paths according to their own personality type or preference. So Yoga, as a whole, as a pure science, is for control of lower vrittis of mind and then seek higher aim of Samadhi. But in its applied aspect it suggests various paths. The essence of all the paths is the same, which is—

- Control of vrittis.
- Striving to attain the ultimate goal of 'Union' with Supreme.
- Balancing of rajas and tamas gunas—because these gunas create all behavioural devitations.

- Establishing the required psychic equilibrium in gunas—

This equilibrium may differ according to a person, his status, his position, his duty. The killing vritti may be tamas and not desirable, but in Geeta, Lord Krishna asks Arjuna to adopt this, because it is his duty—his dharma, at the time.

- Yoga seeks to analyse and sublimate the inner complexes, so that an inner equilibrium is restored in personality.
- Yogic techniques of psycho-therapy may thus change and be adopted to the requirements of person, time and place.
- All Yoga techniques begin with control of vrittis and end with the union with the Supreme being.

Now we come to the specific Yoga technique, here also it is to be remembered that Yoga is the name given to a group or system of methods or techniques, which are applied by the therapist according to the nature of the person, the time and the place. Table 9.2 gives a brief account of the somatogenic and psychogenic techniques of therapy in Yoga.

TABLE 9.2
PSYCHOTHERAPEUTIC TECHNIQUES IN YOGA

Somatogenic	*Psychogenic*	
Shodhan—	1. Yama	
1. Dhouti, basti, neti, Nauli, Kapalbhati, tratak.	2. Niyama	(a) disciplinary exercises
2. Swar—Yoga	3. Asana and mudra	(b) psychosomatic energizing exercises
	4. Pranayam	
	5. Pratyahar	(c) psychic sublimating exercises
	6. Dharna	
	7. Dhyana	(d) Psychic super normal Siddhi exercises
	8. Smadhi	

Somatogenic Practices

(1) Shodhan—Purification of the Body

The basic assumption is 'healthy mind in healthy body'. So purification of the body is given the first and primary importance in Yogic practices. Although the acts are all physical and concern the Sharir or outer solid body—it is meant to purify the mind also. Here only a very brief account of Shodhan practices is being presented.

Shodhan includes six Karmas (acts) —

Dhouti— of four kinds to clear away the stomach of all the waste products and impurities. It is done by mouth region.

Basti— again it is purification of the stomach. It is of two types. An anima like process done through the anal region to clear the stomach of waste products.

Neti, Kapalibbati— these are both done to clear the nasal passage, through nostrils. It makes breathing clear and healthy.

Nauli or Loukiki— it is a very difficult exercise in which the stomach and intestines are made to move from one side to the other. It is supposed to increase bodily fires (Jarharagni).

Tratak— it is a difficult exercise for the eyes. It purifies the eyes. It is to look steadily at any object so long that tears come to the eyes.

All these six karmas are to purify the vital body systems— breathing stomach areas of digestion etc.

Swar Yoga— is the exercise of vocal chords, it is done by the musicians mostly.

All Yoga therapy starts with Shodhan, which directly purifies and energises the body. The psychogenic exercises are meant to purify and energize the nerves and the psyche.

Psychogenic Practices

Varna and Niyama— These are exercises of the psyche and are meant to discipline the person.

Yama— is negative side or the 'don'ts' of behaviour. These are five—

Ahinsa— don't kill or harm others.

Asatya— falsehood—be truthful—don't tell a lie.

Asteya— non-theft—don't steel—don't take other's belongings.

Brahmacharya— abstinence, don't indulge in outward pleasures.

Aparigrah— non-greediness—don't be greedy, don't hoard.

Niyamas are the positive side or 'do-s' of behaviour. These are five—

Shouch— purity of body and of mind.

Santosh— contentment.

Tapa— penance.

Swadhyay— self-study. Self-improvement.

Ishwar pranidhan— resign to the will of the god, surrender to god.

Patanjali has given these ten codes of conduct in his Sutras (II/30-46) and II 33, 34 also prescribes 'opposite practice'. It is in case any obstruction arises in the practice of Yama and Niyam then the opposite practice can be resorted to.

It can be seen that some of these practices are from Atharva veda and followed by Charak also—such as tapa and resigning to god. These practices are meant as preliminary exercises to clear the psyche, so that it can make further advances on its path of ultimate Samadhi. They lead to a moral spiritual transformation—preparing a new mental set—just as the beginning of an uphill task ahead.

The exercise of Yama and Niyama in daily routine, leads to a moral and well-contented life, the psyche is disciplined and the mental set is re-oriented towards higher goals. These are for maintaining better mental health. For cases of mild neuroses or psychoses, these rules pave the way for a more normal and adjusted life.

Psychosomatic Exercises

Asan and Mudra— these are from Hatha Yoga—based on the physiological functions of the body. These exercises are meant to recharge the energies of the psyche. It is said that originally there were 84 lakh asanas, each corresponding to the 84 lakh Yonis or forms which an organism has to undertake to reach the human form—all the evolutionary stages. It is the number of the species of living creatures in the universe and the Asanas are named after the names of those creatures. At present, however, only eighty four asanas are popular and being practised. Each and every asana has its own advantages and efficiency. Asanas are prescribed by the guru according to the needs of the person—his age, health, status etc.

Asanas should be stable and comfortable so that one can stay in one asana upto a required time. Asanas are meant for a person's general health, mental peace and calming of passions.

Asanas have therapeutic value also, for example for relaxation of nerves, energizing the total nervous system these asanas are Sheershasana, Sarvangasana etc. They are also meant to arouse the dormant centres in the human nervous system called Chakras. These psycho-physical systems cause the arousal of different energies and powers.

Mudra— postures— Mudras are highly advanced and technical exercises, only specially trained people can attempt them. They also give rise to special powers and can cure some mental ailments also. Mudras are twenty-five in number.

Some Important Asanas with Therapeutic Value

Sheershasana— This is standing straight on the head with legs and feet up, elbows on earth. After sometime come down slowly without any jerks, first lowering the knees then the thighs. This is a very useful asana for all head problems and memory. It can cure amnesia. But it should be done under the strict supervision of a proper teacher at the initial stages. Later on one can practice it oneself.

Sarvangasana— In this legs are put together and raised without bending them, hands are near the body. When the legs are straight up, raise the trunk with a jerk and support the body with the hands, which should be at the back. The chin presses the portion near the throat. Head and shoulders are touching the ground feet and body are up.

Shavasana— Lying down straight on the back with the hands near the body, relax all the muscles of the body and the joints also. Inhale and exhale effortlessly and smoothly. Hold the eyes balls and speech apparatus, motionless. Don't utter any word, don't see any image. Just watch your breath silently. This can be done for about ten minutes.

These are some of the basic asanas for therapeutic purposes. At first, these should be performed strictly under the supervision of a Yoga teacher. The asanas can improve memory, energize the nervous system. Sarvangasana and Shirshasana are for imparting health and strength to the brain and the nervous system. Acharya Bhadrasena prescribes Ardh sarvangasana, halasana, chakrasana for mental debility. Shavasana is prescribed for agitated patients, for quietening the mind. Then there are asanas for destroying various types of phobias, and for destroying sins of the patients. But the main problem with asanas is that they can be performed by those persons who have mild disorders only. These are not fit for severe cases where the patient has lost his mind the psychotic and also not fit for children.

Pranayam— Pranayam is a basic breathing exercise. It means Pran= breath, ayam=stop or pause, so pause in breathing 'Pranayama is the control of prana and the vital forces of the body. It is the regulation of breath.'

—*Sri Shivananda, Divine Life Society, 1957*

There are five pranadi vayus—viz,

Pran—moves in the heart.

Apan—moves in the sphere of anus.

Saman—moves in the naval region

Udan—moves in the throat region.

Vyan—moves in the whole body.

Pranayam unites pran+apan and takes this united pranapan slowly upwards to the head. It is supposed to awake the sleeping kundalini. By controlling pran and awakening the Kundalini—The Yogi can control omnipresent powers and energies. Pranayam can help controlling the energies and remove all sorts of mental and physical diseases, can improve health invigorate nerves.

Pranayam, asanas and mudras are psycho-physical energizing exercises. According to Yoga, pran and mana breath and mind, are close and exist together. Increase or decrease of one affects the other. Breath is outward and also being physical, is easier to control. By controlling breath we can control mind and its movements. So Pranayama is a basic and preliminary exercise to control the mind. In this way Pranayama can be psychotherapeutic—and can also lead to super-normal powers of the mind.

Looked from other viewpoint, these psycho-physical exercises work in two ways—on one hand energizing the body and on the other hand training and energizing the psyche. By these exercises ego gains control over the body and the nervous system. Ego gains in confidence and energy.

Pratyahar— psychic exercise for sublimating—

This is purely psychological and very difficult. If the Yogi has not mastered the previous stages he cannot gain this step. Pratyahar means 'withdrawal'. Here it means 'a complete withdrawal of mind from Indriya or the sense.' Here senses are alive and working but under the complete control of the master-psyche. They work only when the master commands. This is done in two ways—

- Senses should not be affected by the outside stimuli.
- Senses should not disturb the mind by their messages.

In this stage the Yogi responds only to those stimuli which have spiritual value. Here the lower sensory desires are fully sublimated.

This stage is very valuable for psychotherapy because it helps in breaking the conditioned responses and habits—the whole unconscious gets cleared of rajasik and tamasik vrittis. Pratyahar is semi-directed technique where the patient has to work himself—to do self-analysis free association etc. So the problem is, it can be practised by mildly disturbed patients, like neurotics only—but not on those patients who have lost the sense of reality and have no self control, like psychotics. That is why before coming to this crucial stage all the preliminary preparatory stages have to be mastered.

Pratyahar is a great help in mental health. On one side—the somatic side—it gives the ego mastery over the senses, on the psychological side, it clears the unconscious of all its complexes and sublimates them. And then it paves the way for further stages towards samadhi.

Dharna— Literally means steadiness of mind. When the mind is Fixed on its object—it is dharna. The aim here is to make this period of steadiness longer by practice. Mind is concentrating on one point only. So Dharna has steadiness and concentration, which can come only after much discipline and preparation.

Dhyan— Means contemplation or meditation. Mind has become one unity by now and is concentrating on only one object—which is mostly the Supreme being. At this stage there is duality—that is the Yogi who is meditating and the object meditated upon are two distinct separate entities. But later on a stage comes when this duality vanishes. One who is doing the Dhyan and whose dhyan—the subject and object become one—this is Samadhi.

Samadhi— is a trance like state in which the Yogi forgets everything also. He reaches 'Kaivalya' or the highest state of Yoga—where there are no gunas—they cease to exist. Here the Purush has no more motives to work to act. The kingdom is of soul—there is no manas or mind. This is the stage of liberation, Nirvana or Moksha.

The last three stages described by Patanjali are meant for attaining super powers or siddhis. The general psycho-therapy of Yoga ends with Pratyahar. But some advocates of Yoga are recommending Dharna and Dhyan—mental steadiness and meditation for therapeutic purposes and also for attaining higher mental intellectual powers. For example Mahesh Yogi has given the technique of Transcendental meditation for better mental health. Assagiali of Italy is using meditation under the name Psycho-synthesis.

Importance of Yoga for Modern Life

Yoga is a positive way to mental and physical health. It is a science in the true sense of the word. Yoga is an all comprehensive science which encompasses body, mind and soul into one unity. It will be doing injustice to Yoga if it is confined to the sphere of somatic, psychic or psychosomatic therapy only. It is very practical and above the considerations of religion culture and nationality. All the time foreign thinkers are coming to India, to learn more and more about this wonder science. A prominent psycho-therapist of America came to India to learn about Yoga. Later he took the name Swami Ajaya, Ph.D. He has written a revealing book *Psychotherapy: East and West.*

—A Unifying Paradigun

Swami Ajaya established 'The Himalayan International Institute of Yoga Sciences and Philosophy' in Honesdale, Pennsylvania, U.S.A. A distinguished therapist, Swami Ajaya visited the Dattatreya Temple in Andhra Pradesh and various other centres of Yoga and psychotherapy in India. In his view the Yoga form of therapy is the best therapy for the problems of the world today.

Swami Ajaya says, "Psychological models are built up from particular assumptions. We have to explore new territories that lie beyond the boundaries created by these assumptions that characterise modern psychology and psychotherapy. We have to describe the way in which the various fragmented, partial yet insightful perspectives for understanding human experience can be synthesized in a more comprehensive model of human functioning. This broader perspective can be based on Yoga psychology."

"The East has a tradition of few thousand years of self transformation techniques like Yoga. It is a comprehensive paradigm for modern Psychology."

—Swami Ajaya, 1984

John R. Harvey, a theorist comparing modern behavioural psychology with Yoga psychology noted that "The language of the Yoga Sutras (a basic text of Yoga psychology) is surprisingly similar to that of Skinner." He concluded that, "Behaviour Psychology can be usefully understood by placing it within the broad context of classical Yoga psychology."

—John R. Harvey—a paper in American Psychological Association, Montreal, Sept. 80

Concepts like identification, projection and transference are found in ancient Yoga treatises, as well as in modern depth psychology. But Yoga has extended these concepts far beyond modern psychology's comprehension of their scope. Yoga psychology has also achieved considerable integration of seemingly divergent principles, expounded by the various systems of modern psychology. Both behaviourists and psychoanalysts find something common in Yoga in theory and method.

Stephen A. Applebaum, in his book *Out in Inner Space: A Psychoanalyst Explores the New Therapies*, has compared modern psychological theories to 'the Blind Men and Elephant' story. He says, 'each theory is correct but partial and incomplete. A holistic approach is required to integrate all the diverse viewpoints and this holistic approach can be provided by Yoga.'

Geraldine Coster, Kovoor T. Behanan, Felix Guyot, Hans Jacobs, Abhedananda have all compared Yoga psychotherapy with modern psychoanalysis. They all found Yoga to be much more advanced than modern psycho-analysis.

Geraldine Coster remarks, "......Yoga as followed in the past is a practical method of mind development, quite as practical as analytical therapy and far more practical and closely related to real life." Further more, "I am convinced that the Yoga Sutras of Patanjali do really contain the information that some of the most advanced psychotherapists of the present day are ardently seeking."

—Geraldine Coster, Yoga and Western Psychology, 1957

Behanan, emphasizing the universality of Yoga, says, "Thus in a sense, Yoga may be called "Cosmic therapeutics", and its analysis of mind is coloured by this underlying aim."

—Kovoor T. Behanan in Yoga : A Scientific Evaluation, 1937

Thus practicality and universality are the most outstanding features of Yoga psychotherapy. And as a scientific therapy it is not limited by the shortcomings of religion, caste or culture.

Presented here are the comparison of Yoga psychotherapy to psychoanalysis in the view of Western thinkers.

Yoga and Psychoanalysis

Geraldine Coster has compared Yoga with psychoanalysis and found that Yoga far excelled. She remarks—"Analytical therapy in the West is very new and young experiment. Yoga in the East is a very ancient and mature technique. If the whole matter of moral and social discipline, relaxation, breathing and control of thought by meditation were approached by psycho-therapist in the non-religious and scientific attitude of the student of Yoga, it might well be that this would lead to the discovery of new and valuable psycho-therapeutic methods."

Kovoor T. Behanan comparing Yoga and psychoanalysis, remarks, "Both these approaches, divested of theoretical formulations are in the final analysis, therapeutic systems. To be sure Yoga goes much farther than psycho-analysis, for even fear of death, which is an underlying cause of a mild neurosis in many people, does not assail the Yogin."

—Kovoor T. Behanan in "Yoga : A Scientific Evaluation"

Dr. Hans Jacobs, a psychoanalyst and a pupil of Jung, gives a new light on the relationship between Yoga and modern psychiatric practices. He remarks, "My last case, is to demonstrate perhaps better than any merely theoretical explanation, that it is possible to synthesize the Freudian, the Jungian and the Indian approach. That each of them possesses merits of its own and can in certain therapeutical situations become indispensable. I have not so far had an opportunity of applying to patients anything comparable in intensity with Yoga technique."

—*Hans Jacobs, "Western Psychotherapy and Hindu Sadhna", 1961*

Stekel's psychoanalysis is very near to Yoga. Stekel says that, "psychoanalysis is a training to concentration, a school for observing one's thoughts and the patient must be taught to do this." Yoga's emphasis is also on concentration and observing one's thoughts.

Health and Hygiene Regimen in Yoga

The practice of asanas and mudras, the daily observance of Yama and Niyama codes of conduct lead to a perfect physical and mental health condition. Not only that, it leads to a perfect moral balance and satisfaction which leads to happiness for all. Felix Guyot says, "The general laws of the maintenance of the nervous balance or of its restoration when it is compromised, correspond to what we call in the West, mental hygiene. It follows that the Hatha Yoga training leads not only to a perfect physical condition. It is key to good health and moral balance which leads to a state of happiness." "Such is then the triad at once of the objects and the results of the Hatha Yoga—Health, happiness and prosperity."

Personality Development in Yoga

Yoga is nothing but an art—a technique of personality development. It widens the mental perspective, gives ego strength and control over the lower sensations and passions, resolving unconscious complexes and elevating the conscious to new heights. Swami Akhilananda says, "Indian teachers of Raja Yoga or the psychological method discovered the technique of mental development in its totality—emotional, volitional and cognitive—

as they realized that mere conceptual knowledge does not integrate the total personality."

—Akhilananda, Mental Health and Hindu Psychology, 1952

Shri Yogendra says, "Thousands of years in advance Yoga recognised the full significance of all such issues, namely the need and usefulness of 'the process of sublimation, and has recommended the replacement, deflection or purification of the energy, not only of the sexual impulse but also of the non-sexual mental modifications—Chitta vrittis."

—Shri Yogendra

Thus personality development in Yoga is done through systematic steps, which are—

- Purification of body,
- A strict moral code of conduct,
- Control of senses by the mind,
- Control of Ego over buddhi, manas and senses,
- Purification of unconscious by sublimating the complexes,
- Widening the consciousness by concentration and meditation,
- Elevating the consciousness to higher levels, Super-conscious level.

No psychology or psycho-therapy in the world offers such thorough scientific and systematic programme of personality development.

Attainment of Super Natural Powers or Siddhis

This also is a unique contribution of Yoga of which no parallel exists in the world. It goes beyond and above the scope of psycho-analysis, or other Western Systems of psycho therapy. We may quote Geraldine Coster in this context. "Upto the point reached in the previous chapter, the material of preliminary Yoga and the theory and technique of analytical therapy could be placed side by side and compared, but at this stage, namely the beginning of book III of the Sutras, the science of Yoga begins to pass beyond the confines of analytical therapy, so that the comparison tends to be between Yoga and the future potentialities of that science."

Kovoor T. Behanan has this to say—"In conclusion it might be pointed out that therapeutic similarities exist between psychoanalysis and only the earlier phases of Yoga. The higher stages of Yoga are reached by psychophysical and mental exercises for which psychoanalysis has no parallel. Freud's 'depth psychology' would not be considered deep enough by Yoga."

"Thus while psychotherapy as part of western medicine is still in infancy, Indian Yoga System, which professes the same thing travelled long distance centuries ago."

—*O.P. Jaggi, Yogic and Tantrik Medicine*

In the field of psychotherapy there are many points in favour of Yoga than for any other system—

- Other systems are incomplete, are parts. Yoga is a whole system.
- Yoga goes beyond the point where all systems stop.
- Yoga shows a positive way to mental health and hygiene, not only the negative view of curing the diseases.
- Yoga is all comprehensive encompassing body, mind and soul, where other systems stop at mind only.
- Yoga suggests the way to energize the nervous system and other nerve centres called Chakras—like Kundalini.

Yoga Suggests Methods and Techniques to Boost

Ego-Strength— In all the psychic diseases, most of the damage is caused to the ego and its capacities. The ego gets weak and unable to control its functions. A weak ego is not able to face the reality of the outside world, the demands of the Id and dictates of the Superego. It tries to withdraw from reality, not being able to cope with outside problems and inner complexes. The patient suffers the feelings of inferiority and insufficiency and ultimately there is the shattering of the ego as in schizophrenia. All the systems of psychotherapy in the world aim at making the ego strong and energetic, to be able to face the world and to cope with its inner complexes.

Yoga fulfills this function admirably well. Yoga believes in a composite human personality where there is psychosomatic unity. So Yoga starts its exercises from outside—from the physiological sphere. The daily routine of practice of asanas and mudras, gives a person control over the functions of the body. Pranayama gives control over the vital function of breathing. Thus starting from the gross outside body—the sphere of control of the ego gets wider—it goes to the senses (indriya), buddhi (intelligence) and mana (mind) until by gradual and regular practice the ego is firmly in control of all the affairs—internal as well as external. Here not only the body is toned up and benefitted, the ego strength also goes on increasing. Then with these exercises there is special energy for the nerves and the inner systems also, which further boosts ego-strength.

Yoga comes to the stage of controlling psychic functions, in the last stage of Pratyahar. Ego-strengthened by preliminary exercises, now comes to grips with most difficult task—that of controlling the senses from running after the sense objects. This line discipline is the most strict one—but the most beneficial also. It removes the inner problems and complexes and the Ego is firmly in the saddle — all disorders vanish.

Yoga is the most effective system of psycho-therapy as it makes a three-pronged attack on mental diseases.

All other systems of psycho-therapy deal with one aspect only at the time, such as psycho analysis treats psyche only, while behaviouristic therapy deals with outside behaviour. Some systems deal with emotional problems. But Yoga is unique in this respect. It tries to treat body and psyche and even goes further to the field of soul also. As it treats the total personality and as the attack is from three sides, the results are more effective and more lasting and it also takes comparatively less time. The cure is more efficient, more economic, more complete.

As Dr. H.G. Singh says, "Yoga leads man from abnormality to normality and from normality to super-normality."

Some Criticisms of Yoga

Most of the criticism of this valuable system arise from the misconceptions about Yoga. Here only some points are being taken.

Yoga is for ascetics—Sanyasis only as it teaches non-enjoyment of sense-pleasures or withdrawal from the senses and their objects. It is a wrong concept and based on here-say rather than on facts. Yoga is for all—be it a householder (grihasth) or an ascetic (sanyasi). Its practice helps all. Lord Krishna, in Geeta advocates Yoga for all ages, all ashramas, all varnas, all sexes. Lord Krishna himself, called the Yogiraja or king among Yogis enjoyed grihasthashrama—married many times, but kept all his indiriyas strictly under control of the Atman (Ego).

Yoga is all physical exercises, asanas, mudras, pranayama are all physical. Yes it is true that at the initial stages Yoga teaches physical exercises, but these asanas etc. have two purposes — firstly, keeping the body healthy pure and toned up, and second they lead to the further stages of psychic development. So Yoga is not only physical but also physical since it believes in 'a healthy mind in a healthy body.'

Yoga shows more moral and social considerations than therapeutic ones. That Yoga has moral and social considerations shows it has a much wider scope.

Yoga is a general philosophy—a general view of life, diseases etc. But it cannot treat specific cases. This is a wrong criticism as Western psycho therapists who follow Yoga can vouch for (refer—Hans Jacobs, Geraldine Coster).

Yoga is applicable to milder mental disorders only, and not to severe cases. This is true in a way, because Yoga practices require a certain degree of awareness in the patient. A patient who has lost his mind, is totally deranged, cannot be helped by these. But this is also true that by following health and hygiene regimen of Yoga, a person can keep his mind and his sanity intact and will never have to face insanity.

It can be concluded that Yoga presents a complete programme for self-development for everyone and as such its scope is much wider than merely cure of the mental patients. But mental patients are greatly helped by the relaxation techniques and mental re-orientation taught by Yoga.

Yoga in Modern India

Yoga has attracted the attention of medical men and intellectuals not only in India but all over the world. It is becoming a point of convergence of cultures. Yogasanas have become a part of the daily routine of people throughout the world.

Yoga is a positive science of keeping mind and body healthy. It is developing in various forms and branches. The main source of all being the original 'Yoga Sutra' of Patanjali, they just emphasize certain points, such as Shri Aurobindo, of Pondicherry Ashram emphasised the gradual evolution of a super-conscious by the Sadhnas. Swami Shivananda of Divine Life Society, Rishikesh, gave a comprehensive view of Yoga—for the house-holders as well as the Sanyasi-s. It has become very popular, not only in India, but in foreign lands also.

Transcendental Meditation T.M.

Maharishi Mahesh Yogi founded a brief form of Yoga, which can be called 'Instant Yoga'. This seeks to move away from the long and traditional path of Yoga and make it brief and easy for the fast moving life of today. In this the mind is lead away from all worldly bondages towards the unlimited endless consciousness. According to Mahesh Yogi "Transcendental meditation expands consciousness, develops creative intelligence, clears the power of observation and perception. It gives 'unbounded peace' and man develops in a natural way." Mahesh Yogi describes TM as 'diving down the depths of inner peace' from the superficial levels of mind to the depths of bliss (Anand ka Sagar).

The whole process is very simple indeed and finishes in seven steps. The first two are introductory. The third and fourth are of initiation where a 'mantra' is given to the meditator. The next stage is practising TM under the supervision of the teacher or instructor. Next he sits in individual meditation and gradually increases the time to 20-25 minutes. Now he is trained and goes home to practise daily. There is a follow-up programme also where the progress of the meditator is evaluated and his difficulties are removed. He is asked to report how he feels.

There have been some experimental studies on the effects of TM. These are on the physical changes while the person is in the process of meditation.

Lawrence H. Domash (1977) reports, "On the subjective side the meditator reports physical quietness and repose. Also the steadiness of the thought processes. The bodily sensations may vanish but the consciousness is fully awake, expanded and purified.

During the time of meditation there may be periods when thought processes seem halted. At that time there is clear consciousness and awareness without any object. This period is said to be a period of rest and relaxation and also of deep peace and bliss. After that there is renewed vigour, alertness, energy and mental clarity."

Wallace (R.K. Wallace, 1970) experimentally studied the concurrent physiological processes in TM. He measured the oxygen consumption, exhaling of carbon dioxide, function of the heart, heart-rate and breathing rate. He found a significant decrease in all of these factors. The metabolic rate was reduced by 20 per cent.

Some other researchers studied TM and found that it brought some other changes as well. "The regular practice of TM helped in many types of disorders such as insomnia, blood pressure, stuttering etc." Scientists describe the state of transcendental meditation as 'restful awakeness'. In general there are three states of consciousness—awake, dreamy and deep slumber. The state of 'restful awakeness' found in TM seems to be the fourth state of consciousness.

Yoga Practice and Bio-feedback

The practical side of Yoga is fully scientific. The exercises and asanas of Yoga have been so planned that they strengthen the muscular structure and also give strength to the bones and joints. But this is nothing new—all physical exercises have a similar objective. What is so special about the Yoga exercises is the effect these have on the autonomic system of our body as well as the functions which go on automatically and are vital to life—such as breathing, digestion and autonomic nervous system, endocrine glands etc. According to Indian thinking man has two types of bodies—one this solid apparent Sthool Sharir and the other one not apparent but just like this one—Sukshma Sharir. Yoga seeks to strengthen both these bodies and establish the control of will or ego over both.

Modern science has discovered the technique of bio-feedback. This is a way of controlling biological functions of the body by means of putting the knowledge of their functioning back into them. Here is an example.

EEG— Small electrical waves are present in the brain which can be recorded and studied with the help of electro-encephalograph (EEG). The brain shows different types of waves in different states of activity. Some diseases like epilepsy can also be diagnosed by the help of EEG. Waves are distinguished by their speed. The waves found in sleeping state are known as Delta waves the speed of these Delta waves is 1 to 35 per second. In half-sleep, that is the state between waking and sleep Theta waves are found, the rate of Theta waves is 4 to 7.8 per second. This half a wake, half-asleep stage is the one which can be most creative, when a person can get revolutionary original ideas. There is another state when the mind is awake but completely relaxed, eyes are closed the brain is not working, neither critical nor judging, nor logical. It sees but does not attend, hears but does not understand, in such a state Alfa waves are found. The speed of these waves is 8 to 13 per second. Beta waves are found when brain is active and attending, some intelligent activity is going on or there is some problem to be solved. The speed of these Beta waves is 14 to 30 per second. In the state of relaxation or tension free condition Alfa waves are found and in a state of anxiety the waves vanish.

Yoga seeks to change and refine mental content. In this sense bio-feedback is also a form of Yoga. The Yogi can control start and stop his biological functions at will, he can establish the authority of mind over Sharir. He uses methods of dhyan, self-control, etc. to be healthy and to regain health.

Actually, it is possible to train people in selecting their own brain-waves by means of bio-feedback. It is possible to select the complex electric waves of the brain by the help of electronic apparatus. It is known as feedback apparatus. It is believed that the Theta waves characterize creativity and alfa waves, are for relaxation, by a selection process only Theta and Alfa waves are left. Now these Theta waves are put into an electronic tube where they can produce either sound or light. These sound or light tell the person that now he is in a state of relaxation or creativity. Thus his own biological function gives him information about his mental state, and he can also choose his own mental states. This whole is a complicated process and the description presented here is a much simplified version. In a way bio-feedback also resembles conditioning, but with a difference, in conditioning the reward is tangible in the form of food, in bio-feedback reward is mental peace and productivity.

In Transcendental meditation while Yogi is meditating, Alfa waves have been recorded.

It is heartening to note that new generation of Indian psycho therapists has started returning to its Indian roots. They are trying to find a new awareness and cultural identity.

Neki (J.S. Neki, 1978) has clearly expressed in his paper the dissatisfaction with foreign concepts which are mostly out of context for Indian masses, for example, Edipus and Electra complex. Except a few trained in Western psycho-analysis. What does an average Indian know about Edipus and Electra and about Freud for that matter. We have to find our own concepts born in our own soil. This has given rise to three new trends—

A new leaning towards Shri Madbhagvat Geeta.

A sanction to Guru-shishya tradition in therapeutic situation.

Finding new paradigms for the Indian masses nearly three-fourths of which are illiterate or semi-literate.

The founder of All India Institute of Mental Health Bangalore, (Now NIMHANS) late Shri M.V. Govindaswami's famous saying is—"Mahabharata is a great text-book of psychopathology and Geeta is a great treatise on psycho-therapy". Following Shri Govindaswami many research workers tried to find the pattern of psycho-therapy in Geeta, some names are—

Ramachandra Rao (1962) compared the battle field described in Geeta—Kurukshetra with the battle field of life. Here the person who is surrounded in the conflicts of life— Arjuna— seeks guidance and counselling from an expert, his Guru Krishna, who is not only a friend, but his charioteer also, which symbolically means leading Arjuna in the right direction. Arjuna is filled with anxiety and conflict—shows all signs of neurotic anxiety—perspires, shakes, the bow and arrow fall from his hands and he wants to escape—to run away from the battle field. Now his friend philosopher and guide, his charioteer Krishna gives him the lessons of Karma Yoga—contained in Geeta. Arjuna gets a new insight into things and overcomes his conflicts."

This is how therapy proceeds and should proceed.

Venkoba and Parvati (1974) tried to find a psychosomatic paradigm in Geeta on the basis of which the therapy of both body and mind is possible.

Satyananda (1972) says, "Geeta releases a person from his guilty feelings about the world, resolves his conflicts gives him energy and moral courage, imports to a person an ability and insight to look within oneself." Satyananda remolded the living psychology of Geeta in modern form and developed new methods and techniques in education, prevention and therapy on this basis.

Yoga system is much above other systems since it teaches the patient self-control and a way to follow one's dharma (duty in life) without any fear. It teaches facing and coping life and its problem with confidence and strength and ego-strength.

Ten

Psychotherapy: A Synthesis of Indian and Western

We have just had an idea of the three main systems of Psychotherapy in India, as also the salient features of Indian systems. As has become quite evident by now, there are some basic differences between the two systems viz., Indian and the Western—in their approach, their viewpoint etc. Now the searcher may very well ask the question : Is there a meeting point between the two—can these two widely different trends be ever synthesized? Let us now, try to find out whether this is possible, and if possible how far can this synthesis go.

Psychotherapy

Technically speaking Psychotherapy means treating mental ailments with psychological methods. In the West, it is a very modern and new concept, a product of 20th century, which became popular after Freud. It is the treatment of the 'psyche' by verbal technique or 'talking out' method. Psychotherapy has been designed for disturbed 'psyches' by verbal communications, so that the cause of disturbance comes out in open.

With the help of medical science, Psychiatry, Psychosurgery, Neuro-surgery, Psycho-pharmacology etc. the scope of Psychotherapy has much widened, and it is being treated on par with other therapies such as chemotherapy. Medical science has given its acceptance to Psycho-therapy.

Psychotherapy may be individual therapy, group therapy or multiple therapy according to the number of people taking part in the process. In Indian systems also we find examples of group therapy and multiple therapy in Pujas, havans etc., which are supposed to purify and thus cure all the people taking part in the process.

The common components of any Psychotherapy process either Indian or Western—are—

- One or more person/persons (patients) with some vague awareness of some neglected or mishandled life problem—a person with a disturbed psyche and a weak ego, who finds himself incapable of coping with his problems.
- One or more person/persons, with relative lack of disturbance and withingness to help. This is a person with the task of helping the patient the therapist or Bheshaj (भेषज) in Indian system. The therapists may form a group or a team such as in temple healing in India or a team of specialists as with West.
- The therapist in both the systems—Indian and Western—must be a trained person. The ancient gurus or rishis trained their shishyas for the specific purpose of dealing with mental cases. In Western system a specific training period is required for obtaining a license to practise as a psychotherapist.
- The therapist must have an experience of working with a wide range of mental ailments and the healing methods. In guru-shishya parampara the novice or the trainee shishya learnt by being with his guru all the time. He used to get practical experience of all sorts of ailments and their treatment. There is informal-incidental learning as well as formal verbal instructions. In West also an internship is a must.
- A therapist must have superior intelligence and self-understanding. In ancient India the Atharvanic rishis had to achieve this by their constant Sadhna. They understood and emphathized with their patients. They imparted some of their inner peace to the problem-ridden suffering patients just by an encounter or a touch on the forehead. The Yogin also has the same effect on the people who seek his help—he radiates peace and poise.

Here in the therapists, the patients and their inter-relationships, we find some basic differences in the Indian systems and the Western ones. These are—

- The patients—specially the patients with mental problems

are basically the same throughout all humanity. They are tense, disturbed, with many conflicts and problems, anxiety ridden, with weak and vulnerable ego. They are emotionally charged and sometimes totally deranged. But their basic approach to illness and its treatment are different. Whereas in Western systems the patient's approach is external, objective, matter of fact and even commercialised, in Indian systems it is one of faith. There the therapists are like other professional specialists, and very expensive too. It is considered very fashionable and high brow to say "my therapist.........."

- In Indian systems the approach is one of complete faith as in a guru. Gurus don't demand any fees or anything. The patients coming to him give according to their capacity and their devotion (श्रद्धा). Thus this relation was not commercial at all in ancient systems. But the modern vaidyas or practitioners have made it a commercial affair—that is why the results are not so desirable.
- The attitude of the traditional Indian therapist or rishi is one of synthesizing. His concern is less with proposing or opposing than in exposing—not in many words but in silence may be enlightening. In West, the attitude is one of talking—relax-talk. It is an external process only not one of exploration and silence.
- The therapists in the Western psychotherapy are much qualified, high brow high-income lot. The Indian rishis were not of this type. They were hermits and Sadhaks. As regards the modern day practitioners, Dr. H.G. Singh in his survey (1973-74) found that "most were semi-literate" —"a huge majority fall in low income group." He further observes that, "The reason for their poverty may be that the majority does not charge any remuneration for treatment, they do it on altruistic basis." In temples also the Mahantas do not demand any fees. But there are offerings of a set nature (चढ़ावा) which are given mostly voluntarily by the family of the patient.
- To the Western therapist learning, professional skills and competition are more important, while the Indian guru is

uneffected by personal desires. He is calm, magnanimous, and ocean of mercy, and without any sort of personal motive whatsoever. To him healing is not professional, it is Sadhna-worship-or way to God.

As far as synthesis of the two is concerned one cannot foresee a trained Western therapist behaving like a guru or rishi of modern times. One cannot turn the clock back—but has to move forward. We have to have more and more professionally trained psychotherapists. But these therapists must have changed values and attitudes, having the patient's welfare as their highest motive. An ideal situation can be when the therapists are government employees, paid and supported by the government or some welfare agency, so that their relationship with the patients is totally free of all financial and commercial considerations. There is a question of personalities also. During training itself the therapists must try and develop calm and serene personalities.

The Goals of Psychotherapy

According to Alvin R. Mahren the general goals of psychotherapy are—

- Reduction of psycho-pathological condition—It means—
  - (a) Reduction in symptoms which may be concrete, such as ticks or convulsions, it may also mean, changes in life styles and attitudes of the patient.
  - (b) Reduction of defences—so that the patient may be free to express himself and open up.
- Reduction of Psychological pain and suffering—which means—
  - (a) Reduced anxiety.
  - (b) Reduced hostility.
  - (c) Reduced meaninglessness.
- Increased level of pleasure—a general sense of contentment and fulfillment—ability to enjoy oneself.
- Increased experiencing—enhanced sensibilities, and sense of being alive every moment.
- Better self-relationships—which means—
  - (a) Increased acceptance of self.
  - (b) Increased inner-directedness.

(c) Living more richly within oneself.
(d) Finding meaningfulness in life.

- Better external relationships—which means—
(a) Improvement in personal relationships.
(b) More closeness in interpersonal relationships.
(c) Increased competence of functioning.
(d) Increased ability to adjust to one's environment.
(e) Increased social commitments.

These are universally accepted goals and no one can have any quarrel with them. Only thing is that these are not so specifically stated in Indian systems, which aim at a complete and healthy being. Indian systems are more spiritually oriented not socially oriented. They seek the harmony of the individual with himself (आत्मन्) the Supreme-Self (परमात्मन्) and the whole universe (जगत्). Actually Indian systems are more broad base. These are oriented towards all living beings—seeking the welfare of all living beings in all forms—plants animals and men. Some examples of social orientation are found in group therapy or samoohika chikitsa—where groups of patients with similar symptoms are treated together in a group as in Bhaya (fear or phobia) or unmad (hysteria). Another such example is Utarna or transfer, which is very different from 'transfer' found in psycho-analysis given by Freud.

Transfer is a form of directive therapy found in Atharva veda. It is a process of transferring or sending the symptoms of the ailments to other objects or things. For example, the main symptom of fever is 'a sensation of heat, of burning'. In a mantra of Atharva veda it is said, 'O fever, why are you giving me (the patient) trouble by burning me. Go to the ocean and drown yourself to quench your heat.' The heat or burning sensation, which is doing harm to the patient is to be transferred to the ocean, which can never be harmed by the fever.

Priyaratha Arsh in his Atharvediya Mantra Vidya (1942) has given a scientific explanation for Utarna. Arsh says that the elements or waste products which are harmful to the patient are transferred to some such suitable place, object or living being, where these elements can do no harm, or can rather be more useful and helpful. Arsh gives the example of Utarna in a patient of jaundice. The patient of jaundice gets his skin pale, this palour is transferred or requested to be transferred to turmeric plants (haldi) to make them all the more rich in yellow colour. It may also be transferred to the parrot or other yellow things. In the same way the transfer of grahs, sharp and pap etc. are also tried with the help of mantras and rituals. Bloomfield has also given a description of the process of transfer.

This idea of exchange of symptoms or the elements is unique to Atharva veda. In the light of modern psychotherapy, it can also be called a form of suggestion. The therapist gives the suggestion and the patient believes that his symptoms are going away, because these have been transferred to other objects, plants, birds or animals.

The Main Therapies of Western System

The main therapies of the Western System may be described as forming three major groups—

- Bio-psychological development therapies which correspond to the Freudian System.
- Psychological actualising psychotherapies which include client centred and existential therapies also, which emphasize the 'self'.
- Reconstructive therapies which are based on learning therapy. These are also known as behaviour therapies.

All these therapies have uniformity of goals, which may be stated as—

- removing the interferences and blocks in the process of development of self or personality.
- restoring personality as an intact unit.
- leaning to face the problems or live with problems.

The data of psycho-therapy are—

- **external** outward physical such as postures, voice etc.
- **internal** concepts, thinking cognitive processes. In depth psychology the data are more deep seated, profound. It seeks the resolution of basic problems at their deep roots while the behavioural approach concerns itself with more external behavioural problems.

In actualizing approach the basic data are coping, feeling, reaching, behaving experiencing etc. It believes in the on-goingness of the present. It also seeks a high degree of emotional stability and flexibility.

The reconstructive approach is based on learning theories. Here the attempt is to re-educate the patient and to restructure his behaviour patterns.

We can find the common points between the Indian systems and these main systems. Let us take depth psychology first. It seeks to reach the deeper roots of the problems. The Indian systems also try to solve the problems of mental nature, by going deep into them, to enable the patient himself to look within, to go deep inside, to reach back in to Antakarna or inner self. The psychological actualizing systems come nearer to the Indian systems, because both are concerned with coping, feeling, reaching and experiencing. Both believe in actualizing the self and finding a meaningfulness in life.

As far as the reconstructive approach is concerned Indian systems also believe in reconstruction. It also seek to re-educate and restructure, but this is not at the behavioural level. This re-educating and restructuring is sought at the inner level.

Swami Akhilananda says, "Western psychotherapies of various schools have been trying to solve the mental problems of people. Yet, in spite of their attempts and noble contributions, they lack something—which can be given by India."

—Swami Akhilananda

Actually we have to reach at a point of symbiosis-a synthesis between the two, so that the suffering mankind may be rid of its mental problems.

Mental problems are very often the result of misplaced, mishandled and mismanaged emotional states. Naturally, the cure for such emotional disturbances lies in correcting and reforming emotional responses.

"The traditional Indian systems such as Ayurveda, Yoga, Dhyan etc. can help in establishing marvellous control over many mental ailments." G.N. Reddy.

Satvalekar refers to many sayings in Atharva veda as "I release". These sayings indicate instances of verbal therapy. The examples of such therapy are

Atharva Veda 2.10.1 क्षेत्रियात् त्वां मुन्चामि। I release you from illness.

Atharva Veda 2.10.1 अनागसं ब्राह्मणा त्वां कृणोमि। I make you guiltless.

Atharva Veda 2.10.5 तासु त्वान्तर्जरत्वा दधामि। I make you of a long life.

Atharva Veda 2.10.6 ग्राह्याश्चोद मुक्था। Now you are free from the grahi ailment.

All these mantras are meant to console the patient, to increase his ego-strength, to help him gain a real and firm confidence in himself and thus to restore his mental health. In Atharva Veda we also find means for uplifting of emotions, increase of mental powers and curing the patient of all types of mental disabilities which arise out of a sense of guilt (Pap bhawna). According to 'Atharva veda, not only mental ailments but physical ailments also arise due to a sense of guilt and mental weakness, which can be cured by reforming emotions, by increasing mental powers and by increase in the level of self confidence of the patient.'

This is the latest research finding on Indian systems like Ayurveda, Yoga etc.

Prof. Carl R. Rogers in Counselling Psychotherapy says, "During therapy the patient must develop his own insight, think of his previous states." But Rogers concluded that, "Directive motivating signals are not very successful during therapy. These are usually incomplete or totally rejected."

These words come from a very successful and renowned therapist who practised client-centred therapy. Even he had to admit that "the directive motivating signals are not very successful during therapy." Here the Indian systems can come to help. These "directive motivating signals" are given in a different way in Indian systems.

Firstly, there are very strong suggestions from a person of prestige and authority—a guru or priest who says, in various ways, "I release you from these ailments." Then there are suggestive mantras which produce a long lasting effect on patient's mind. Lastly there are havan puja and other ritualistic performances. These all combine to create an atmosphere, where the patient is put into a sort of hypnotic trance. He receives all suggestions for release from the ailments during this trance. When he wakes up from this trance, he is a new and transformed person. These are directive motivating signals. There are other suggestions which may be considered 'directive and motivating'. Some examples are—

- Atharva Veda 3.30.3 वाचं बदत शान्तिवाम्– Speak gently and sweetly as harsh words or speech is the cause of mental agony to self and others, sweet words give peace of mind.
- Abnormalities arising out of the unfulfilled sex desires—here the suggestion given is :
  To satisfy natural urges in natural ways and not to over-indulge in sensory pleasures. Kama or sex desire has been treated in a very natural way, so that there is no guilt feeling attached to normal healthy sex life.
- For hallucinatory insanity or unmad—there are other external means such as burning of herbs and incenses etc. The patient sits or lies in a closed room. Small mustard seeds (राई) and red chillies are burnt here. The smoke and the strong pungent smell is supposed to remove all inertia from the nerve fibers and the mind is relieved of all false illusions.
- For excitable patients camphor, sandal wood, ghee and other aromatic herbs are burnt. They produce a fine fragrant atmosphere, the smoke goes upto brain and makes the tissues strong there. This atmosphere also gives a pleasant feeling of peace and tranquility to the patient, soothing his nerves and calming him down.
- There are various other suggestions and auto-suggestions given in Mantra vidya in Atharva Veda. Mantra vidya in itself is a sort of suggestion to the patient, to console him and to build up his self-confidence. Mantra vidya generally includes—
- *Mantra*— Small Sanskrit verses to be chanted by the priest and sometimes by the patient also.
- *Abhichar or rituals*— They combine behavioural as well as medicinal methods. These rituals are the means to some pre-meditated goals. They often lead to a complete upliftment of emotions. These rituals create an emotionally charged atmosphere, which envelopes the patient, his family, his friends and the whole neighbourhood. The rituals help in purging the individual, throwing away the emotions which act negatively and create emotions which are conducive to life. The new emotions give a new bent

to life and a renewed will to live. Now these patients are able to cope with their life problems. They can face any natural or man made calamities with calm and poise. The rituals are for uplifting morale—creating a fearlessness and optimism in life. These are negative or escapist. The rituals as given in the vedas are never negative, for causing harm to others or pessimistic, for escaping from life.

Here are two sutras from Atharva Veda with commentary by Satavalekar

पवमाना आर्त्या वि।
शन्नः पापकृत्या कि।। अर्थव सू॰। मं॰[2]

One who has virtue is away from troubles and ailments. It also means the man who is strong with moral and mental strength, is away from sins. Cleanliness and virtuosity are removers of illness. "Make your body clean with water and mind clean with truth." These two examples must suffice to show how simple rules of life like bath with water and truthful behaviour lead to mental and physical health, according to Indian systems.

Indian systems, although spiritually oriented are free from religion and religious dogmas. Indian systems start from inner preparedness and awareness and then lead to action. It is in juxta position to the Behaviour. Therapy which starts with modifying overt behaviour and believes that outward changes will lead to changes in inner values and attitudes. The goal of all Indian systems is cleansing the consciousness, elevating it to higher levels, leading to super conscious states in some cases. It is above rational since it transcends reason also.

The Nature of the Self

Of all the Western Systems of psychotherapy Jung comes nearest to the Indian concept of the self. The self to him "represents the sum total of conscious and unconscious existence." It is "the ultimate experience of the psyche." But as compared to Indian concept it is too narrow. Jung himself said (Psychology and religion, 1938) that he borrowed the term from Indian Philosophy. In Indian system the term 'self' stands for 'Atman' आत्मन्. The Atman resides in every living being—vegetation, animal life and mankind. The Jivas or living beings are grouped on the basis of their relative consciousness, some within the same group may be more conscious than the others.

'Atman' is an eternal all pervading entity. It is the experience of all that goes on. 'Atman' signifies universal consciousness, while Jungian 'self' corresponds to the subtle body 'Antha-karna' अन्तःकरण in Indian terms. Antah-karana is conditioned while the Atman is unconditioned. This self if covered and conditioned by individual's propensities. The individual is unaware of the true nature and existence of self in him. In Jung, the self has unconscious component and is completely dependent on it. This is a narrow and deterministic concept. It may lead to boredom, sterility and hopelessness. There is a sense of meaninglessness from which all thinking men tend to suffer. This vague sense of meaninglessness is found in all the cases of neurosis of the present day—

Jung—Integration of Personality, 1939.

Jung—Modern Man in Search of a Soul.

In Indian concept of self such hopelessness and meaninglessness does not arise. This concept leads to a sense of oneness with the cosmos, and a sense of purpose in life.

The Psychological Constitution of Man

The man has an inner soul, an outer condition or body (upadhi). Inner soul cannot be rationally perceived. Body has different degrees of manifestations—the gross (स्थूल), the subtle (सूक्ष्म). Both of these are material, though of different density. Brain, sense-organs, nervous system are all real and material. All mental activity takes place in this body. There are nerve-centres known as Chakras which can be aroused and controlled by the Yogins. Mental centres are co-ordinated in the centre of nervepath-Sushumna. The lowest of mental centres are the five elements.

The human vertebral column, by itself, turns the mind upwards. The centres of nerve or mental activity are these Chakras. These can be known by introspection. The lowest Chakra lies at the base of the Spinal column मूलाधार चक्र Muladhar Chakra. At the highest is the Sahasrara Chakra (thousand petalled lotus) which lies close to the summit of the head. One main Chakra is between the brows, where tilak or bindi is put. It is the centre for meditation. Yogins arouse these Chakras one by one and go up to the highest level of mental energy. According to this system, mind operates through two channels—right — Ida (इड़ा) left Pingala (पिंगला) which combine with the main nerve channels. The material body is constituted by heredity. Inheritence refers to this gross body not to the mental receptacle, which is independent of material elements. The gross body is instrument for action, it envelops the inner invisible substance, by which it is filled, much as a vessel is filled by water—Vivek Chudamani - Shankara.

The soul (Jiva or Jivatma) lives inside the subtle body. It is the medium of experience. It leaves the body at death and is subject to rebirth. After death a new consciousness arises, according to the mental tendency of the departed. It is the same consciousness and not yet the same. The individual soul evolves and is alone responsible for its evolution. In this way man is the creator of his fate. Indian system is not deterministic. The laws of cause and effect condition man to time and space, which create predispositions. But man can also exercise his free will and can with purposeful effort, undo what he has done. He possesses a vast range of spiritual resources, which he can utilize for evolving further up. The bodies comprise the three gunas—satva, rajas and tamas — in various combinations. The one within is free of these three gunas. It is pure consciousness (chit) which seeks to be united with the cosmic consciousness. Once the man frees himself of his egohood, and to the degree that he is capable of identifying himself with the supreme, he attains its knowledge — sat, power—chit and bliss — ananda, Swami Vivekananda - Woodroffe.

The Westerners decry this theory as mere metaphysical phantasizing — the subjective mental images with no objective reality or truth in them. It is a fact that there are no proofs in any objective scientific sense. These are just experiences which had profound effects on the individuals who had them as also on mankind in general. According to Indian doctrine everyone, who follows a proper procedure, can reach the same insights by the spiritual exercises or Sadhna. The practices generally known as Yoga are not merely physical gymnastics. These are pre-requisites for the co-ordination of mind and body and for the attainment of higher levels of consciousness.

Good and Evil, God and Demon

These are seen as two extremes of human nature. The basic attitude of Judas-Christian tradition is that God and man are separated by an unbridgable gulf. All the thinkers, from Plato onwards state that it is not possible to accomplish a real transformation of human nature. The psychotherapists right from Freud and Jung admit the influence of the demoniac powers in modern man and in modern civilization. Jung in his essay on contemporary events (1946) says that, 'the idea that a truly liberated man (jivanmukta) can bring his weight to bear against the demons, is foreign to these conception.' To Indians it is an accepted conception. Here the aim is not to bring about a solution of the problem of good and evil in man but accepting both and reaching higher levels. Here concentration is something more than Salvation, it is complete liberation from the bonds of conditioned existence.

Concentration

Only a concentrated mind can peep into the inner-most recesses of its own mind. Concentration is a pre-requisite for all creative and successful pursuits of people such as painter, poet, surgeon or any other proficient operation. Concentration leads to self-discovery. But man is afraid of discovering himself, he tries to avoid inner demons—his fears and anxieties. The Western therapies show no way out of this dilemma. They suggest, 'Bring out the demons to the surface and then they can be tamed.'

The psychoanalysts object to concentration as it may be a form of repression. But a closer look reveals both the processes to be very similar. The process of concentration resembles the analytical method of free association. In both the mind is made acquainted with itself, watching one's thoughts leads to an intimate knowledge of the mind, its conflicts and contradictions, and then there is a progressive awakening to what was as yet unperceived. In concentration, Dhyan, the mental activity is slowed down. The more the inner layers are exposed to the light the more the inner determinants of mental processes will manifest themselves and then can be controlled. The doors of higher consciousness are opened and the mental processes are no longer dispersed by emotional conflicts. The mental powers are united by and directed from one focal point — the self. Now the whole mental apparatus is put under perfect control and latent potentialities awakened.

Here we can see the difference between Indian and Western systems. While in the Western systems the objectivity only produces a multiplicity of long dead and past thoughts, a firm attention or dhyana opens up the perennial supply of knowledge, in fact a higher state of consciousness is reached. Self is now contented in its own self and pure bliss results. He knows his innermost self deeply now and this is the ultimate aim of all Indian systems— "know thyself" आत्मनंविद्धि.

This idea is very near to the existential psychotherapy, where more emphasis is put on 'immediate' 'now' 'on-going' processes. The 'being' is the foundation on which the structure of 'becoming' stands.

A synthesis is possible if the two ideas come a bit closer— knowing oneself and becoming are quite akin to each other.

Suggestion

Most of the practical aspects of Indian systems are ignored or ridiculed as being mere auto-suggestions or suggestions such as pooja, havana, mantras, charms etc. But what is the harm in auto-suggestion? The investigations of Nancy School have shown that auto-suggestion plays its part in mental life, and can be applied to mental problems also. So both systems can accept ant-suggestion as one of the methods of mental healing.

In Indian system the Gyan or superior knowledge is restricted to the select few — the elite or enlightened ones, and the rest have to follow these enlightened seers or rishis. These elevated ones keep themselves at a distance from the masses. This is not democratic. Look at the Western systems, where on principle, all knowledge should be accessible to all. But, does this democratization or 'reaching out' to all, lead to an accumulation of knowledge — yes, if information is taken to mean knowledge— not if knowledge means deeper wisdom. Reaching out to all has diluted pure knowledge — it is atomized — an atomization of life itself.

Diet

In mental healing in India, diet also counts as an important factor, as it is contended that there is a close relation between the clarity of mind and the condition of the body. There are no general prescriptions, for diet depends on habit, kind of occupation, climate, bodily and mental disposition, economic status etc. Food suggested is mostly vegetarian and simple for the mental patients. It is a strong belief that the food produced without bloodshed is purer. Here the Western ideas of getting proteins, hydrocarbons or vitamins is not so important as the inner attitude or Bhava of taking food for the sake of sustaining life. The therapists also advise that food, medicines or any other things consumed by the patient are to be prepared by the near and dear ones like mother, sister, wife so that the well wishes are mixed with the food consumed and medicines also become more effective.

Here a synthesis can be reached by bringing together the two approaches — of purity and bhava. Indian and scientific dietetics of the West. A combination of the two can provide full and wholesome new insight into the problem.

Neuropsychology

Neuropsychology is a very recent development which seeks to find out in the relationship between the working of the nervous system and mental functions. Latest researches in neuropsychology have led to many new ideas such as autonomic immunity system—which works on the physical level but affects mental states specially emotional behaviour. A neuropharmacologist at National Institute of Mental Health (U.K.) Cadence Pert (1973) has done research on Neuropeptides which can control feelings and emotions. These drugs are called psychoactive drugs since they arouse and work on mental functions. These may be external or internal secretious.

INDORFIN is an internal secretion having the same effect as morphine. Similarly scientists have found Neuro-transmitters which are in a way the independent units of consciousness. These units transmit messages in electro-chemical form within the nervous system. The better the working of these neuro-transmitters, the better the level of awareness in the individual.

In India there is a Combined Therapy Program (CRX) initiated by Swami Rama (of Himalayan Institute Hospital Trust, Jolly Grant, Dehradun). The program, pioneered by Swami Rama, in the late sixties, at Menninger Foundation USA showed that the mind has remarkable control over the autonomic nervous system. Swami Rama created a difference of 10 degrees F in his palm at two different points and consciously produced delta waves, the sign of deep sleep while he was fully awake. Many other aspects of body activity like heart-beat and pumping function of the heart were similarly controlled. Thus now an attempt is on to bring together bio-feedback, Yoga, acrobic exercise, nutrition and breathing relaxation skills. Similarly ayurvedic techniques can be applied. All these modalities are aimed at creating self-awareness on all levels, body, breath, energy, emotions and mind. This can give a better understanding of body-mind relationship.

Ayurveda also offers cleansing and rejuvenation techniques like Panch Karma. According to Ayurveda many illnesses result from the build up of toxins in the body so the cleansing regimen becomes necessary. Yoga therapy is for developing self-awareness. It also focusses on the mind-body-breath relationship and self-healing and self-transformation.

Biofeedback is another technique with a purpose to develop control of autonomic processes. The first step is to develop an awareness of the different functions of the autonomic system such as breathing, heart-rate, blood pressure muscle, tension. Then he is trained to gradually control these functions, and thus the abnormalities get corrected by themselves.

In this way there are many attempts at the holistic approach to health and life which combine the Indian and Western techniques, and this a good sign for the future when a synthesis of the two systems can be possible.

Mental Health

Mental health is the positive aspect of therapy, which suggests ways and means to ward off illness, adopt a life style where mental diseases get no chance to attack people—a life style which is free of tensions, anxieties conflicts and stress which give rise to mental problems.

Atharva Veda suggest two ways to mental health — One increase in self confidence and ego-strength, and various ritualistic performances like pooja, havana, mantra.

Greatest importance is attached to cleanliness, both of body and the mind. "Clean your body with water, and mind with truth."

Atharva Veda gives a detailed program for mental health and hygiene, as also for improvement and better integration of personality. This program is as follows—

- *Medha Vardhan*— Improving memory and learning power. Medha means retentive capacity of the mind. For improving memory and retentive processes some devices are suggested—
  - *Sankalpa*— Self-determination, vowing to oneself that he will retain this wisdom in memory.
  - *Tapa*— Means penances but here it means very hard labour. This is done in the form of exercises and repetitions of the learned material. Vedas were committed to memory.
  - *Suggestion*— By self or by others, in the form of havana, pooja, prayers etc. to attain better mental powers.

Improvement in memory and learning process naturally lead to better mental health.

- *Paushtikarni*— It means making strong, gaining Atma-bal and building up ego-strength. It refers to both physical and psychical aspects. It is well known fact in modern psycho-pathology that when the ego becomes weak, it falls prey to various types of mental illnesses. The ego has to be strong to face the realities of the outside world, as well as to cope with its own Vrittis (Id and Super-ego in Psycho-analysis). All psychotherapies seek to strengthen the ego, to make it more integrated so that it is able to control all its faculties. Various devices are given to make the ego strong such as—
- *Gaining more and more knowledge*, for knowledge is strength, it leads to more self confidence more knowledge gives one more power.
- *Self-control*— To gain Atma-bal, one has to control one's own senses and establish full mastery over the Indriyas.

- Sweet speech—Atharva Veda 3.30.2 says वाचं वबूत शान्तिवाम्। Use gentle and sweet speech, as harsh words cause mental agony. Sweet words give pleasure and contentment to the speaker as well as to the listeners. Sweet and gentle words are great promoters of metal health.
- Auto-suggestion works miraculously in this respect. The person repeatedly says to himself "I'll do..... "I am becoming strong and radiant like the sun..." An energetic ego is the foundation of mental health.

- *Samanasayani*— This refers to social integration and harmony. Man is a member of a social group. There must be integration and harmony between man and his group and better inter-relations among the various groups. Social disharmony and disintegration are detrimental to mental health of all its members.

Atharva Veda suggests devices to check social disintegration and create harmony is three broad social groups viz., the family, the friends and other small groups and the nation or the whole country. The word 'Manas' or mind occurs many times in the Smansayani mantras because social integration also depends on 'mind'. The devices suggested are common poojas, performing rituals, havana prayers etc. and coming together in assemblies (सभा).

Mental Health and Ayurveda

Ayurveda is the ancient 'science of life.' It is not just a system of medicine but also gives ways to maintain physical and mental health for a happy healthy living and to prevent occurance of illnesses. Ayurveda describes life as a four dimensional entity comprised of Sharir (body), indriya (senses), satva or manas (mind) and atma (soul). The integration, in a right manner of all these four in an individual is essential to perform all the duties and actions in life.

The principal objectives of Ayurveda are to maintain the health of a healthy person, and to give relief to those persons who suffer from various kinds of diseases.

As stated earlier Ayurveda is psychosomatic in its approach

the physical and mental aspects always go hand in hand. For physical health, a balance of bodily humours vata, pitta and kapha is essential, in the same way for mental health, the gunas or vrittis, satva, rajas and tamas must be in harmony with each other. Excess of one leads to diminishing of the other and this imbalance causes problems and disorders. To maintain good mental health Ayurveda suggests—

- A balance of bodily humours by proper diet and life style observing dincarya and ritucharya.
- A balance of gunas by exercising control (चित्तवृत्ति निरोध).
- Sadvrat (सद्व्रत) or proper behaviour in all respects and all circumstances.

Sushrut Samhita devotes a full chapter (Utt./64) to the aim of preservation of health. Mantra, japa, shantikarma, pooja, prarthana and havana have been suggested for maintaining mental health.

The tridiscordance theory of Ayurveda works both on the physical and psychical levels. It is a holistic approach both soma and psyche form the two aspects of the same coin.

Mental Health and Yoga

Yoga is the science of mind. It is the highest product of Indian Psychology. The origin of all forms of Yoga are the yoga-sutras of Patanjali. From the very beginning it is psychological in nature as it starts with Chittavritti-nirodh. Yoga teaches control for mental health. It starts from the body level and goes upto the highest level of mental achievement that is samadhi.

The yogic methods can be applied for the prevention of mental illnesses. By the method of Yoga, the inner complex can be analysed and sublimated and mental equilibrium can be attained. Actually this equilibrium or harmony is the state of mental health. But it is not static. It is creative and dynamic, it moves a step a head of other systems. It seeks to bring about a surge of new fresh mental awareness—a sense of being one with existence itself — elevating consciousness to higher levels.

Yoga has eight limbs or sections — Ashtanga viz., Yama, Niyama, Asan, Pranayama, Pratyahar, Dharna, Dhyan and Samadhi. Yama and Niyama are the rules for normal healthy living. From right living to right thoughts, actions and behaviour result. Asan and Prannayam release muscles and give new 'Prana' and energy. Pranayam also frees life and its vital processes from the wasteful charge of emotions. Pratyahar gives redirection to life force. The three stages after Pratyahar, dharna, dhyan and samadhi are for mental discipline. They elevate man to self-transcendence as also detachment from this world.

These stages are not for common people. The ordinary men and women can achieve a higher mental level, right living, right behaviour and action just by following the first four or five steps of Yoga.

Thus mental health in Yoga is very positive and creative concept. It is for release of creative potential of man, for self-actualization, for living a whole (समग्र) and a realised (समाहित) being.

Metal Tensions in Indian Systems

According to all the Indian systems mental tensions are the main blocks in the way of mental health. Various ways are suggested to cope with mental tensions.

Tensions arise due to Pragyapradh (प्रज्ञापराध) or transgressions of the Pragya intellect or mind. It means when the person knows he is doing something he should not do, and is not doing something which he should do then there is a sense of guilt and shame within him. Due to guilty conscience whole of his mental life is affected. Pap and manas-pap are the causes of tensions and to ward off these tensions some means are suggested such as sweekarokti or confession — before the guru or priest or deity. Prayashchitas are procedures for penances which include japa, tapa, bali, tyag and dan. Atharva Veda gives details of prayashchittani. There are more than fifty prayashchittani mantras in Atharva Veda. They deal mostly with the expiation of pap bhavna or guilty feeling. "Whatever sublimates or catherises pap is prayashchitta. Prayashchitta means doing tapa to expiate pap as a voluntary decision — the person who is tense due to guilt takes it upon himself to make for or condone for his own wrong doings. It's purpose is to purify ego by sublimating or throwing away of pap bhavna in a sort of purging".

In the psychology department of Calcutta University Ram

Nath Kundu and Geeta Bhaumik did a study on murderers entitled 'Personality Qualities of Murderers'. They found that most of the murderers were aggressive personalities and also suffered from severe tensions.

Tension may also arise from boredom and frustration. The fast-moving, impatient, instant living, dejected and pessimistic persons also tend to suffer from tensions. The modern live-wire executives are the potential victims of tensions.

Tensions are caused by a feeling of emptiness, purposelessness and meaninglessness in life. The people who lead a positive constructive meaningful life are less likely to have tensions.

Tension is a disease of modern times, even small children and adolescents can be gripped by tensions. There are tensions due to broken families, neglect of the children, no proper attention paid to them, because both the parents are very busy. There may be other emotional disturbances to cause tensions in children such as very strict discipline, faulty relationships, separation from some much-loved person—grandfather, grandmother, etc. The adolescents may suffer tensions because of social or financial constrains, family conflicts, high level of aspiration, cut-throat competition, job expectations, unemployment etc.

In Gulbarga Government General Hospital (Karnataka State) from April 76 to Feb. 78, a study of suicide cases was carried on. Of the 44 cases studied 22 per cent were victims of mental diseases, 8 cases of depression and 2 psycho-paths.

Indian systems provide various measures toward off mental tensions. First are the positive measures that is, adopting a life-style in which tensions do not arise. Second is providing such social and familial security that the small children and adolescents do not feel lonely and insecure and fall prey to tensions. In Atharva Veda, hydrotherapy is suggested as a cure for tensions, Drinking lots of cold water, bathing in open water like river or lake relieves tensions. Water is very effective in reducing physical and mental fatigue. It makes one active and alert and also cheerful. Living a natural life, in close proximity of nature—water, rivers, mountains, forests greenery, relieves tensions. Ayurveda suggests gaman (environmental change) and chittaprasadan (recreation) for relieving the tensions. Besides these, Shanti karma or propitiatory rites may be performed to relieve individual or group tensions. Here some ritualistic ceremonies havana, pooja etc. are performed along with mantras. Some ghee and aromatic herbs are burnt, cooling things like khus or sharbat and cooling baths with curds, turmeric and oil are used—all these have calming and soothing effect on nerves and relieve tensions.

In Yoga, the regular following of Yama and Niyama itself ensures a tension-free existence, since the person is doing, what he knows he should be doing. The Yamas —don'ts—are five—*himsa, asatya, steya, a-brahmacharya* and *parigraha.* The five Niyamas or 'do-s' are — *shoucha* (purity), *Santosh* (contentment), *tapa* (self-mortification), *swadhyaya* (study) and *ishwar pranidhana* (submitting to god). These ten are the codes for good behaviour, meant to discipline the individual—to give a direction to the mental set.

The Yoga suggests various asans for relief in tension. The asanas are physical exercises in the form of bodily postures. These exercises are good for general health, peace of mind and calming of nerves. Some of the Asans suggested for imparting health to the brain and nervous system are Shirshasan, Sarvangasan, Dhanurvakrasan, Paschimothanasan, Ardhamatsyendrasan and Shavasan.

There have been many experimental studies of Shirshasan and Shavasan, to show that they really cause a change in the brain waves, agitated waves are quietened down.

Thus Indian systems have many measures to relieve the tensions not to suppress but to calm them down by various methods. Western systems can adopt these simple measures which do not require any drugs or any expensive equipment. Studies in this direction have already begun—Yogasanas are being put to experimental tests to know how far these can really affect physical processes such as brain waves, breathing intake of oxygen, muscular tensions, blood-pressure, GSR electric skin response etc.

Relationship Between Indian Systems and Western Systems

At stated earlier also, psychoanalysis of Freud and Jung comes very near to Indian systems, specially Yoga. Psychoanalysis digs up one's past. Yoga takes into accounts the individual's entire biological past which has been built into the system by the process of evolution. What man is, in fact, sums up his entire evolutionary history. Take the Yogasanas which are supposed to be eighty-four lakhs (84 lacs). These asanas represent the 84 lacs species found on earth and are named after the species such as matsyasana—is like fish. This way Yoga goes to the phylogenetic past while psychoanalysis goes to ontogenetic or individual past or at the most collective past as in Jung.

To psychoanalysis of Freud, the unconscious is a seething couldron of excitements and tensions. Life has tension—discharge rhythm built-in. But the channels of discharge must be socially and ethically justifiable. Basic to Freudian psychoanalysis, and many modern variants of its techniques are the concepts of unconscious and its probings and draining out. It is meant so as to free ego of its libidinal infantile conditioning. Yoga too has evolved a large body of such techniques in its eight limbs or Ashtang (अष्टांग). Patanjali's Rajayoga gives eight techniques — known as Ashtang. Of these the first five are preparatory and the last three are for releasing of creative potential of man, for self-actualization and for living a whole (समग्र) and realised (समाहित) being.

To Yoga as to psychoanalysis, it is the dawn of new awareness that brings about mind's healing. Therapy to both is the process of rebuilding life on a plane of new consciousness, although this new consciousness is much more profound in Yoga, than in psychoanalysis. This new consciousness is wider and elevates one to higher levels. In psycho-analysis it is more on objective, surface level. Bridges can be built up on this aspect in the two systems.

To psychoanalysis it is the complete new orientation of the mind that frees it from infantile fears and complexes. To the Indian systems, it is the realization that individual is not an isolated bit of existence—it is one with it — a part of it that delivers him from the dread of life. These two concepts can come together without going into the philosophy or meta-physics. New orientation is common to both.

In a way, the following are also very near to the Indian systems—

C.G. Jung— To him integration of personality is the method for cure. Man must find his soul in its own wholeness, which is now torn into conscious and unconscious minds -- each with its own divergent laws. Man must become one and be at peace with himself, before he can be at peace with the world. This is Samagra yoga—wholeness.

Behaviour therapy has now advanced beyond Watson. Its main modern exponent is Eyesanck. To behaviour theory the basic assumption is: 'all behaviour is learnt behaviour'. Therefore all sickness abnormality etc. are also learnt. To overcome sickness, man must learn, unlearn and relearn. The techniques for this are conditioning, de-conditioning and re-conditioning. Operant conditioning is also one of the techniques. In truth Eyesanck seems to believe that all ailments arise from wrong living and they can be corrected through right living. The cure here is correction or relearning. Yoga also confirms that the remedy for wrong living is right living. Start living a rich and full life. Yoga thus is a technique for self-improvement.

Carl Rogers, in his client-centred therapy, gives activity programs for improvement of his clients. The Atharvedic and Ayurvedic systems also give activity programs in the form of ritualistic performances like pooja, hawana etc.

Erich Fromm was an existential humanist who attempted to bridge the chasm between two divergent views about man—that is man's own power to grow to evolve and his mental sickness—which exposes a desire to avoid his responsibility. Every man has a basic responsibility towards himself—towards his own life, that is to go forward—evolve to reach upto higher goals. But man is also a shirker—he wants to avoid responsibilities and in the process develops reaction mechanisms Psychological, psychosomatic and even somatic disorders are the results of this shirking on man's part. The humanistic philosophy of Fromm is centered around man and his strength. The main aim of man is to develop and to achieve greatest mental strength. His chief virtue is self-realization, not obedience. God is a symbol of one's own powers, which one tries to realize in life. God is not a force or determination—it is not power over man. It is the outer manifestation of man's inner self.

Modern Western Psychotherapy is turning more and more towards values, towards developing a philosophy of life and life styles where values are given importance. Two types of values are mentioned: External values, such as ideas, feelings, people around and material objects, and Internal values as ego, systems, self-systems and core systems. These are built around the self. The role of a counsellor lies in helping a client develop a mature philosophy of life imbibing these values.

One can compare the Indian systems here. These systems are value laden and are built around the Atman or self. They also seek to integrate material as well as moral and spiritual values around the self. They seek more and more expansion of the self so as to elevate it to higher levels of consciousness. This is thus the meeting point of Indian and Western systems.

The new therapists are also searching for meanings. A Viennese neurologist Victor Frankl postulated a strong need for 'god', similar to biological needs of hunger and thirst. He stresses man's striving for meanings—meaning to life, meaning to this world, etc., Frankl asserts that the human personality (DAS GEISTIGE) has laws which go beyond psychological laws, and are concerned with man's ideals and responsible behaviours. The similarity with Indian systems is evident. Here also the search is on for meanings. In Indian systems also the laws governing Atman go beyond the psychological laws of Buddhi, etc.

Logo-therapy is a form of therapy devoted to discovering the central purpose and meaning of life (Logo = meaning). Here the client develops self-understanding which leads to self-change and self-improvement. This is Gyan Yoga of Geeta.

Existential psychology deals with existence itself. It is based on elan vita or surge of life which may be equated with 'Prana' of Indian systems. Jean Paul Sartre, the main exponent of existentialism, say "To be able to live well, one must start to live and to throw of the useless accretions (debris) of reason". Indian concept also views the mental processes of perception intelligence etc. as burdens at one stage. To reach further this burden is to be shed off.

The new system of Yoga or any other Indian concept, has to bring down its ideas to the common man. To a common man Samadhi is not so important. It is an achievement of the chosen few not for everybody. What is really important to common man is an abiding peace of mind and healthy inter-personal relationships.

Latest Trends in Psychotherapy

Marshall Edelson M.D. in his *Socio-therapy and Psychotherapy,* (1970, Univ. of Chicago Press) says - The therapist has to arouse in the patient an active interest in his own physical and psychological survival. In the treatment of ego-failure, it is not resistance to the uncovering of conflicts between the sub-systems of personality, that should be the focus of psycho-therapeutic attention, but rather the resistances that interfere with the recovery of ego functioning —denial or falsification of reality, attitudes of omnipotence, apathy, aloofness, withdrawal, regression, etc. Pathological behaviour according to Talcott Parsons (1951) means deviant behaviour. It may range from passive alienation from values and norms, evasion and withdrawal or ritualistic compliance, or compulsive and joyless performance to active alienation, in challanging and flouting values, responsibility and expectations. To cope with this type of deviant behaviour Indian systems start with internal and move to external. They focus more and more upon the internal integration of personality. Internal changes make the deviant person also value-oriented and social oriented.

The main problem in both the therapy systems is development of a mature and developing consciousness. In the young child there are rudimentary feelings which are channelised through parental demands and punishments. In the older child or adolescent these demands become internalised. He also seeks sanctions from his teachers and peers. He is more social oriented. For the mature adult the consciousness is built around his self—his self system values and ego system values. He gives selected response to various external demands according to his own value systems, and as far as he is not able to follow his own value systems normal guilt responses result. These guilt responses cause most of the deviant and abnormal behaviour.

The main problem of any psychotherapy is handling of this guilt and relieving the patient from the pressures and tensions caused by guilt. The famous therapist and Existential thinker has this to say about handling of guilt in therapy, Dr. Rollo May (in Existence Ch. II. 1959)-

- Release clients' tensions with a relationship characterized by acceptance on client's part.

— Help him see the origin of his guilt — the suggested ways to do this are—
  (a) Let him admit to guilt — sweekarokti in Indian systems.
  (b) Let him see motives — why he is feeling so—internal observation (अवलोकन).
  (c) Cut rationalizations.
  (d) Transform neurotic — repressed guilt to normal, tolerable level.

— Now, utilize the gap between his self-image and his own actual self—a further motivation to grow.

This type of therapy consists in assisting the client to make a decision—a vow or Vrata in Indian systems. Also, it seeks to develop a more stable and mature value structure. Swami Akhilananda in his "Mental health and Hindu Psychology" also lays stress on this on this aspect of Indian therapies. These systems help the individual to purge himself of all feelings of guilt and then build up a new value system in which he has a healthy acceptance of himself and then he is motivated to transform himself not only to a normal but to an above normal even super-normal being.

The Indian systems are criticised as being impractical, too much of spirituality and beyond the reach of the common man. As far as spirituality is concerned it is true, Indian systems are full of spiritual wisdom—they seek well being of body mind and soul. A holistic view of the man who is not just body and mind, who seeks something 'More', who transcends body and mind and seeks super-consciousness. But the charges of being 'impractical' or 'beyond the reach of common man' are not true. We can take up some examples. The Yama's and Niyama's of Yoga system are very practical, down to earth, and touch the life of man, from lowest to the highest. They are common rules—do's and dont's of every day life and are also very simple which anyone and everyone can follow. Or take the dictum in Atharva Veda—'Purify your body with water and your mind with truth'. This is very simple, very practical and within the reach of everyone, who wants it. There is noting difficult or mysterious about it.

In fact, Indian systems of Psychotherapy try to follow a 'Madhyam marg' or middle way. See diagram. This is the Madhyam marg of Gautam the Buddha also. Madhyam marg means the middle way. Man must satisfy his material needs upto a certain extent—not starving, nor over-indulging. Similarly he must satisfy his spiritual urges also, but must not go to the extreme, only upto a certain extent. In this way, the maximum satisfaction can be reached only when the materialistic and spiritual satisfaction are in balance. This seems to be not only the best but also 'the only' solution of man's problems. Shri Krishna also gives the same advice to Arjuna in Geeta: "Let the indriyas go to their subjects, but control them from within." This way the satisfaction will be from the lowest to the highest levels from indriyas to mind to higher consciousness.

Mukti-freedom

Freedom is the core of man's spiritual reality. The concept of 'Mukti' (liberation) is unique to Indian thought. Man is not bound by his past, he can break the bondage (बन्धन) of life. Mukti is not just liberation, denial or salvation. It is liberation from lower desires. It is the realization of the core of one's being. Yoga and other systems are built on the faith that Mukti-freedom from bondage—is attainable in life. It frees man from repression and intra-psychic conflicts. It is a process of enrichment of life which deepens, expands, illuminates and intensifies consciousness and adds new dimensions to it.

The recent development of Psycho-synthesis adds a new dimension—the noetic or spiritual to the bio-psyshic already accepted "Bio-psycho-noe-synthesis'. Roberto Assagioli, an Italian psycho-therapist, who belongs to Psycho-synthesis Research Foundation, Greenville, Delaware, is an exponent of psycho-synthesis. He says, man is more than body and mind, he is spiritual also. Even West has begun to realize the spiritual core of human nature. 'Psychology and psychotherapy has to work within the framework of scientific psychology. But it is time, it starts widening its own horizons.'

Psycho-synthesis says, going to the dead past is dangerous to mental health. Man may be stuck to the past. Man must seek to realize his higher nature. It is close to Yoga in that it teaches that klesha (क्लेश) is caused by the suppression of higher nature and being stuck to lower nature. The ills of negative living—of mental agony and suppression can be overcome by positive living. The example can be found in overcoming hatred by love.

Indian systems show the way to self-improvement and self-realization through positive living, positive thinking. It can be called a science of spiritual self-engineering. "You set your own goals, choose your own path and proceed on it. There is no barrier or bondage in your path to self-realization. Only sky is the limit for you, so fly high."

In Mahabharata is it said—

याह गिच्छेच्च भवितुं त्याह, भवति पुरुषः/महा. शान्ति पर्व 299/32

Man become what he chooses to become.

Indian systems of psychotherapy lead man from darkness to light from negativity to positive thinking and positive living. Atharva Veda seeks to join man to his time place situation and environment. It gives constructive outlook in life. It teaches that man can be healthy and happy if he practises mental non-violence not hurting any one, even in the thoughts and mind. With such mental non-violence, there can be no anxiety. There must be no anxiety, no conflict, no guilt feelings, if one is performing one's duty.

Conclusion

Here we have seen the general goals of psychotherapy which are common to both and which are unique to each. For future psychotherapy there can be combined and agreed upon goals which are acceptable to the modern scientific viewpoint.

There are problems in both the systems o psychotherapy—Indian as well as Western. We have seen some of these problems. The main problems can be summed up as—that the Western systems are searching for something 'more', something 'higher'. They seek meaning and purpose in life. The Indian systems on the other hand lack the down to earth objective scientific footing. They are based on thousands of years of experience of the rishis, no doubt—but these have to be tested in the light of modern science.

A synthesis of the two will mean removing or solving the problems of both in a constructive way so that both can come together and work in better co-operation in future, for the welfare of the suffering mankind.

Indian systems can have far reaching consequences for the Western systems in—

Body— In psycho-somatic medicine and bio-feedback Indian system specially Yoga can show the way. The autonomic processes of the body like breathing and heart-beat can be brought under control by Yoga practices.

- Yogic asanas. These asanas are not mere physical exercises. Physical exercises draw 'prana' out of the body, while the Asanas send it inside and distribute it evenly in the whole body.
- As Maharishi Raman has shown, abnormal powers or siddhis can be achieved by the Yogic asanas.
- Pranayama is a breathing exercise, which along with the asanas and psycho-therapy can improve even psychotic cases, cases of depression also showed improvement, with pranayama.
- Tension—Yogic asanas are great relievers of tensions such as shavasana which is recommended by modern Psychiatrists also.

Mind— Indian systems show the ways to channelize the vast mental energy to higher goals of life.

So the need of the hour is an integrated approach of Indian and Western methods of psycho-therapy as is being done in the field of medicine. The best of both the systems are to be combined—and this combination is possible. Roberto Assagioli's Psychosynthesis may very well show the way in this direction.

Eleven

Conclusions: Salient Features of Indian Psychotherapic Systems

Psychotherapy in Indian has been overdominated by Western concepts, our therapists are trained mostly in Western tradition which is not relevant to our own culture and traditions. It is heartening to note that the new generation of Indian psychotherapists after 60's have started getting unhappy and disgruntled with Western ideas, concepts and methods. They are demanding ideas and concepts which have relevance for Indian masses. They are trying to seek new paradigms to work on—and new avenues to explore. But they are still groping in the dark—although some light has started coming now. (Neki, 1972).

It is a common knowledge that we have a veritable treasure house lying buried in thousands of years of debris. There are invaluable gems waiting to be explored in the depths of our past—our scriptures—veda—upanishads and our cultural traditions. But nobody seems to have the courage to dive deep in this ocean and find the pearls of wisdom, sown there by our learned men the Rishis in the past. Our Western educated friends, the modern experts in psychotherapy are deterred by two major factors. Firstly there is the non-availability or near extinction of old authentic texts. Some perished with time, some were taken out of the country by foreigners; some are still kept hidden from the public eye by the descendents of owners of these texts. So the basic texts are near impossible to get. The second problem is the language—Sanskrit is no longer a used language. Any scholar who wishes to explore the basic texts, of course provided these are available, has first to master Sanskrit then only he/she can understand what lies in those ancient texts written on palm leaves. Again even the masters of Sanskrit differ among themselves about the meanings and interpretation of those small axiomatic stanzas, known as Sutras. These sutras can have scores of interpretations. Thus causing confusion among the new researchers.

Still, there have been admirable efforts on the part of Indian and foreign scholars to translate, compile and redact the old Samhitas. They are becoming more approachable now with their Hindi and English versions. Research is going on in the field of ancient psychotherapy at various centres in India and abroad also. Some main centres of research are—NIMHANS Bangalore, Gurukul Kangri Vishvavidyalaya, Hardwar, Shanti Kunj—Brahmavarchas Sansthan at Kankhal, Maharishi Mahesh Yogi's centres at various places in India and abroad, Divine Life Society of India—to name only a few of them. Then there are the newly opened and spreading Ayurvedic Colleges all over India—doing some sort of research—but mainly on medicines. Among the individual researchers the most noteworthy names are Swami Akhilananda, Swami Ajaya of USA and Dr. H.G. Singh of GKV, Hardwar.

In the present work, discussions of systems of Psychotherapy in ancient India, have been confined to the three main systems only, namely, the Atharva vedic system, the Ayurvedic system and Yoga. Some minor systems have been incorporated within these three large systems. Jain and Bouddha systems have not been taken separately as these are branches of the main Ayurvedic System only.

One important system is Unani System. It was used and popularized by the Muslim invaders and later rulers. They brought famous Hakims from Iran, Arab etc. with them. It is also very popular today in India. But it has not been included in the present work due to two reasons. First of all, Unani system did not originate in India. It has its roots in Arabia and Persia. Secondly the Unani system is not an ancient system, in the sense in which Atharva veda is ancient. It is comparatively new owing its origin to Greek medicine.

Here some salient features common to all the Indian systems of psychotherapy will be presented. Upto now we deal with the individual systems and their characteristic qualities. What we propose to take up now are the characteristics shared by all Indian systems. These very characteristics distinguish Indian systems from other systems of modern psycho-therapy.

Salient Features of Indian Systems of Psychotherapy

(1) Indian System is the Oldest in the World— The origin of Indian system is almost ageless. It goes to the times when the Aryans were establishing themselves as agriculturalists. They were afraid of nature and of diseases and sought to get rid of these diseases. Atharva veda is the oldest available record of therapy, both somatic and psychic in the world. The date of Atharva veda has been put at 2000 BC. Thus, Indian psycho-therapy is at least four thousand years old. This is oldest in the world.

(2) The Continuity of the System— Indian system of psycho-therapy is the only one system in the world with a continuity at least four thousand years. It started with Atharva Veda and is still alive and kicking. Dr. H.G. Singh in his survey conducted in 70's found 170 practitioners in northern parts of Uttar Pradesh and East Rajasthan alone. They are found elsewhere also, mostly in the South-Kerala. They are spread over rural and urban areas.

(3) The Basic Unity of the System— We have seen in the previous chapters that all the systems and authorities right from Atharva veda, Ayurveda, Charak Sushruta, Vagabhatta, Patanjali in Yoga Sutras all differ from each other in their own special way. But still one finds a common thread running through all of them. This shows unity in diversity, their fundamental unity. At the very core they are all Indian.

(4) Indian System is a Dynamic System— We have seen that the Indian systems like Ayurveda and Yoga have been going on for thousands of years and there is a continuity in them. But the systems are not static. They are dynamic in the sense that they have been changing with times. In the systems many practices are discarded, many new ones have been added, some have been modified but the basic system remains the same—as the waters go on changing but the river remains the same.

(5) All Indian Systems of Psychotherapy are Spiritually Oriented— These systems have an objective of treating the body, the mind and the soul. These three are considered a composite unit of human personality and no cure is considered complete if it does not go up to the soul. The basic aim is having a healthy body and the healthy mind which lead to the ultimate goal of salvation of the soul.

(6) The theoretical and practical sides of the systems run side by side. Theoretical side gives basic concepts like normality, abnormality, causes, symptoms, diagnosis etc. The practical side deals with different techniques like mantra vidya. The older texts abound in theoretical side because practical training was imparted from guru to shishya and was oral and was kept strictly secret for fear of misuse by quacks. Atharva veda and Yoga are rich on practical side while Ayurveda abounds in principles and theory. The present day practitioners are good in practical side but are poor on theoretical side. Systems may be rich in one aspect and not so good in other aspect, but both the sides are found together in all the systems.

(7) The Concept of Normality and Abnormality is Common to all Systems— Indian systems are based on the assumption that the psychic personality has two aspects—Purush and Prakriti. Purush is pure inner self. Prakriti or nature is composed of three gunas—sattva, rajas and tamas. Sattva is pure while rajas and tamas can get corrupted and vary in degrees. Normal state is when the three gunas are balanced. But as soon as the balance gets disturbed, abnormality starts. So normality and abnormality are a matter of degree of deviation of these gunas.

(8) The General Etiological Factor in Psychic Disorders is Believed to be the Past Behaviour of the Person Himself— (Bhoot= past)— that is how the name Bhoot vidya was given to the study of mental disorders. Psychic disorders are mostly psycho-genic or functional. There are psychosomatic disorders also but mostly these are functional. There are definite tests and diagnostic techniques to determine if the disorder is somatic or psychogenic. These are scientific diagnostic tests like the clinical tests found in modern psychotherapy. These are described in detail in Ayurveda specially Charak.

(9) The Basic Approach of all Indian Psychotherapy is Psychogenic— The therapies are psychological in nature—they may use some outside materials as in havan and ritualistic ceremonies. Sometimes medicines may also be given as in unmad.

The psychogenic therapy started from Atharva Veda itself and has gone upto yoga and even in the vaidyas ojhas sayanas of today. The examples of psychogenic therapy are mantra, tantra, havan, prayashchit, gaman etc. Yoga is a simple ideal psychogenic approach. These psychogenic therapies have been used on nearly 30 kinds of mental disorders, ranging from acute insanity—unmad, to milder cases of anger, fear, bad dreams etc. Because these methods do not have to use many material aids, their range of applicability is very wide.

(10) Indian Psychotherapy is Cheaper— This type of therapy is much cheaper compared to other modern psycho-therapies. Firstly because it makes the least use of medicines and other material aids. Secondly it does not have to use the costly apparatuses for diagnosis and treatment and lastly because there is no long and expensive training of the therapist. The therapist makes use of home made medicines obtained from herbs etc. He may use some thread to tie on, red powder and turmeric power some grains of rice etc. Even when the ritualistic therapy or drama takes place, the expense is very negligible. Apparatuses are not used at all and the training of the therapist is in guru-shishya parampara—where the teacher imparts training orally without taking any fees. The therapist does not charge any fees from the patients also. Whatever they want to give, they offer to the deity (*chadhava*).

(11) The Spectrum of Indian Psychotherapy is Very Vast— Indian Psychotherapy starts with removing the abnormal symptoms from the patient's behaviour, thus bringing equilibrium and normalcy back. This is the objective of all other therapies in the world. What is special about the Indian systems is that they do not stop at bringing back the normalcy, they go farther than that. They aim at improving the total personality—moving him/her towards higher goals. In Yoga, there are practices for expanding and elevating the consciousness, for imparting supernatural powers and leading from conscious to super conscious state— Samadhi. It is a sort of cosmic psychosynthesis or being joined with the cosmic superpower on psychic level.

(12) All the systems of Indian psychotherapy have positive and negative sides. The negative side means curative that is,

treating the disease which has already attacked. The positive side is the side of mental health and hygiene, where the do's and don'ts of maintaining good health are laid down. Emphasis is always on cleanliness (shouch) of both body and mind which leads to bodily and mental health. Moreover the utmost emphasis is laid on a moral and social conduct, which helps in better adjustment in social surroundings and thus, to personal satisfaction and better mental health.

(13) Indian systems never teach running away from the problems of life—they teach doing one's assigned duty in this world, with courage and self-confidence. They try to infuse a new orientation in the patient and raise his Atma-bal.

(14) Indian systems of psycho-therapy may be—

(i) Individual or group therapies.
(ii) Directive non-directive or semi-directive therapies.
(iii) By one therapist or by a battery of therapists.
(iv) One technique or multi-technique therapies.
(v) Symptomatic or dynamic therapies.

(i) Individual or Group Therapies— Although individual therapies out number the group therapies, still group therapies are there. Individual therapies are sadesh, santvana, sweekarokti, japa, tapa etc. The examples of group therapies are—havan where the family or larger social group may participate. Utarna, prarthana, parivarik punarshikshan, gayan (songs), nritya (dance), sir hilana (convulsive shocks) etc. Even to this day we have examples of group-therapy in India at Dattatreya temple at Gulbarga A.P., Balaji temple near Jaipur and Pushkarji Ajmer.

(ii) Directive, Semi-directive or Not-directive Therapies— In directive therapy, the therapist is active while the patient follows him passively. Important directive therapies are—sadesh (suggestion), samvashi karan (hypnosis), ritualistic therapies, mantra and tantra etc.

In non-directive therapy, the patient is active. He conducts the activity or performs and the therapist directs from behind the curtain only. The examples of non-directive therapies are sankalp, japa, tapa, vrat, sweekarokti, prayashchita etc.

In semi-directive therapies the roles of the patient and the therapists are equal and keep changing. Sometimes one being more active than the other and vice versa. The examples of semi-directive therapies are—havan, prarthna, mangal karma, shanti karma etc.

(iii) By One Therapist or A Battery of Therapists— In most cases of psychotherapy one single therapist conducts the whole affair. But there are therapies in which a group of therapists work with different functions, for example in 'sayana' system, in vogue in rural areas of North India—UP, Haryana, Rajasthan, there is a group of therapists or sayanas. The chief 'sayana' conducts the show, one person plays an instrument, mostly a drum, someone sings, the third one may be moving his head convulsively, a fourth one talks to the patient, some other one may be talking to other family members. All are specialists in their functions and their activities are co-ordinated to reach a goal. At Balaji temple near Jaipur also there is a group of Mahantas. In Atharva Veda one finds the examples of transference and havan by a group of rishis.

(iv) One Technique or Multi-technique Therapies— In the total process of therapy sometimes only one technique is used and at other times more than one techniques may be combined. In chronic and complex cases usually multiple techniques are applied as in the case of sayana system, cited above, song, dance, sir hilana, bateheet, sankalp are all combined. In older times examples of mantra prarthana and havan etc. being together are common. The example of single technique is gaman for cases of depression, or prayashchit and tapa may be used singly.

(v) Symptomatic and Deep Root or Dynamic Therapies— Most of the Indian psychotherapies do not stop at curing symptoms only. They try to go deeper and try to remove the roots of the disease. They provide depth cure. Swami Akhilananda has said, "Along with the therapeutic value of Indian psychology, there is a dynamic effect on the development of personality." Indian systems do not leave the patient after cure. They lead him forward, towards better mental and physical health towards higher levels of mental life.

(15) Indian Psychotherapy is not only Environment Friendly it is Universe Friendly— Indian systems try to cure the disease without harming anything in this whole universe—any living being any entity—be they river or mountain on ocean. Take the example of Utarna (transference). It is supposed that the disease is given to others—but if one goes a little deeper one finds that the disease is given where it can do no harm. It can rather benefit to whom it is given. As in Jaundice—the disease is transferred to the turmeric plant which can get a richer yellow now. In Atharva veda there is a Sutra which says, "O fever, why do you trouble me (the patient). Please go to the ocean quench your thirst and become cool."

So Indian psychotherapy, while curing one, does not harm to other—it rather tries to help other animate and inanimate objects. Havan therapy, it is said, purifies the whole environment and thus helps the community.

On the basis of above discussion, it can be concluded that Indian system of psycho-therapy is an independent and original system. It has many distinctive characteristics of its own. It is economical and spiritually oriented. It is also scientific, not in the sense of laboratory tests, but in the sense that its findings have stood the test of time—of ages and thousands of years. It has stood the test of experience also in successfully curing the maladies of mind, in suggesting preventive measures and in positively leading to better mental health conditions.

Our systems are indigenous and original and independent of any outside influence. They have reached the highest point ever reached by any therapy in the world in achieving a more synthesized personality.

One point of caution here—that these systems have to be modernized. In spite of all the special characteristics, Indian systems need a modern scientific touch. Scientific investigations and research must make them uptodate and be of relevance to the modern world of Psychotherapy. If Indian spiritual tradition combines with the scientific outlook of the west, a new path may be opened for psychotherapy of future.

"If our science of mental health is to become more effective psycho-therapists will have to balance their knowledge of psychological concepts and techniques with a contemplative awareness—an awareness that exercises itself day after day in quiet openness."

Conclusion

We have reached the end of the present narrative and face the rather hard task of concluding this whole thing. Actually this work is nothing but an exercise in summarizing the collected data. We have touched the shores of Indian thought, which is like a deep large ocean of wisdom. One can gather the pebbles from here and there, but can never aspire to encompass the whole. It is very deep, very profound. People just scrach the surface, look at the shinning brilliance of wisdom and think they have discovered it. "Eureka ! Eureka !!" they cry in glee. But have they found the real thing. No. They are dazzled by the shine. For the real thing one has to dive deep, to go below the surface, beyond the obvious, to reach the deepest levels. These levels were reached by our ancient seers—actually these rishis were the authors and the originators of these thoughts. Even these rishis managed to get just a glimpse of the 'real'. Because all this thought and wisdom is not the work of some one mind. These concepts have been accumulated all through the ages. This wisdom and reality is beyond the reach of common people and specially those people for whom surface reality and objectivity are the criteria for science. In our land, in this age also there have been seers and sages like Shri Adi Shankaracharya, Raman Maharishi, Shri Aurobindo etc. who tasted the real nectar of Indian thought and simplified and imparted it for the benefit of common man. But these great men and many more like them—touched only some particular aspects. They presented some view points—but the 'real' thing was still beyond reach. The real is a "whole".

The present work is a humble to find some gems of wisdom pertaining to psychotherapy from this vast ocean of Indian thought. It seemed a necessity in the present time when Indian psychotherapy seems to be shrouded in mystery and witchcraft. It was essential to dispel misconceptions regarding Indian systems. The misconception seems to have been caused by the name भूत-विद्या Bhoot-vidya given to ancient form of mental treatment in both Atharva veda and Ayurveda. Then there are modern practitioners like Ojhas or the Sayanas who practise various tricks to dope simple public. Our systems have to be brought to the notice of public who wants to know more about the indigenous forms. And this work is a step in that direction.

But this task has been a formidable one, due to so many hurdles in the way. First of all there is a question of time-gap—a gap of some four to five thousand years—even by a mild estimate. These long ages naturally brought about many changes in the social structure. Many concepts beliefs norms and life-style of those days—of a simple agriculture based society became irrelevant in the highly technical society of today. Secondly, in Indian thought, right from the time of the Vedas, all learning is found in a jumbled mixed-up form. Metaphysics and philosophy, ethics and logic, psychology and sociology, politics and economics and the systems of medicine, all together form a large mass of learning. In today's trend of specialization, any one, who wants to go back in time and find some facts there—the task becomes almost impossible. The task ahead for him/her is to extricate the required facts from the jumbled up mass something like picking grains from a big heap of chafe. The, these facts are not organized and found at one place, in one chapter. They lie scattered here and there—if symptoms are in chapter two, treatment is found in chapter eleven. Only a very keen eye and a discerning mind can find the relevant facts in such confusing conditions.

One more difficulty is the language. Even if one is quite well-versed in Sanskrit—the language of all ancient treatises of India, one is not quite successful in getting what one wants. The mantra-sutra technique found in all old literature presents the great task of interpretations. The mantras have to be expanded and interpreted to reach any valid meanings. These may be interpreted in different ways by different people. The ancient commentators also differed in their commentaries (भाष्य) of the same Samhitas, and that is how the different branches or Shakhas of Vedas developed. The opinions are so diverse sometimes that one fails to find the way in all this chaos.

Well, in spite of all the problems and difficulties the task is completed for the present—and only for the present, mind you. For a great future lies ahead and one can foresee a surge of interest in our own systems. This work has been possible with the help of various books commentaries on Vedas, Ayurveda and Yoga, available in Hindi and English. Going to various commentaries and references helped in arriving at the common and agreed points. In case of differences of opinion, one had to rely on either majority or most logical and relevant views. The present author expresses deep gratitude to all the authors and commentators, who made reaching out to ancient texts possible. This is an open and inviting field, waiting for more and more research.

Now in conclusion, one can give a brief account of the matter presented here. After an introductory chapter, the next two chapters give a glimpse into the main systems of modern Western psychotherapy like—psychoanalysis, behaviouristic psychotherapy and humanistic—existential systems; and then, into the three main Indian systems of psycho-therapy viz., Atharva Veda, Ayurveda and Yoga. Only those Indian systems have been presented which were born and developed in India. Unani system of medicine which became popular during Muslim rule in India, and is still prevalent in Northern India, is not taken up, because it was not born in India, although it developed in the indigenous soil. Similarly Jain and Bouddh systems were actually the offshoots of Vedic and Ayurvedic systems. Vagabhatta who is one of the Brihad-trayi (the Big three) had incorporated some of the Bouddha concepts in his systems, such as Aparajita vidya.

Next, the three main systems of Indian psychotherapy have been dealt in detail—the Vedas are given in some detail—just to introduce to the general public and to dispel some of the misconceptions regarding old scriptures. Then the Atharva Veda is introduced along with Atharvediya psychotherapy. Ayurveda—the science of life—comes next. Then treatment of mental diseases in Ayurveda is presented. Ayurveda is a vast system containing the holistic treatment of body, mind and soul. It required a more comprehensive description, with the details of all the mental and psycho-somatic diseases and their treatment.

Last to appear is Yoga system with a general introduction, and then Yogic psychotherapy in some details. Yoga also is a comprehensive and holistic system, which needs a much more detailed treatment than has been possible within the confines of this book. Yoga has some very effective techniques for development of mental powers and for mental health. It gives some very useful relaxation techniques which are being adopted by psycho-therapists today.

Some salient features of Indian systems have been presented in some detail in the next chapter. Then there is an attempt to put forward the common points of these two diverse systems of psychotherapy, viz., Indian and Western. The two systems are basically different in their approach and goal. While the Indian systems are spiritually oriented, the Western systems are more worldly oriented. The Indian systems vouch for an individualistic goal of Moksha or liberation from all worldly bondage and upliftment of the 'self' of Atman. The Western systems, on the other hand, seek liberation of man from the inner demons—his own unconscious conflicts and anxieties. The idea of better adjustment to one's social group—the family, the neighbours, the peer group and the larger community, runs side by side in both the systems. The Indian systems have wider horizons they seek oneness of man with the cosmos or the whole creation (सृष्टि-जगत्).

Next comes the question can there be any convergence of these two divergent systems—is any sort of synthesis possible? Yes, there is a ray of hope—a chance for such a synthesis to take place. The attempts are on way to integrate the two and arrive at a combined comprehensive programme of psychotherapy and mental health. An integrated approach is the need of the hour, which can avoid the pitfalls of both and incorporate the merits and positive points of both the systems. Modern educated trained psychotherapists should enter into the practice of psychotherapy. Indian system of psychotherapy is very much alive even today, but it has fallen into the hands of either low educated vaidyas or mahantas or quacks like Sayanas and Ojhas. They have no knowledge of modern science or modern methodology. If trained psychotherapists come into the practice field, along with the indigenous practitioners and learn their practices they can utilize and apply them in better scientific and improvised ways. Such combined efforts can bring about the much needed synthesis of these two systems and open the way for better mental health of mankind in future.

"East and West need each other. Each is richer in some goods, poorer in others. The West cannot afford to neglect the gifts which wise men from East may bring. The gifts are based on the results of centuries of experience and spiritual experiment, as truly as science is based on the work of centuries of physical experiment."

Edgar Sheffield Brightman, quoted by Swami Akhilananda in Hindu Psychology.

One bright point for future synthesized Psychotherapy is : while Western psychotherapy stops at normality, Indian psychotherapy moves ahead to seek the goal of supernormality. Indian psycho-therapy can also play a great role in relaxation techniques and attainment of inner mental peace. It is inner mental peace of the individual which can pave the way for establishment of peace in the whole cosmos. So we end with the prayer :

सर्वे भवन्तु सुखिनः सर्वे सन्तु निरामयः
सर्वे भद्राणि पश्न्तु माकश्चित दुखभाक भवेत।

Bibliography

1. Acharya Bhadra Sen, *Yoga and Swasthya*, Yogic Vyayam Sangh, Ajmer, Sam. 2008.
2. Acharya, Pt. Sri Ram Sharma, Vangamaya, 41, "Jeevem Sharadam Shatam", Shanti Kunj, Hardwar.
3. Agehananda Bharti, *The Tantrik Tradition*, London : Rider 1965 Paperback edition, Doubleday, New York, 1970.
4. Akhilananda Swami, *Mental Health and Hindu Psychology*, George Allen and Unwin Ltd., London, 1952.
5. Apte, V.S., *Sanskrit English Dictionary*, Motilal Banarsi Das, Delhi, 1963.
6. Arsh, P., *Vedic Manovigyan*.
7. Arsh, P., *Atharvediya Chikitsa Shastra*, Arya Sarvadeshik Sabha, Delhi.
8. Arsh, P., *Atharva Vediya Mantra Vidya*, Gurukul Kangri Press, Hardwar, Samvat 1999.
9. *Atharva veda Samhita*, Ed. S.P. Pandit 1895. Trs. W.D. Whitney and C.R. Lanman, Harvard Oriental Series.
10. Assagioli, Robert, *Psycho-synthesis*, Hobbs Dorman and Co. Inc. New York.
11. Atreya, B. L., Article I *Bhartiya Manovigyan*, Akhil Bhartiya Darshan Parishad, Faridabad, 1963.
12. Atrideva Gupta, *Ashtang Sangraha Part I*, Nirnaya Sagar Press, Bombay, 1951.
13. Bernard Theos, *Hatha Yoga*, Rider, London.
14. Bernard, Theos, *Heaven Lies Within Us*, Rider London.
15. Bloomfield, M., *The Atharva Veda*, Grundriss.
16. Boiling G.M. and Negelain J.V. Parishishthas of Atharva veda, Leipzig, 1910.
17. Boss, Mildred: *A Psychiatrist Discovers India*. Translated from German to English by Henry A. Frey. M.A. Rupa and Co. Delhi, 1966.

18. Brown, J.F., *Psychodynamics of Abnormal Behaviour.* McGraw Hill Co. Inc. London, 1940.
19. Brightman, Edgar Sheffield, *Hindu Psychology,* by Swami Abhilananda, Routledge and Kegan Paul Ltd., London, 1960.
20. Coleman, James C., *Abnormal Psychology and Modern Life,* Latest edition.
21. Coster, Geraldine, *Yoga and Western Psychology.* Oxford University Press, London, 1957.
22. Dawson, W.S., *Aids to Psychiatry,* 1944.
23. Das Gupta, S.N., *Yoga as Philosophy and Religion,* K. Paul, Trench Trubner, London, 1924, New York : Dutton, 1924.
24. Drake, R.M., *Abnormal Psychology,* Little field, Adams and Co., Paterson, New Jersey, 1959.
25. Drever, James, *A Dictionary of Psychology,* Penguin Books Ltd., 1952.
26. *Encylopaedia Americana* Vol. 22 'Psychotherapy'.
27. Erich Lindermann, *"Guilt" The Encyclopaedia of Mental Health,* New York.
28. Felix Guyot, Yoga : The Science of Health, Rider and Co., London.
29. Freud S., New Introductory Lectures of Psychoanalysis Hogarth Press Ltd., London, 1949.
30. Griffith, *The Hymns of Atharva Veda.*
31. Gulab Kunverba Society, *Charak Samhita,* 1949, Gulab Kunverba Society, Jamnagar.
32. Hans Jacobs, *Western Psychotherapy and Hindu Sadhna,* George Alien and Unwin Ltd. London, 1961.
33. Harper, Robert A., *Psychoanalysis and Psychotherapy,* Prentic Hall Inc. Englewood Cliffs, N. J., 1965.
34. Henry Lefever, *The Vedik Idea of Sin.*
35. Indra Devi, *Forever Young Forever Healthy,* A. Thomas Preston, England.
36. Jean Vanenne, *Yoga and the Hindu Tradition,* (French) Trans. Motilal Banarsi Dass, Delhi, 1989.
37. Joshi K. S., *Yoga and Nature Cure therapy,* Sterling Publishers Pvt. Ltd., New Delhi, 1991.
38. Kapali Shastri T. V., *Further Lights, The Vedas and the Tantra,* Shri Aurobindo Ashram Press, Pondicherry, 1951.

39. Karambelkar, V.W., *The Atharvedic Civilization*, Nagpur University Press, Nagpur, 1959.
40. Karambelkar, V.W. *Atharva Veda and the Ayurveda*, Usha Karambelkar, Nagpur, 1961.
41. Kenneth E. Appel and Harod H. Marris, Jr. "Psychiatry" in *Encyclopedia of Mental Health*.
42. Korchin, Sheldon J., *Modern Clinical Psychology* 1989 edition, 'Basic Books Inc.', New York.
43. Kovoor T. Behanan, *Yoga: A Scientific Evaluation*, Dover Pub. Inc., New York, 1937.
44. K. Sadashiv Sharma, "Manas Prakriti", Hindi Magazine *Sachitra Ayurveda*, 1965.
45. Krishamurti, *At the Feet - of the Master*. The Theosophical Society Adyar, India.
46. Lannoy, Richard, *The Speaking Tree: A Study of Indian Culture and Society*, Oxford University Press, London and New York, 1971.
47. Max Muller, *The Vedas*. Sushil Gupta, Calcutta, 1956.
48. Max Muller, *The Sacred Books of the East*, Vol. XIII, Hymns of Atharva Veda Motilal Banarsi Dass, Delhi, 1964.
49. Nagar, S.D., *Pranik Chikitsa*.
50. O.P. Jaggi, *Yogic and Tantrik Medicine in History of Science and Technology in India*, Vol. V. Atma Ram and Sons, Delhi.
51. Page, James D., *Abnormal Psychology*, McGrow Hill London, 1947.
52. Pathak, Dr. Balakrishna Amarji, *Manas Rog Vigyan*. Shri Vaidya Nath Ayurveda Bhawan, Jhansi, Fourth Edition, 1983.
53. Pandey K.N. and G.N. Chaturvedi, *Charak Samhita*, Vol. I, Chaukhamba Vidya Bhawan, Varanasi, 1961.
54. Radha Kant Dev Bhadure. *Shabd Kalpadrum*, Hindi Dic. Baptist Mission Press, Calcutta, 1886.
55. Ramacharaka, *Gyan Yoga*, L. N. Fowler, London.
56. Ramacharaka, *Fourteen Lessons in Yoga Philosophy*, L.N. Fowler, London.
57. Rapaport, Robert N., *Social Anthropology and Mental Health*, The Encyclopedia of Mental Health, New York.
58. Ray P. and H. N. Gupta, *Charak Samhita*, National Institute of Sciences of India, New Delhi, 1965.

59. Rees, John R., *World Mental Health*, The Encyclopedia of Mental Health, New York.
60. Richards, T.W., *Modern Clinical Psychology*, McGrow Hill, London, 1946.
61. Rotter, John R., *Clinical Psychology*, Prentice Hall of India, New Delhi, 1964.
62. Satavalekar S.D., *Atharva Veda ka Subodh* Bhasya Swadhyay Mandal, Pardi, Surat, 1958.
63. Satavalekar, S.D., *Vedic Chikitsa Shastra*, as above 1958.
64. Shaffer and Lazarus, *Fundamental Concepts in Clinical Psycho*, McGrow Hill Pub. Kogakusha, Tokyo, 1952.
65. Sharma R.C., Atharva Veda Samhita, Sayan Bhasya, Kand VI, Mathura.
66. Shastri, R.G., *Vedon Men Ayurveda*, Ayurvedic Anusandhan Trust, Delhi, 1956.
67. Shende, N.J., *The Religion and Philosophy of Atharva Veda*. Oriental Research Institute, Pune, 1952.
68. Shukla, J.P., *Mansik Rog Vigyan*, Sudha nidhi Press, Prayag.
69. Singh, H.G., *Psychotherapy in India*, 1977, H.P. Bhargava, Agra.
70. *Srimad Bhagwat Geeta*—Translated in English, Harward Press, 1944.
71. Swami Ajaya, Ph.D., *Psychotherapy: East and West*, 1948, Publisher : The Himalayan International Institute of Yoga Sciences and Philosophy, Honesdale, Pennsylvania, U.S.A.
72. Sri Shivananda, *Practical Guide to Students of Yoga*, Divine Life Society Hongkong, 1957.
73. Swami Shivananda, *Karma Yoga*, The Divine Life Society, Rishikesh.
74. Tucci, Giuseppe, *The Theory and Practice of the Mandula with Special Reference to the Modern Psychology of the Unconscious*. Translated by A.H. Brodrck, Rider, London, 1969.
75. Vaid, Bapalal, "Ayurveda men Manas Shestra", Hindi Magazine *Sachitra Ayurveda*, 1965.
76. Vasu, S.C., *The Gheranda Samhita—A Treatise on Hatha Yoga*, Bombay Theosophical Society Pub. Fund, Bombay, 1895.
77. Vedalankar, B.D., *Vedic Swapna Vigyan*, Gurukul Kangri Press, Hardwar.
78. Vidyalankar, Atrideva Gupta, *Charak Samhita*, Shanti Prakashan, Varanasi, 1964.

79. Vishvakarma, Dr. Hiralal and Upendra Nath Dwivedi, *Atharva Chikitsa Vigyan*, Krishna Dass Academy, Varanasi.
80. Weigel, J.A. *Psychiatry in General Practice*, Elsevier Pub. Co., London, 1958.
81. Whitney, W.D., *Atharva Veda Samhita*, Motilal Banarsi Dass, New Delhi, 1962.
82. Winternitz, *A History of Indian Literature*.
83. Williams, Monier, *Sanskrit English Dictionary*, Motilal Banarsi Dass, Delhi, 1963.
84. William James, *On vital Reserves*.
85. Wood, Ernest, *Yoga*, Penguin Books, London.
86. Yogendra, *Sri Yoga Magazine*, Sept. Oct. 1933.
87. Yogendra, *Sri Hatha Yoga Simplified*, The Yoga Institute, Bombay, 1959.
88. *The Yoda Upanishads*, Translated by T. R. Shrinivasa Ayyangar, Edited by Pandit A. Mahadeva Shastri, Adyar Library, Madras, 1920.
89. *The Yoga System of Patanjali*, Translated by J.H. Woods, Harvard, Oriental Series Vol., 17, 1913, Reprinted, 1972.
90. *Yogic Therapy* by Swami Shivananda Saraswati, Umachal Yogashrama, Kamakhya, Gauhati, 10, Assam.
91. *Yoga Samhita* by H. H. Swami Shivananda Maharaj of Divine Life Society, Rishikesh.
92. *Yogic Therapy: Its Basic Principles and Methods* by Swami Kuvalayananda and Dr. S.L. Vinekar.

Index